# The Bennett Playbill

*To my grandchildren:*
*Amanda, Timothy, Cynthia,*
*Markey, Lisa, Parker,*
*Felix, Victoria, Samantha,*
*and those who follow.*

# Acknowledgments

In the preparation of this book we are indebted to a great number of people who cheerfully contributed their time and efforts with unstinting generosity. A list of them all would be impractical, but we are especially grateful to George Abbott, Diana Anderson, Mrs. G. M. Anderson, Julio Averill, Geoffrey Barr, Samuel N. Behrman, Binnie Bernstein, Romney Brent, Virginia Carrick, Molly Caulfield, James Coco, John T. Coulter, Carmen Dirigo, Chester Erskine, Donald Farber, Mr. and Mrs. Ben Finney, Gary Garth, Margalo Gillmore, Alec Blasco-Ibanez, James Ross Kibbee, Mr. and Mrs. Milne B. Kibbee, Sr., Milne Kibbee, Jr., Wallace Kibbee, Jill ("Scotty") Leask, Joshua Logan, Elizabeth Loughlin, George Minor, Mrs. Harry Morrison, Victor I. Morrison, Jr., Margaret Mower, Patricia O'Connell, Susan Palmer, Jim Parish, Mrs. Osgood Perkins, Robert G. Pitkin, Peter Plant, Mary Pritchett, William Roerick, Mary Cohan Ronkin, Mrs. John Steinbeck, St. John Terrell, Ted Tiller, Mrs. Wendell L. Willkie.

Research was incalculably aided by Louis A. Rachow, Librarian, Walter Hampden Memorial Library at The Players; Staff of the Theater Collection, Lincoln Center Library of the Performing Arts; Glory Robertson, West India Reference Library, Institute of Jamaica, Kingston, Jamaica, W. I.; Mrs. Gladys Hansen, San Francisco Public Library;

Mrs. Adelaide A. Nixdorf, Free Library of Philadelphia; Mary Ann Jensen, Curator of The William Seymour Theater Collection, Princeton University Library; Sam Pearce, Curator of the Theater Collection, Museum of the City of New York; Mrs. Dorothy Crawford, Sterling Memorial Library, Yale University; Allan R. Ottley, California State Library; Staff of Howard Tilton Memorial Library, Tulane University.

# *Preface*

"And what did your father do, Miss Bennett?"

It seemed unaccountable to have to explain who my father was and what he did, but recently I was asked that question by a journalist. On second thought, I don't know why I should have been amused or surprised. Though my father, Richard Bennett, was a distinguished and celebrated actor in the American theater for more than half a century, it's undoubtedly a fact that some of his distinctions have diminished with the passage of time; to others if not, understandably, to me. Suddenly, through the eyes of a newcomer, it is clear that we and our fellow players fade in the minds of those unfamiliar with "dealers in magic and spells."

In any case, that passing incident was not the mainspring that began to shape this book. The catalyst was of a far more personal nature. I'm the proud mother of four children and, at this writing, the doting grandmother of nine, and it occurred to me that if any of them were questioned about their forebears, they'd be better equipped to give some knowledgeable answers with a written record at hand.

My hope is to revive for them something of the family's theatrical flavor, a heritage that by no means began with my father. He was only the first member of his family to pursue an acting career, but on my mother's side I represent the fifth generation in the theater. The Morrisons and Woods of my maternal ancestry are threaded through the fabric of the theater on both sides of the Atlantic, beginning almost two hundred years ago and continuing in an unbroken line to the present day. Their members can be counted among the strolling players at the fairs and in the courtyards of England in the late eighteenth century; the classic Pantomimes of London's Drury Lane Theater; the thriving New Orleans theaters during the American Civil War; the grass roots houses of Midwest America, which incubated my father's blazing talents; Broadway to the turn of the century and beyond; through the silence and sound of Hollywood's motion picture industry, golden years in which my sister Constance and I were privileged to flourish. At present it seems we've come full cycle, for today I'm working in a serialized drama on television called *Dark Shadows,* which might be termed an "electronic stock company."

I can scarcely remember a time when the theater was not a part of my life, either as a spectator or a participant, when the lowering of the houselights did not impart a thrilling sense of anticipation. A love of the performing arts, a respect for its people, a sense of enchantment, are all part of a cherished legacy left to me by my parents, a legacy which I'd like to share with the generations that follow mine.

Also, there are some plain, old-fashioned truths I'd like to pass on to them, though come to think of it, nobody has asked for them lately.

Moving to a more personal level, I'm not at all unaware of the interest that has been generated in the human problems of my family's history. There's no doubt about it; like every other family we've had our fair share of public and private controversy, tragedy, and fun and laughter, to say nothing of a rather generous helping of weaknesses, foibles, and excesses.

Retrospection is rather like looking through the wrong end of a telescope; scenes, events and figures seem to recede into a distant and shadowy corridor of the mind, and sometimes, the memory becomes more precious than the event itself. I can only say I've tried to bring some of the players to life, and to evoke something of the theatrical climate in which they performed their comedies and tragedies, both personal and professional. Whether they were claimed by celebrity or obscurity, the figures that people this book lived and died in the service of an honorable trade, and each contributed something to the theatrical framework of his time.

My only desire has been to share the chronicles of one family in the theater, for whatever value and interest it may have for my children, my grandchildren, and those members beyond them, yet unborn. I like to think of our family traditions as a not inconsiderable inheritance. I hope they will think so, too.

JOAN BENNETT

*New York City*
*January 1970*

*We are vagabonds to the heart*
*and we are not ashamed of it!*

RICHARD   BENNETT

*The Bennett Playbill*

# 1

"You mustn't mind them, they're just acting like Bennetts!" has been a much-used phrase among our friends and enemies as long as I can remember. I suppose it's true that we are a volatile, temperamental breed and have managed to invite wonder, admiration, amusement and hostility in fairly equal measure, both publicly and privately, throughout the family history.

For the actor, however, confidence and effrontery, both synonomous with temperament, are indispensable attributes whether they're acquired or built into his chemistry. The theater not only attracts people with those attributes but, by its very nature, insists upon them.

On one hand the world behind the footlights or the movie screen is an enchanted, if distant, realm of instant glamor, cardboard battles, learned-by-heart nobilities, IBM virtues and emotions of operatic proportions. Spectators know it is only a charming game or diversion in which they are touched, engrossed, amused or bored, as the case may be, for a few fleeting hours. Beyond those externals, however, the performing art is a rigid, strict and jealous disciplinarian in which its practitioners daily throw themselves into the arena to reap approval or censure each time they make an entrance to open their mouths. It's an art that is both selfish and generous, for it affords a deeper despair, a quicker hope, a grander gesture, a larger vanity, and more grinding failure or prodigal success than is to be found in most any other. In such a fiercely demanding and competitive trade, temperament is a kind of occupational disease or hazardous by-product of the actor's terrain. I'm neither advocating nor excusing it, but it's a subject that's bound to come up from time to time in these pages.

In addition to ample temperament and independent behavior, one of the things that attracted attention to the family through the years was our marriage and divorce rate. It's really nothing to boast about but we seem to have had a cheerful proclivity for adding to the national statistics. Among my parents, Richard Bennett and Adrienne Morrison, my sisters Constance and Barbara, and me, we've managed fourteen marriages and eleven divorces.

Someone once wrote that the Bennetts were like a forest fire; the minute the flames were put out in one spot, they'd pop up in another. In retrospect, a period beginning in 1920 seemed a particularly active time in which the Bennetts were "acting like Bennetts."

The early part of the year no one paid much attention to us—except in the newspapers. In January, Constance's first marriage to a young University of Virginia student, Chester Moorehead, was annulled. The petition charged "both were underage and neither had the consent of their parents," which met the issue all right, if somewhat mildly.

Then Father, who was on a national tour of Andreyev's *He Who Gets Slapped* for the New York Theater Guild, started a running battle with the critics in each city. He'd been doing that for years, of course, but in the final stages of the tour he escalated the war. Once again he aroused enmity among the theater's reviewers, added longer lines at the box office, and reinforced his already sizable reputation for instant controversy. The contribution to his personal satisfaction was enormous.

I don't know what first triggered his violent dislike for

dramatic critics, for he was a brilliant actor who was rarely reviewed with anything but high praise and admiration. Nevertheless, he responded to them with total recoil. Their vigil on opening night was referred to as "The Death Watch," and he wasn't above alluding to their doubtful birth and blighted ancestry, or to quote him more directly, "those bastards!" Frequently they were designated "intellectual pygmies" or "mental degenerates." In his view, the public was the only critic whose opinion was worth a damn.

"I am making an earnest appeal," he said, at the height of his road campaign, "for dramatic criticism that is written by someone who understands the theater. You cannot expect a man to be able to lay out a sewer in the morning and judge a Gainesborough at night, any more than it's possible for him to cover a baseball game in the afternoon and act as a dramatic critic in the evening. But that's what is happening!" And he added, if not quite accurately, "I speak as one who has never received a bad criticism. Those who would be critics should go to school to learn the art. I would not abolish the critic, mind you, I would educate him!"

Thoroughly refreshed from "The Crusades," Father returned to us in New York, and things went along rather smoothly after that, with few dramatic disruptions. One or two little brushfires maybe, but nothing serious. I was about to finish at Miss Hopkins's School for Girls in Manhattan with an eye to attending St. Margaret's in Waterbury, Connecticut, as a boarding student in the fall; Mother closed in Channing Pollock's play, *The Fool,* for the summer; Constance and her new beau, Philip Plant, had gone to neutral corners to wait for the next emotional round.

Meanwhile my sister Barbara, the quiet one, had been diligently studying since the previous year at the famous Denishawn Dancing School in Peterborough, New Hampshire, where Martha Graham was one of the young instructors. Barbara had shown considerable talent for dance, and although she didn't seem particularly driven by ambition for a career, she'd worked very hard at her training. Father thought the rigors and strict discipline of a dancing school wouldn't be amiss, even if Mother wasn't very keen on the idea, and they let Barbara stay at Denishawn until it was time to enroll her in a finishing school in Paris in the fall of 1923.

Mother and Father prepared for a trip to Europe that summer with no premonition of things to come. I was scheduled for summer camp when Miss Hopkins's let out, Barbara was happy and busy at Denishawn, and in June they took Constance to Rome where Father was to do a movie with Lionel Barrymore. During the filming of *The Eternal City,* they were guests at the wedding of Lionel and Irene Fenwick, who had been Father's leading lady more than a dozen years before. It was a restful, tranquil summer until they got home. Nobody could find Barbara. Scheduled to enroll at the school in Paris, she'd taken a ship bound for France as planned, but the Denishawn Dance Company just happened to be aboard on its way to an engagement in England. Instead of going to Bordeaux, she disembarked at Plymouth and went to London as a full-fledged member of the Denishawn company. The eruptions were splendidly Bennett-like, until they finally found her, and she was brought home in disgrace.

Things were reasonably calm after that, and by early September I was conjugating French verbs at St. Margaret's in Connecticut and struggling nearsightedly with the dark evils of mathematics. Most everything else in the way of studies I could manage easily, but math would forever remain an incomprehensible mystery. I remember that later on I had to have special instruction to get through it. With barely fluttering colors, I finally passed the course, but only because the math teacher had a large crush on my matinee-idol father.

On the last day of September, there came a really staggering blow to all of us. Mother and Father separated. Outwardly, it seemed quite an amicable arrangement. Father called it "a little experiment in marital separation due to personality differences." He and Barbara took an apartment on West Fifty-eighth Street and Mother moved to East Fifty-fourth, taking Constance with her. Except for weekends, I stayed at St. Margaret's, heartbroken. When Constance had married Chester Moorehead two years before, she'd taken Mother's wedding ring for the ceremony but when the marriage was annulled, she couldn't get the ring off her finger and had to have it cut off by whatever expert did that kind of thing. To me, cutting that wedding ring somehow became the cause and symbol of my parents' separation. At the age of thirteen, it seemed a patently clear and logical reason.

While Mother had little comment, Father had a lot to say on the subject, mostly to the newspapers. "I left her," he declared, "because I couldn't bear seeing my children do what the children of today are doing; racing around unchaperoned, madly running the pace of the times. After all, a father worries for his children. So, my wife suggested that since it worried me so, I go away and live by myself. It's a wonderful success. When we meet, we're all glad to see each other, and we're all on our good behavior. They are romance to me because I see them less often, and I am a more romantic figure to them because I'm not around the house being unpleasant and fretful." There was more than a hint of anguish behind that brave façade. Asked if a divorce was in the offing, he snorted, "Of course not! Any man would be a damn fool to divorce a woman like Adrienne Morrison!"

The truth of the matter was my long-suffering mother had had enough. There was no single reason that prompted their separation after twenty years, only a gradual erosion of her spirit. Delightful and endearing as he was, living with Richard Bennett was like living with a tidal wave. He was a colossus, a stormy spirit filled with thunder and lightning, brilliantly gifted, proud, vain and intractable, and powerless to be anything else. Nor, as one of the world's most attractive men, could he help his attraction for other women. Overbearing and puritanical about the women in his own family, he exercised no such restrictions for others.

Mother had waited until Constance, Barbara and I were well on the way to young adulthood before she broke up the nest, and when the time came, in her usual gentle way, she simply withdrew and summed it all up in a single quiet comment. "You see, Mr. Bennett is a genius, and geniuses should be segregated."

The Bennett's separation provided a series of headlines for a week. Father called it a "temporary personality difference," the newspapers referred to it as a "six block divorce." At the time, it seemed incomprehensible to me that two people who loved each other as much as my parents did could be separated and still be able to function in the world as though nothing had happened. They dined frequently together and continued to share family problems. Less than three weeks after the break, Father opened in a new play, and Barbara made her Broadway debut in the same production. I was terribly puzzled and confused by it all and didn't realize until later, of course, that beneath Mother's circumspection and Father's bravado, there was a chronic ache.

Despite the surface calm, my sisters weren't immune either. The situation increased Constance's unrest, already at fever heat. Phil Plant was ever present and ever ready for the next skirmish. Their romance was off one day, on the next; they quarreled violently, then had frequent reconciliations. Barbara simply retreated and continued to perfume the world with her innate sweetness, although her occasional youthful protests and abrupt expressions of hostility always seemed surprising. For me, there was nothing left to do but stay in Connecticut at St. Margaret's and keep right on conjugating French verbs.

Their separation now seems a particularly distressing time, aside from the personal unhappiness it brought, for so many elements in their lives conspired to make it a lasting and rewarding relationship. Both were passionately devoted to the theater, both were privileged with gifts of beauty and ability, and they were deeply in love.

Actually, they'd met some years before they finally worked together. At the age of fourteen, during Mother's first season in the theater, she remembered a young actor named Richard Bennett who came backstage to pay his respects to her father, Lewis Morrison. At that point, Grandfather was one of the most successful actor-managers in the American theater, and he'd introduced Mother that season as Juliet in his own touring repertory company. Their backstage visitor, then in his midtwenties, had been engaged in the theater as a juvenile leading man for five or six years, mainly in smaller companies in the Midwest. Their meeting was casual and courteous, and not particularly memorable for either of the Morrisons or the young and handsome Mr. Bennett. The year was 1897.

Neither Father nor the Morrison side of my family may have been aware of it then, but the decade before the turn of the century marked important transitions in the American stage. It brought the death of Edwin Booth, the last significant exponent of the "grand manner" in acting. Also, it introduced the new realistic drama and the "well-made" play, which established the material as supreme over the star performer. Other influences were being felt in the profession with the ascendance of the Frohman dynasty, an enterprise that would transform the American theater and be an important force in the professional lives of my parents.

Early in the eighteen-nineties, the remarkable Frohman brothers, Daniel, Charles and Gustave, had already begun the operations that would make them the world's foremost theatrical magnates. By then nearly all of the old stars were gone or passing from view and Charles Frohman, particularly, realized that along with the passing of those great stars was the passing of the system that had created them. In the previous era, the stars had made themselves, and like my grandfather, Lewis Morrison, had risen from the ranks after years of service. But Frohman believed that the new generation of theatergoers wanted young people, new popular names, someone to talk about. He knew that the strongest aid a play could have was a magnetic personality, and he became one of the theater's first "starmakers." By the late eighteen-nineties his star machine was operating at full capacity. William Gillette and John Drew were under his management, he'd made a star of Maude Adams, and he was seeking new plays for Ethel Barrymore, the brilliant young actress who had enchanted London playgoers a short time before.

Charles Frohman had heard reports of the rising young actor, Richard Bennett, from his brother, Gus. At a time when Charles was looking for a new juvenile leading man for *The Proper Caper* in 1897, Father was committed to another producer, A. L. Erlanger, who agreed to release him for the greater prestige of playing in a Frohman production. The opening of *The Proper Caper* at the Madison Square Theater in New York marked the beginning of Father's association with "C. F.," as Charles was affectionately known, and he remained under that banner for almost seventeen years. At the outset, Father must have known it was a great opportunity for any young actor of the time. Eventually, it was one that cemented his princely position in the American theater.

Once asked for his definition of a leading actor, Frohman had said, "There is a world of actors, but too few leading actors. If, in casting a play, you can find an actor who looks the part you have in mind for him, be thankful. If you can find an actor who can act the part, be very thankful. And if you can find an actor who can both look and act the part, get down on your knees and thank God!"

Soon after joining the Frohman ranks, there was talk in the profession that Richard Bennett was being groomed as John Drew's successor. Though not yet a star, with each succeeding production, it was apparent that he could fill Frohman's description of the ideal actor, and he went from one play to another with little interruption. In January of 1898, Father was playing *The White Heather* with the formidable, imperious Rose Coghlan, and under Frohman's guidance, he went through a series of plays for the next two seasons. It was a day of short runs, very brief when compared to the eight-year engagement of *My Fair Lady*. A run of one-hundred performances was generally considered satisfactory, and a stay of fifty or sixty performances was by no means a calamity.

From *The White Heather,* Father went into *Sweet and Twenty,* starring Annie O'Neill; *His Excellency, the Governor,* whose cast included Mae Robson, Guy Standing, and Frohman's new ingenue, Ethel Barrymore; *Her Atonement* at the Academy of Music; *Twelve Months Later,* a distinct flop; *At the White Horse Tavern,* a huge success. Between appearances in New York he either toured on the road or played stock all summer.

Throughout those early Frohman years, Father showed other facets in his work besides talent and diligent care in his portrayals. It was surpassingly clear that he projected across the footlights a fatal attraction for the ladies. A handsome, virile man with blue-gray eyes, a determined chin, a firm and generous mouth, and a magnificent speaking voice, his good looks were only part of the fascination. Some called it sex appeal, others called it animal magnetism, but whatever the label of that glandular quality $X$, he breathed it out like a hot wind. The female "oh's" and "ah's" trailed him wherever he went, and his matinees were mobbed by flushed, agreeable ladies who fairly quivered in his presence. I must admit, he was often extremely charitable in rewarding their attentions, individually, and the demand was never more than he could supply. Nor were the matinee matrons the only ones who fell under the spell. Teenagers were not at all immune. Not long ago, Jane Wyatt told me that as children, when we rode the same school bus, the girls would argue each morning about who was going to sit next to the Bennett sisters, because their father was "that divine Richard Bennett." As a specialist in matters feminine, Father would always have an embarrassment of riches.

A matinee idol at the turn of the century was defined generally as a good-looking actor who drew a great many impressionable ladies of varying ages to matinee performances. His ability as an actor was not as important as his handsome features, an impeccable wardrobe, and a thrilling voice. If he was shrewd, he developed certain stage mannerisms that became trademarks and could angle his profile at any moment, provided the lighting was right, in a fascinating awareness of his power to charm. Some of the breed could act, some could not. Richard Bennett could and considered acting ability much more important than handsomeness. He hated the label "matinee idol," but like it or not, he was tagged with it for years to come.

In September of 1900, Father was appearing at the Lyceum Theater in *The Royal Family,* starring the petite comedienne, Annie Russell, and included in the cast was Mabel Adrienne Morrison. Since the time they'd met three years before, Mother's career had bloomed in New York, too. Always attracted to beauty and ability, Charles Frohman had found engagements for her in several of his productions. Frohman and my Grandfather Morrison had been acquainted for a number of years, since 1882 when Grandfather appeared as Creon in C. F.'s production of *Oedipus Tyrannus.* It was he who introduced his daughter to the theater's foremost producer. Mother said later, "Fate and Frohman cast me in *The Royal Family."*

From the beginning, Father called her "Mab," and though later she changed her name to Adrienne for professional reasons, he used the abbreviation for Mabel throughout their lifetimes. She was seventeen, Father was twenty-eight, and he wasted no time in turning on his fascinating power to please. Soon it was obvious that Miss Morrison and Mr. Bennett were "keeping company."

I adored my father, but he was the most opinionated of men and almost always turned out to be the hero, both on stage and off. He later wrote in his memoirs, "She was a beautiful creature, vivacious, brilliant, sloe-eyed. They were brown eyes that set you all aglow. Born in the theater and of it, with no small opinion of her ideas, she was much used to being indulged in all things. Abnormally stage-struck, but why shouldn't she be? Her family tree showed a straight line in the theater for four generations. But I soon found out that she had a definite leaning toward the uptown Blue Book. She was much younger than I, and had more strings to her bow than any girl I'd ever met. To be brief, I became the favored escort in her eyes, though why I couldn't make out, for she was socially bent. She was smart—and talk? I could listen to her for hours, watching fire spring into her brown eyes."

It's not very likely that Father ever listened to anybody "for hours." He loved conversation, particularly his own, and had a phenomenal command of the language. Self-educated, he had a lifelong passion and respect for learning and the English language, and his habit of reading everything in sight had been developed in the early lonely years of traveling on the road. Nightly, he dipped into the *Oxford Concise Dictionary* and a thesaurus, both of which he kept by his bedside.

In any case, it's small wonder that he was attracted to Mother's exotic beauty. Despite his view that she was spoiled and indulged, she was a person of extreme gentleness, quiet and soft-spoken, though there were times when the calm reserve could be deadly and when forced to it, she held her ground with steely resolve. As a foil to her energetic suitor, they were invaluable qualities. My mother was also a person of high intelligence, with a wry and delicious sense of humor. Totally endearing and sympathetic to anyone else's troubles, people just naturally gravitated to her all of her life.

Mab introduced Richard to her father at the Lyceum's backstage, one night after a performance of *The Royal*

*Family.* The occasion for showing off onstage was usually reserved for relatives or VIP's, and Father's performance was wildly overacted that evening. Grandfather was restrained and dignified, said nothing about his excesses onstage but courteously complimented him on his performance. Father beamed and laid it on thick. "I'm glad to meet you, Mr. Morrison, though you may not remember me, we've met before. I've always thought of you as one of the great artists of our day, they don't make them like you any more. Go to the theater today and what do you see? A lot of namby-pambies, the spawn of brick-layers and scavengers, all copying the English style. Our poor present-day hams have no insides. But think of being the confrere of Booth, O'Neill, Salvini, Cushman and Jefferson, the giants of the theater! Think of being permitted even to live in their day!"

"Yes," Grandfather replied, and left.

As time went by, Father began to make noises like a possessive male. If, he declared, his relationship with Mab was going to have any meaning or future, then she'd have to give up the theater. There couldn't possibly be two careers going at the same time, there were too many examples in the business of people splitting up over professional differences. Furthermore, she'd shown distressing signs of moving in New York society circles. Father was always terribly scornful of people who were, in his words, "socially bent," and the "infiltrations of socialites with ambitions to elevate the stage" sent him into a rage. "The stage cannot be elevated," he said, "it must be let alone. There is only one aristocracy, and that's talent! Our breed is a helluva lot nobler than anything you'll find in that damn Blue Book!"

Despite his declarations, Mother never had social pretensions. As a young and beautiful actress, she was often invited to social functions which she accepted because they gave her pleasure. With no effort, she made herself extremely popular with the young society set of the time, and Father simply was stung by the competition. He was right in one thing, however; she did have strong ambitions for the theater.

Quietly and reluctantly, she withdrew from his insistent demands to leave the theater and by the time *The Royal Family* closed, the coolness between them was palpable. His other conquests had been far more agreeable and pliable, and angered by the rebuff, he swore vengeance and predicted she'd be sorry. He couldn't wait to get out of town, immediately accepted a road tour of *His Excellency, the Governor* in the early weeks of 1901, and went steaming off in a widening wake of resentment. Father really asked for very little. All he wanted was to have his own way in everything.

# 2

When Mother's rejected suitor left New York to go on tour, he sulked all the way to the Midwest. Determined to forget Mab Morrison, however, by the time he reached San Francisco he was his irrepressible self again. During the run there, he met an adoring seventeen-year-old music student named Grena Heller, and within a week and a half of their meeting they were married. The move, of course, was designed to drown Mab in despair, but there was only indifferent silence from the Morrison camp in the East. She was far too busy in a new Frohman production to give much thought to Richard's antics.

To his surprise and delight, Grena Heller turned out to be a very superior young lady and to his credit, he paid her an affectionate tribute when years later he wrote of their brief life together. "San Francisco . . . I was young, I had a job, I was independent. What madness of romance might not lurk behind this freedom, even the right to choose my own bondage. I did. We played the old Bush Street Theater for three weeks. At the end of ten days I had wooed and married a girl with blue-black hair, beautiful brown eyes and a peach-bloom complexion. Always, she had a sweet, tolerant outlook on life; a noble motherly person, though there was no issue from our union. Our life was uneventful. My road life drifted us apart. I meet her often now, we are good friends and I am beholden to her for much. I still hold in my heart a thankful affection for Grena."

Born in San Francisco, Grena was attending music school when she and Father were married, and although their fleeting marriage brought divorce in 1903, it's obvious there was never ill feeling between them. When they separated, long before the divorce, Grena went to France to continue her musical studies in piano, theory and composition, and returned to the United States in 1905 to take a temporary job as art critic on *The New York American,* later *The Journal-American.* She soon gave preference to her musical background, however, and became the newspaper's music critic, a post she held for forty years, using the professional name of Grena Bennett. She was passionately dedicated to the idea of presenting American singers in American opera houses at a time when only foreign singers seemed to be acceptable to the public, and she used her column as a battering ram.

These things, of course, I didn't know until much later, for Father never mentioned Grena Bennett that I can remember. Years afterward, at a time when I was returning home from Europe in 1927, she introduced herself to me on shipboard and said, "I once was married to your father." I remember it as a slightly awkward moment, and thought it curious that this smiling and pleasant middle-aged woman, a total stranger to me, had been an important, if brief, part of my father's life.

In November of 1902, Father went into a play called *Imprudence* with Mae Robson, Annie Adams (in his words, "Maude's Ma"), and William Faversham, one of the great leading men in the Frohman stable. Father remembered that as a particularly compatible company. Behind the backstage banter, however, he was greatly annoyed that Mab Morrison was not in New York that season. She was out on tour with her father's company of *Faust* in the role of Marguerite, but he went to see her older sister, Rosabel, who was starring in

New York in *The Deserted Bride* and thought her "a first-rate actress."

By the late spring of 1903, Mother and Grandfather had returned from the road tour, and the family congregated at Morrison Manor, Grandfather's summer home in Peekskill, New York. Mother's nineteen-year-old brother, Victor Jago, came up from his studies at Princeton and spent much of the time playing chess with his father. Uncle Victor never had much to say about his youth, except that he and Grandfather never got on well together. He lightly laid it to the fact that "I always beat the old man at chess!" Underneath was the truth that, except for Rosabel, Mother and Victor had had a lonely childhood in what amounted to a motherless home. The long separations enforced by the profession, their parents' divorce, and a stepmother for whom they had little affection, all contributed to the loneliness and friction. Uncle Victor was absolutely determined to have no part of a profession that inspired so much unhappiness. In 1905 he joined the United States Marine Corps in which he had a long and distinguished career.

Early that summer, Father invited himself to Morrison Manor. Bravely, he took the train to Peekskill, hired a horse-drawn rig at the station and drove the dirt road to the house, grimly determined to pay court whether Mab liked it or not. Mother, with perfect, unruffled calm, greeted him on the veranda, and her father shook his hand and "seemed the perfect center of that perfect house, courteous, restrained in every gesture."

In the garden, Richard made amends and the result of their meeting in that flowery setting was a reconciliation. He seemed not quite so intractable about her theatrical career and she, too, promised some concessions. Besides, who could resist the irresistible? Previous differences vanished and they announced their engagement that afternoon. Earlier in the year his divorce from Grena Bennett had been set in motion, and they had only to wait until he was legally free.

In the meantime, he was committed for a season of stock in Chicago for the summer, and reluctantly he left Mab at Morrison Manor.

In late September, he returned to New York for a play with a Boer War setting, *The Best of Friends,* with Lionel Barrymore playing the role of his father, although Lionel was six years younger than he. Father recalled, "He portrayed an old war general with an elaborate makeup and two pounds of crepe hair. Every time I gave him a cue he was in a different spot onstage, picking crepe hair out of his eyes, nose and mouth, swearing loud enough to be heard by all present, though the audience thought it was part of his character. Those false eyebrows and whiskers began to diminish and by the end of the run, Lionel was wearing a chin-piece only. It hurt his performance; without the whiskers he picked up all his cues on time, and left out the profanity."

During the run, Father's legal obstacles were cleared away and he and Mother were married November 8, 1903. His schedule allowed no time for elaborate plans and the wedding was a brief ceremony in Jersey City, New Jersey.

After they'd settled into an apartment in Manhattan, Father opened on December twenty-ninth in *The Other Girl,* with Lionel Barrymore and Elsie de Wolfe, the future Lady Mendl. It was so successful that Frohman was prompted to organize a long road tour, beginning in March. By then, Mother had had enough enforced inactivity and accepted a part in *Miss Hobbs,* a comedy starring Annie Russell. Father erupted like a volcano. Mother stood her ground. He reasoned, threatened, thundered, and did his best, which was very good indeed, to dissuade her. It was their first, but by no means last, battle royal. At the height of the conflict, Grandfather Morrison arrived and Father turned on him with language more forceful than refined. First he invited him to keep his oar out, then recited a long list of his wife's childhood grievances, accused him of substituting affluence for love, and enlarged on his unfitness as a parent, all of which ended with, "Take your daughter home and help her to a career, which seems to be her greatest desire! I'm through!"

If Father was through, Grandfather was not. For once in his life, he forgot he was a proper Victorian and punched his son-in-law squarely in the nose. The drawing of blood brought instant remorse from all three and they fell weeping into each other's arms. That emotional climax, however, did nothing to solve the problem. Father remained grim, Mother signed the contract for *Miss Hobbs,* and Grandfather went back to *Faust,* which was playing Brooklyn. Finally they agreed that Mother would accompany Father on tour for three weeks before she was due in New York for her first rehearsals. "I loved her then," Father wrote later, "would always love her no matter what she did. I do to this day, after a thousand battles lost and a thousand battles won. Yet I well know she was the devil's own when she released her temper, and no one knew when that would be or what would cause it!"

His road tour opened in Baltimore and in the middle of the first week, Elsie de Wolfe was stricken with bronchitis, too sick to play the following performance. With no understudy, the play was in trouble. Mother rushed to the rescue and offered to take over the part until Miss de Wolfe's recovery. Father was thrown into a dilemma between upholding the traditions of the theater and upholding his masculine pride. Privately, he phoned Frohman in New York and asked him if Mother could substitute for the ailing leading lady, and C. F. said it would be fine if she could get up in the part in time, but to Mother he reported that Mr. Frohman was in Boston and couldn't be reached. With time running out, he told her, perhaps they'd have to cancel after all until Elsie was better. Within an hour, Bob Everley, the stage manager, rushed in with a telegram from Frohman that read:

That did it. Mother swept out of the hotel and into the theater to start work with the stage manager for the evening's ordeal, taking her luggage and leaving Father with a backward look, which he described as "cold and hostile as a diamond-back rattler's."

She spent the entire day studying feverishly and going over the stage positions with the cast, while Father took refuge in the nearest saloon for most of the afternoon. Eventually he steered an unsteady course for the theater, lurched into his dressing room, and fell sound asleep on the floor. When he was roused by the half-hour warning call, he found a note on his dressing table. "I looked in your dressing room. There is a drunk on the floor. I hope he doesn't disgrace himself."

The difficulty of playing a two-hour performance under those circumstances can only be imagined. Playgoers that night were treated to the sight of a hungover leading man and a distraught, pinch-hitting leading lady who both adored and hated each other and played beautiful love scenes together with no signs of domestic conflict. Somehow, a lifetime later, the curtain fell on the final act and they stood together, hand in hand at the curtain calls, bowing and smiling graciously upon Baltimore's citizens while hissing ugly little phrases at each other through clenched teeth.

Fortunately, the agony was not prolonged. Elsie de Wolfe recovered enough to play the following night, as sometimes actresses will do when an understudy appears, and Mother left Baltimore on the next train headed for New York and rehearsals for *Miss Hobbs*.

Philadelphia . . . Cleveland . . . Chicago, and then he called her in Peekskill. She said sweetly, "All I ask is that you stay away from me. I won't grieve if it's forever," and hung up. Omaha . . . San Francisco . . . Los Angeles . . . Denver. Like a small boy he bought *The New York Times* just to see her name in the theater ads. All through the season, he tried to make peace with her, himself, and a profession that would pit a wife against her husband. Although as time went by he learned to live with it, he never really got used to the idea of her having a career, though perversely, he was terribly proud of her successes. To him, a woman's place was in the home; he was very old-fashioned about that. Perhaps, he thought, the Elizabethan theater had the right idea after all. No women in the theater! (Except out front on matinee day.)

After the run of *Miss Hobbs,* which ended early in June, Mother went to Peekskill to rest for the summer, alternating between dread and joy; she was pregnant. She let the months go by without telling him, still stung by his repeated objections to her acting career, and disquieted by the all too frequent reports of his increasing drinking habits. Yet it was almost impossible to resist him and the reams of lyric poetry he sent her along the way. Already having begun the pattern she would follow for years, she succumbed, and Father came racing as soon as the tour ended, wild with joy, puffed with pride, and at the same time sobered by his new responsibilities.

The baby was born in New York City, October 22, 1904, although even as I write this, I know she'd never quite forgive me for noting the exact date. They named her Constance Campbell Bennett, a namesake of Sarah Campbell's, a long-ago strolling player who was our great-grandmother. Constance was born in the middle of a thunderstorm and later said it was prophetic, the first signal of a stormy life.

Father worshipped the traditions of the family and loved the role of parent best of all. He worried, fretted, stormed, bragged and made loud father noises all of his life. He adored all of us, and with each one, fatherhood reduced him to a tower of gelatin. Although he hated being thought sentimental, he wasn't above recording his sentiments when

Constance was born, and I know he expected them to be seen by other eyes than his. "I sneaked over to the bassinette. There she lay, yelling her lungs out. She seemed to me at that moment to be mostly voice and little pink fists. I remember hearing someone say that a baby who keeps its fists closed will turn out to be a good fighter. There's a lot to those old sayings! I stood there looking at my daughter and felt a strange mixture of happiness and loneliness. Here was something tiny that must be trained and molded into understanding, tolerance, yet free as sunshine and rain. To have, to hold, to let go, that was my job at any sacrifice and at any cost. Of one thing I was certain; I had another responsibility, a creation of my own, something that really belonged to Mab and me. It was wonderful."

By the fall of the next year, 1905, Mother was heading for one of the biggest successes of the season and of her career. Over Father's objections, though not quite so strenuous as before, Charles Frohman chose her to play the leading role of the Indian girl in Edwin Milton Royle's *The Squaw Man,* a melodrama of the Wyoming frontier. At one time Royle had been an acting colleague of Edwin Booth's, and he and C. F. selected a distinguished cast headed by William Faversham. Also among its members, the cast listed Theodore Roberts, George Fawcett, Selena Royle (the author's daughter), and Mitchell Lewis. The play opened October 23, 1905, and was a solid hit. Edwin Royle was lauded for his natural, realistic writing, Faversham for his surprisingly powerful acting, and Mother for her beauty and sensitive portrayal of the courageous Indian girl. *The Squaw Man* settled in for a long run at Wallack's Theater.

Father, though somewhat nettled by the competition and the thought that Mother would be devoting less time to him and Constance, was proud of her reviews nonetheless. She neglected neither of them, of course, since her hours at the theater were exactly the same as his, and their theaters only a few blocks apart.

A month after Mother's big success, Father was in his own when he opened at the Lyceum in a delightful comedy by Charles Klein, *The Lion and the Mouse*. Two hits in the family, three with Constance, was enough to bring their differences to a halt and serenity came once more to the Bennetts. It was so serene that Mother discovered she was pregnant again. Actors George Fawcett and Theodore Roberts, who, in one scene, carried her offstage each night in *The Squaw Man*, noted that she got a little heavier as the weeks passed. It was obvious she could no longer play the Indian maiden, and she withdrew from the play.

An expanding family needed room to expand in and they began looking for a suitable house. Eventually, they found it in Palisades, New Jersey, just across the Hudson River from Manhattan. The house needed some attention before they could move into it, and Father was in his element there. In whatever spare time he had available he arranged and rearranged, puttered and fumed and had a grand time redoing the place, while Mother followed behind him, quietly and tastefully putting things back in order. Within two months their preparations came to a halt, however, with the news that Father was to be sent to England for the London opening of *The Lion and the Mouse*. That meant decorating plans had to be suspended, and of course, the new baby would be born in England, but it was too good an opportunity to refuse, since a London success meant new prestige for any actor whose star was rising.

Producer Oliver Morosco, who'd borrowed Father from Frohman, began to prepare for the opening in May at the Duke of York Theater. Everyone was supremely confident of repeating the New York success and Father, counting on a long run, leased a house in St. John's Wood for a year and bundled the family onto the *S. S. Baltic*. Constance made a great hit on the way over by taking her first steps and learning to walk on the rolling decks of the ship.

May 22, 1906, *The Lion and the Mouse* was first introduced to London audiences. They didn't give a damn. Although Father made a great impression in the role of Jefferson Ryder and the rest of the company was lauded for its skill, the box office drooped and the play closed after a five-week run. Almost before they knew it, the Bennetts were packing up to go home.

Father didn't brood long over the London failure, for there were too many prospects to distract him when the family returned home. The new baby was due in a month, the new house still needed attention before they could move in, and C. F. would have a new play for him.

His arrangement with Frohman at the time was a flexible one in some ways, and not at all in others. His contract allowed him to work for other producers when there was no place for him in the "home" productions, but Frohman only granted permission for the loan-out when he thought the part was right for his actor. Although a quiet, gentle man, he was the supreme dictator in his own organization and guided his charges with the power of a benevolent despot. They obeyed because he had an uncanny theatrical sense of what was right. In the Frohman productions an actor, particularly a supporting actor, was assigned to a role; it wasn't offered to him.

When Father returned from England there were two manuscripts waiting for him. One was *The Judge and the Jury,* the other *The Hypocrites,* by the English author Henry Arthur Jones. He disliked both of them, considered them only secondary parts, and not enough of a challenge to his capabilities. He wrote to a friend on the production staff, "I'm afraid C. F. has no confidence in me." Of the two submitted, the part in the Jones play was the least distasteful, but the other was bad from a dozen points of his view. He decided to make a stand, and exchanged the following correspondence with Charles Frohman.

July 28, 1906

My Dear Gov,

I would not care to play either of the parts Mr. Seymour submitted, they are unpleasant and insincere. I suppose this will mean the forfeiture of my contract, but I would *pre-*

*fer that* to playing parts in which I cannot do myself justice. I do not want to give offense and hope you will understand my import. Perhaps I am too ambitious but I prefer to stand or fall by my own judgment in this matter. Thanking you very kindly for past favors, I am

> Very truly,
> Richard Bennett

July 28, 1906

Richard Bennett, Esq.
Lyceum Theater
Dear Sir:—
I have no intention of releasing you from your contract. My idea in making contracts is to have my artists keep them, the same as they expect from me. My only purpose in giving you your choice of the two parts was that I know they both stand out and I wanted to give you an opportunity of choosing the one you liked best; this I do not usually do.

> Yours very truly,
> C. F.

Father went into rehearsals the first of August for *The Hypocrites,* just a week after moving into the new home, and it was none too soon. Mother was very close to the birth of her second child.

My sister, Barbara Jane, was born in the Palisades house on August 13, 1906. Father pronounced her "an absolutely perfect specimen of femininity, eyes like her mother's and heartbreakingly beautiful. I thought for awhile there was something wrong with her because she almost never cried, but I guess I was just used to Constance." He took great delight in telling everyone that she'd been delivered by Dr. Victor Pedersen, America's leading authority on contraception. "Unless you can turn them out like I do," he said, "put that name down where you can find it!"

For Mother, the time of her great happiness in Barbara's birth would also be one of the deepest sorrow. Her father died five days later in Yonkers, New York.

On the opening night of his new play, August 30, 1906, Father was in a terrible state. He hated the role of the juvenile, Lennard Wilmore, and predicted instant failure for himself and the play. He worried about Mother and the deep effect of her father's death, news which he'd kept from her until she'd recovered from Barbara's birth. His father-in-law was dead, and in spite of their melodramatic scene two years before, he'd felt real affection for him. All told, opening a new play was going to be an ordeal. Doris Keane, his leading lady, doped him with coffee and smelling salts, while he doped himself from the bottle under his dressing table.

It was a wildly enthusiastic opening night. The next morning, Father was painfully aware of his poor judgment and had to admit that Frohman had been right again. *The New York Mail* called it "a biting satire," and noted:

> Richard Bennett rises to stellar heights. There are subtleties in the character that demand higher art and he is fully equal to the task, never failing to draw the lines truly.

C. F. quietly gave him costar billing with his leading lady for the first time.

*The Hypocrites* ran solidly into February of 1907, a handsome run for the period, six months, with a road tour planned for August. For the tour, Frohman agreed to let him play the role of the vicar, Henry Linnell, which was a more interesting part than the juvenile he'd played before. However, there were ominous signs of new complications. "Mrs. Bennett," he told a friend, "is beginning to feel an urge to elevate the stage."

C. F. was delighted to know Mother was available again and immediately offered her the Doris Keane part for the run of the tour. Father gave a fleeting thought to homicide.

August thirty-first, Mother and Father began the tour at the Powers Theater in New York, then traveled until the Christmas Holidays, accompanied by Constance, Barbara and a nurse. Domestically, it was something less than idyllic. Father had become possessed with the idea that he was a greatly misunderstood, downtrodden husband, deprived of every vestige of respect and the solely male right to provide for his family. He even entertained the thought that Mab was poisoning the minds of his children against him, quite certain he could "see it in their eyes." It didn't matter that Constance wasn't quite three and Barbara was just a year old, he could see it anyway. In any case, he thought, it wasn't right to turn his children against him. It was more apparent every day, not so much in Barbara, but in Constance. "Why, she twists out of my embrace and skids away with the affection of a cockroach!" he told Mother.

His imagined injuries merely stemmed from the natures of his two daughters; Barbara a quiet introvert and Constance, even then, a conniving and delightful tomboy who created battles for the pure joy of fighting her way out of them. She'd given them quite a time during the period when she learned to talk, by absolutely refusing to do so. She laughed, mumbled, yelled and cried, but wouldn't utter a single intelligible word. Father spent a great many apoplectic hours trying to get her to say something—anything! But she wouldn't. She waited until she got damned good and ready, then astounded everyone with a ringing, flawless rendition of *Twinkle, Twinkle, Little Star*. From then on, he couldn't shut her up.

The Bennetts returned from touring in *The Hypocrites* during the final week of 1907, and Mother involved herself in settling Constance and Barbara into a less eventful routine in Palisades, while Father extracted a promise from her that she wouldn't think of "elevating the stage," at least for awhile. Since it hadn't been an altogether tranquil tour, she agreed, in order to keep the peace, and accepted no engagements for the entire year of 1908.

Until September of that year, Father was engaged in a series of distinct failures. In January, he opened at the Savoy Theater in *Twenty Days in the Shade*, undistinguished except for Pauline Frederick; then there were *Going Some*, not distinguished by anything, and *Diana of Dobsons,* which was never mentioned in the house. He occupied himself with all kinds of activities outside the theater to keep from brooding over his run of bad luck. He gardened, wrote poetry, and because aerial ballooning was a popular pastime at the moment, took it up with a vengeance. Once, drifting over the countryside near Palisades, New Jersey, the balloon suddenly descended and the trailing ropes of the carriage struck an electric high-wire. The balloon crashed on the property that neighbored the Bennetts's, strewing debris all over the area. Luckily, Father and his copilot walked away from the crash with only a few minor bruises and a couple of damaged egos, but it caused great commotion and attracted an anxious crowd, the police, an ambulance and a newspaper reporter. Mother came rushing frantically to the scene at a moment when Father was just congratulating himself on having escaped an untimely death. At the sight of him standing there in one piece amid the wreckage, she marched up to him, said, "Well, you've certainly made a spectacle of yourself!" and left.

Life was seldom dull. He started home one night from the theater lugging a box of baby barley that Mother needed for a special formula. To get to Palisades from the theater district, he went first by streetcar, then by ferry across the Hudson River. Always on those late night journeys, he carried a gun. He was crazy about firearms and carried them around with masculine arrogance, insisting that there was not an unremote possibility of being robbed. Also, they were used on occasion as effective props for his personal melodramatics. In any case, the streetcar stopped a block short of the Hudson River Ferry, which had rung the first warning bell for departure. A milk wagon had broken down in the streetcar's path and the passengers joined in an effort to push the wagon off the car rails. In his eagerness to help, Father fell over the milkman, scattering milk bottles and baby barley in every direction, while the gun fell out of his pocket and clattered across the pavement. He picked it up and turned to confront the milkman who, mistaking his motives, threw a bottle of milk at him which missed, broke with a crash and splattered an innocent citizen standing nearby. The fight was on, with all three of them engaged in a first-rate swinging match. The ferry departed. The police arrived. In short order, they were taken to the nearest jail and booked for disturbing the peace, conspiring against the public welfare, willful destruction of property, and resisting an officer of the law. Father was given an added demerit for carrying a gun without a license.

The cells that night were already filled to capacity, so the battling trio was allowed to sit in the sergeant's duty room where they played pinochle all night and ended as the best of friends. The next morning, they banded together against the law, refused to give any information or accuse one another, and the charges were dropped. Fortunately the judge was a theatergoer who recognized Father and made arrangements to issue him a gun license. By then, of course, a good deal of time had elapsed and Father's first act after he was released that morning was to call Mother, who he knew would be frantic with worry.

"Where have you been?" she demanded.

"In jail."

"What for?"

"Disturbing the peace, destroying property, resisting arrest, and carrying a gun without a license."

"Oh, thank God," she replied, "I thought you were with another woman!"

Chafing under the monotony of a string of bad plays, Father frequently found diversion in the delightful company of John and Lionel Barrymore, at a time when the brothers shared a dormer apartment in the Carnegie Hall Building. The apartment had a long, narrow trunk room that ran its length and was used for dumping everything from old programs to old razor blades, and old laundry which neither Barrymore remembered to send out to be washed. If one needed a clean shirt, he bought it, and the pile in the trunk room grew daily. Father's bulldog, Romeo, who was devoted to Lionel, one day rummaged through the pile and reduced it to shreds, thereby solving the laundry problem.

One of the more colorful features of the Barrymore's apartment was a timeworn bathtub that, from the look of it, had been used for everything in the world except bathing. Frequently it was used as a sort of repulsive refrigerator for milk, beer and soft drinks. One evening Lionel decided the time had come for the luxury of a proper bath instead of his usual shower, but Father and John, in a splendid gesture toward hygiene, urged him to paint it first and they came up with an old can of quick-drying enamel from the trunk room. Under Romeo's supervision, Lionel painted away at the bathtub, and charmed with the idea of restoring it to a pristine loveliness, he gave it a second coat for good measure. Several hours passed quickly with the help of a generous supply of brandy, and then John and Father heard the not unmusical sounds of running water and Lionel's baritone, followed by a contented silence. Suddenly, an unearthly shriek issued from the bathroom. Interrupted with a glass in midair, the other two rushed in to find Lionel covered with great patches of white enamel, frantically trying to peel them off various parts of his anatomy, and yelling like a banshee. All three set to with a will. They rubbed, scraped and pulled, but came away with little but Lionel's hide, which was beginning to look like Romeo's dinner. Then Father had the brilliant idea of soaking the enamel in brandy, so they tried that, lacing a few carefully chosen spots from time to time, and swilling a great deal in between. John decided it was just a waste of bad brandy and declared that turpentine was the only answer. There was an old tin of it in the trunk room and why not try? By this time, Lionel was willing to try anything. Mr. Bennett agreed it was the only solution and helpfully poured the whole tin of turpentine over the enameled Mr. Barrymore. Lionel fainted and was out of his current play for a week, swathed in cotton and linseed oil.

By the late fall of 1908, Father was approaching what would be a conspicuous milestone in his career. Increasingly discouraged by a running streak of bad plays, from time to time he appealed to Charles Frohman to rescue him. C. F. not only rescued him, but gave him a role that catapulted him to stardom opposite one of the theater's most lustrous and enchanting figures.

*What Every Woman Knows* had come from James Barrie's graceful pen expressly for the incomparable Maude Adams, who was at the zenith of her remarkable career. One of the most revered of actresses, she'd already made herself an idol with the American public in three previous Barrie plays: *The Little Minister, Alice Sit by the Fire* and the immortal *Peter Pan.* The public's affection for her developed into an exalted love affair, without precedent.

Maude Adams cared for nothing in the world but the theater, and at the end of her long career she could take pride in the extraordinary fact that she'd never missed a single performance. C. F. was a firm believer in wrapping his female stars in veils of mystery and that, plus her own inherent shyness, built around her a legend of elfin elusiveness. Both her talents and her legends made her the best box-office attraction in the country. To work with Miss Adams, of course, meant great prestige for any actor, and Charles Frohman gave Father that opportunity when he handed him the plum role of John Shand in *What Every Woman Knows,* a part originated in London by Gerald du Maurier.

Rehearsals were called early in October, but the first few days lost their splendor because Miss Adams was absent. The Frohman company worked through the fourth day of rehearsals, when, at last, the star arrived, led into the theater on the arm of the producer. Spontaneously, the company rose to a man and applauded and even the stage and house crews came forward to greet her. The men nearly knocked her down helping her off with her wrap, a long old-fashioned brown coat, frayed at the edges, which she always wore to rehearsals as a good luck charm. She shook hands all around and said simply, "You make me so happy." Father didn't know how the others felt, they were British, and a number of them had played in the London company, but he was moved to write later, "It was thrilling . . . a small-town Hoosier country boy, now the leading man of Maude Adams, the most distinguished position I had ever held in the theater."

During rehearsals, symptoms of the famous Bennett temperament began to manifest themselves. One day Charles Frohman sat out in front watching a rehearsal as two actors went calmly through a scene, while offstage, in a dark corner, Father thumbed frantically through his manuscript. With an approaching entrance cue, he'd suddenly lost his place. The cue came and went, there was a pause and finally the director, dripping with sarcasm, asked if Mr. Bennett perhaps had lost his vocal powers altogether. Our hero jumped to his feet and pitched the manuscript clear across the footlights, missing his target by a hair. The director glowered, Maude Adams laughed, and Frohman merely grinned and cautioned him not to damage the manuscript, at least until he'd learned the part. Father admitted later that was exactly the way to handle temperament, and rehearsals proceeded on a calmer note.

For many years the role of John Shand remained Father's favorite and I think he felt it was a part challenging enough even for his craving. He worked very hard on the Scottish accent the part required, particularly after Frohman accused him of vacillating between a lower-class accent and an educated one. It had to be a combination of both and still have clarity for the listener, and he solved it by a singular device. First he went to the Brooklyn waterfront and found a Scottish longshoreman with a sizable thirst, apparently an easy assignment, then he got him drunk and listened by the hour to the slurring results. In rehearsing it himself, Father discovered that the Scottish dialect was produced by an imaginary block, or glottal stop, in the throat. He modified that by seeking the company of David Torrence, a Scottish actor in the company who'd attended the University of Edinburgh, and engaged him in endless conversation on long walks. Torrence wearied of such talkative meetings, and no doubt wondered at the sudden interest in what he had to say, but unknown to him, Father was soaking up his educated "burr" for the character of John Shand. The result produced a perfectly authentic accent and, afterward, many playgoers were convinced that he was a native Scot instead of a Hoosier from Bennett's Switch.

*What Every Woman Knows* was a stunning success. The day before its New York premiere at the Empire Theater, Richard Bennett had been eclipsed by Maude Adams, but the day after, he was sharing top honors with the beloved star in one of the most triumphal hits in a decade. At the final curtain of the first performance on December 23, 1908, the company took seventeen curtain calls. Critics unanimously heaped superlatives on the play and its players. Father was described as "an actor of the very finest intelligence," and his John Shand as "a rare achievement."

Professionally, it was wholly gratifying for Father, and in recalling the time later, he wrote,

Everything conspired to make my two years with Maude Adams the most rewarding to me. In the first place, there is only one James Barrie, and even he is not likely to write a second play in a lifetime to match *What Every Woman Knows.* It is his monument.

Then, the association with Miss Adams meant more than I can say. People who have never worked with her don't know what an inspiration and a sustaining force she is. She invigorates her fellow actors and the effect of her power is felt. She is severe with her colleagues, but also with herself. One can't be associated with such a big, clean, wholesome life without deriving some benefit from it.

After the first season, the Empire closed for the summer hiatus and Father went to San Francisco and Los Angeles for a season with the Morosco Stock Company, where he played with Charles Ruggles, Fay Bainter, then just beginning her career, and an assistant electrician who played small parts, Harold Lloyd. Barrie's play was due to reopen its fall season of 1909 in October; then, after a few weeks in New York, it was scheduled for a long road tour and Father hurried back from California just in time to make the brushup rehearsals. When he returned, he was in high spirits, looking forward to another season with Miss Adams and delighted to be with his family again. Both Mother and Father were preoccupied at that time; he was acting, she was pregnant.

It was absolutely first-rate news for Father. At last, he thought, a son, an image and perpetuation of himself. Constance and Barbara, of course, were perfectly divine children; exceptional in every way, brilliant, remarkably beautiful, although Constance was a trifle assertive and pleasure-loving, perhaps, and Barbara somewhat introverted. But a son! Mother also agreed that a boy would be nice, though she didn't really care as long as the baby was healthy. They even agreed on the name of John in connection with his role of John Shand in the current hit. Father's pleasure in the tour was diminished somewhat, however, for it meant he'd be away when John was expected in February of the following year of 1910.

Their calculation turned out to be a trifle premature. I was born in February as expected, the twenty-seventh, but I wasn't at all what they'd anticipated. Like Barbara, I was also born in the house in Palisades, New Jersey, and as a child, I was convinced she and I had entered the world at the same time simply because we were born in the same bed. It didn't matter that she was four years older than I, that's what *I* thought anyway, and I clung to the idea for a long time.

Father left the company in Bangor, Maine, on his day off, a Sunday, and hurried home to be with Mother. So the day wouldn't be a total loss, my birth was induced to coincide with his trip home, which proves that actresses are among the most accommodating people on earth. I guess I was forgiven for emerging as a female since father declared later I was "a rosebud blooming in the sun and it was love at first sight." As for my name, Maude Adams's Scottish-accented pronunciation of "John" was very close to "Joan" and the matter was settled in that way. For the record, it's Joan Geraldine, a namesake for the Bennetts's lawyer, Gerald Stalter. Father left immediately for the Chicago opening and from there was bound for the West Coast, so we didn't meet again for five months.

Everywhere it played, *What Every Woman Knows* met the same thunderous welcome. From then on, Father was everybody's favorite juvenile, the fair-haired boy, and he rode the crest of popularity for years. As his own star rose, however, his disenchantment with Maude Adams began to rise toward the end of the tour, while his self-regard remained undamaged. When introduced once as Miss Adams's leading man, he replied, "I beg your pardon, sir, I am not Miss Adams's leading man, I am her costar!" Which, indeed, he was. Privately, he referred to her as "a very much over-rated actress." Which, indeed, she was not.

His irritations stemmed from the fact that, as a perfectionist, she never stopped fiddling with the play or the performances, which resulted in a state of constant change. Although Father wasn't at all above making improvements, he would have preferred to "freeze" the show to avoid inconsistencies in the playing. Miss Adams would never speak to him directly about what she wanted or what bothered her, but instead went quietly to Frohman and wondered if "Mr. Bennett would mind trying" this or that. Frohman passed the requests on to the director, who gave them to the stage manager, who in turn gave them to Father. Although he always complied, it brought him close to the bursting point. What nettled him even more was that Miss Adams declined to play a third season. The play could have run a dozen seasons, but she'd had enough of the role of Maggie Wylie, and although Father hated giving up his beloved John Shand, he wouldn't play it with anyone else.

Despite his disappointment, he always carried the highest regard for Maude Adams as a professional artist. Personally, it was another matter. He never hesitated to show his irreverance for even the most distinguished figures, in or out of the theater, and one of his favorite indoor sports was shattering idols.

After *What Every Woman Knows,* Miss Adams appeared in Edmond Rostand's symbolic French drama, *Chantecler.* Originally written for the great French actor, Coquelin, Frohman had bought it as a vehicle for Otis Skinner, and there was a hint that he was considering Richard Bennett for it if Skinner refused. But Maude Adams liked the play and Frohman agreed to give it to her. A satire on society, *Chantecler's* characters were barnyard animals, and she assumed the male feathers and strut of the title role. On her opening night in January of 1911, Father sent her what became one of the most famous greetings in theatrical history.

I CONGRATULATE YOU ON THE REALIZATION OF YOUR FONDEST AMBITION. AT LAST YOU ARE YOUR OWN LEADING MAN.

# 3

As I look back on our childhood I know, of course, it was governed and influenced by the theater from the very beginning. We learned the theater's parlance when we learned to speak and we knew almost no one other than theatrical people, for by its very nature it is an insular profession. Sometimes we were without one parent or the other, sometimes they were both absent on tour, and during those periods, there was a good friend of Mother's who came to stay with us, an actress and writer named Norma Mitchell. Louise Closser Hale, a fine actress and another family friend who lived nearby, also came to visit from time to time when our parents were on the road. Always, there was a governess or housekeeper to look after our daily needs, and once there was even an English "nanny" when they were fashionable. Father thought it ridiculous and accused Mother of coddling us, but she was determined to see we had at least some social graces, even if it killed him. I was a mother's girl and always threw a fit when she left for a tour, and though I loved Father, too, he scared the life out of me.

Frequently we were taken on tour with them, which was always a delight to us, although the chief problem for Mother was our education. It was an easy matter to find a governess to travel with us but the question of piano lessons posed a problem when the company remained only a week, or less, in each city. She solved the difficulty by traveling with a dummy piano keyboard which had the further advantage of allowing us to practice silently without disturbing other guests in the hotels, which must have been a positive blessing.

The Bennett troupe often traveled by car. We smuggled our pets into the back seat, which held a weird assortment of luggage, baskets of kittens, a bird cage, a turtle and once, a bowl of goldfish. Father gave an absolute "No!" when it came to my fish, but after a big fuss he finally relented. (I could cry on cue in those days.) In any case, I was fiddling with the lid Father had improvised for the fishbowl, when the car gave a sudden lurch, most of the water splashed out and took the goldfish with it. They flopped frantically all over the back seat. Father brought the car to a screeching halt, stuffed the fish back into the bowl and presented them to an astonished housewife at the nearest farm.

Quite often, even as very small children, we were taken to the theater to watch either performances or rehearsals, as long as we stayed on our good behavior. After *What Every Woman Knows,* Father did a play called *The Brass Bottle* in the fall of 1910, an English fantasy in which he played a young man who bought an antique vase, complete with its own magical genie. Thinking it would amuse six-year-old Constance, he took her to a dress rehearsal at the Lyceum Theater one day on the promise that she maintain absolute silence, particularly since Mr. Frohman himself would be present. The rehearsal went along without a hitch, up to a point where the genie, played by actor Edwin Stevens, made his first entrance through a puff of smoke. Apparently, he was an altogether too genteel spirit for an expert in magical matters. Bursting with righteous indignation, Constance rose from her box seat and in a tone better suited to Yankee Stadium, declared, "That's no genie!" The company froze into a group of living statues and even Father was rendered speechless, but Charles Frohman smiled, walked over to the box, and said, "And why isn't he?" Warming to her subject, she told him what most everyone knew, that genies were rough, terribly unpleasant, and had claws and long teeth. Some of them were good and some were bad, but all of them were extremely ugly. It was the very first thing one noticed about them. C. F. had to admit that his personal knowledge of genies was somewhat limited, and asked if she had a suggestion. Of course, she had. To look like a real genie, he would have to be a lot uglier.

The rehearsal continued without further interruption from my sister, the six-year-old critic, and later Frohman did make some changes in the genie's costume and makeup. After the final scene, he told Constance he thought she should be paid for her help as a technical advisor, and said he'd give her a dollar for each year of her life. "How old are you?" he asked. "Seven!" she lied easily. The next week there was a pay envelope at the theater with her name on it containing seven dollars. It was the only time in her life, to my knowledge, that Constance advanced her age rather than subtracted from it.

But even with my sister's help as the youngest salaried director in the theater, *The Brass Bottle* was a failure. Father's name went up on the marquee as the star, and came right back down again. The scenery went to Cain's Warehouse, a kind of scenic graveyard for flops, and "going to Cain's" was a synonym for a play's closing. The single virtue of the production was in introducing to the American public a talented young actress named Irene Fenwick, the future Mrs. Lionel Barrymore.

Constance's first forays into the theatrical world had no effect whatever at the time. Only later did her theatrical ambitions take hold when, at the age of ten, she suffered her first attack of stage fever. It was a time of great anxiety for Mother, who resisted all of her supplications to appear before the footlights. Her principal argument was based on the logical reasoning that she could apply herself more diligently to her lessons in the afternoon, if allowed to perform at night.

When that took no effect, she cast around for a more com-
pelling argument and came up with a capital idea. She
wrote a letter on Hotel Ansonia stationery, where we were
staying at the time, and sent it to herself.

Dear Miss Bennett—
Won't you come over to the Liberty theater and try a
new leading part, and I wouldn't get any Body else. We
have a Starr part for you called the Kidnaped Child it is
a great part and just your tipe. Please come if your Mother
will let you—

Yours verry truly
Douglas FairBanks

Douglas Fairbanks, Sr., wasn't an especially ideal choice
of conspirators. After a few successful Broadway appearances,
he'd gone to Hollywood to play his first small part in movies
for D. W. Griffith, and it wasn't altogether likely that he'd
carried away a supply of Ansonia Hotel stationery. So it was
back to the ignominious drudgery of school without the in-
spirational evenings in the theater. She really didn't need
them, anyway, for she was a quick student with an amazingly
retentive memory. Even as a small child, Constance remembered every word of a story and made corrections the next
time around if a syllable was changed. Later she could reel
off names, dates, places and statistics with the speed and
accuracy of a computer, invaluable for political arguments
of which, eventually, we had a good many.

She looked like a da Vinci angel but, demonlike, generated enough energy to light up Manhattan. Aggressive and
assertive, she played with boys more often than girls and
could beat them at their own games nine times out of ten.
And she wasn't above bringing Father down to her size,
either. Barbara remembered one Christmas morning when
we all three scrambled down the stairs and rushed to the
tree. Apparently Santa had lingered, however, and we caught
a fleeting glimpse of him in his red suit, lurking in the hall.
Barbara and I were terrified and hung back, but Constance

marched right up to him, planted a small fist on each hip, and gave him hell for malingering. "Why have you stayed here all night?" she demanded. "You should be on your way taking care of the other children, mister!"

I loved her, but as a child, I was scared to death of her. I had none of her dynamism, nor Barbara's deep-seated emotionalism that kept Mother and Father always wondering what would happen next. Barbara must have been awed by our older sister, too, for even though she was closer to Constance's age than mine, she hung back with me and we shared each other's company by the hour in childish games. Our favorite was a paper dollhouse we made ourselves by cutting out a whole houseful of rooms from the slick home-furnishing magazine of the time and pasting them in a big scrapbook. To fill the house we cut out figures to represent members of the family and the household staff. I remember it was a very real world, and we played at it with solemn concentration. We used to play "office," too, at Father's big desk, swinging our legs toward each other through the kneehole on either side and spending hours at weighty conversations on the telephone. Barbara was a marvelous playmate, but she had her own private, intense world that sometimes even I couldn't penetrate.

In the years that followed *What Every Woman Knows,* Father's position in the American theater established him to a point where he could choose his own plays. Sometimes he chose wisely, sometimes not, but in either case he began to select more interesting, varied roles than he'd been playing as standard juveniles.

Mother and Father appeared together in *The Deep Purple,* a moving melodrama by Paul Armstrong from which no one expected much, but it ran ten months and closed finally in May of 1911. *Passersby* by Haddon Chambers was his next and in Pittsburgh, Mother confounded Father again by filling in at the last minute for the leading lady who'd been injured in a fall. Frohman wired her his thanks and Father, relenting a little, told a reporter, "I am prouder than if I had been nominated over Roosevelt for President." From him it was a real accolade, since he thought Theodore Roosevelt was the greatest man of his time.

In November of 1912, Father tried his first venture as an actor-manager and produced *The Stronger Claim* by Margaret Turnbull, which opened in Washington, D. C. It was a modern religious drama and something of a problem play in more ways than one; it laid an egg. A wildly funny farce followed, *Stop Thief,* which had been produced unsuccessfully once before. The author, Carlyle Moore, approached Father and George M. Cohan to doctor the script, and talked producer Sam Harris into giving it a new production. They rewrote during the rehearsals and in three weeks, they'd come up with the comedy hit of the 1912–1913 season. Then Father prepared himself to rock the country back on its heels.

My father had a passionate dedication to all aspects of the theater, not just the areas of acting. He believed that the theater could be used as a force for good, that it had something to say and was obligated to say it. His first concern, of course, was to entertain, but he saw no reason why audiences shouldn't be made to think while they were being amused or moved, and he went drastically out on a limb to prove his theories about purposeful drama.

While playing *Passersby* in Pittsburgh, Father had dined with Pennsylvania's State Senator Flinn, and they'd discussed a bill then before the Pennsylvania legislature providing that applicants for marriage licenses must be proven free from venereal disease before a license could be issued. Senator Flinn's bill had been partially inspired, he told Father, by a French play called *Les Avaries,* or in its recent English translation, *Damaged Goods.* A serious and clinical study of hereditary syphilis by Eugene Brieux, today the play might seem very tame stuff, but then it was a highly inflammable subject even for impolite society. Syphilis was referred to, if at all, as a "social disease," or "the red plague."

The senator's bill was having a tough time in the legislative forums of Pennsylvania. As early as 1906, Dr. August von Wasserman announced the discovery of detecting syphilis by blood tests, and although recognized as an infallible method, it was largely ignored by society and most legislators until much later.

The discussion of Eugene Brieux's play and the problems of Senator Flinn's legislation piqued Father's interest, and he searched Pittsburgh's book stores until he found a copy. It was the last one of an order of five, the other four having been bought by the senator for distribution in his campaign. From the moment Father finished reading it, the idea of producing *Damaged Goods* became a driving obsession. Subject matter aside, it had been written by a playwright who was known as "the French Ibsen" and who had been lauded by George Bernard Shaw as "incomparably the greatest writer France has produced since Moliere." Father also recognized the worth of its theatricality, and through Brieux's American representative, optioned the play for five hundred dollars.

He knew that prejudice stalked in his path, but he prepared himself to do battle. The failure of the Pennsylvania legislature to pass the proposed bill only spurred him further, and by the time he returned to New York he was in a lather. Singlehandedly, he became a kind of circulating library for *Damaged Goods*. A friend at The Lamb's, an actor's social club, told him, "It's an interesting play to read, Dick, but it's too revolutionary. It's not for the stage." Father's reply was one he would repeat often in the next two years. "The hell it's not! I intend to stage it. Seen on the printed page the play may be forgotten; in the living presence of the theater, it never will!"

On tour again with another play, he made himself a national distributor of Brieux's ideas, and in every city he got the same reactions of shock and disapproval, sometimes from women's clubs, the clergy or social leaders, often from his own colleagues. He went through a year of combat, stumping the country, until the first ray of encouragement appeared in Chicago, where he was asked to speak at a men's service club. After an hour's harangue on his favorite subject, the dean of one of Chicago's leading churches approached him, expressed his interest and asked to borrow a copy of the play. Once he'd read it, the dean put the play into circulation in his own parish and preached a sermon on its theme. Father was delighted and announced gleefully, "The first shot has been fired!"

Back in New York once again, he began more positive preparations. He needed a theater, actors and some backing. Charles Frohman was horrified, turned it down cold and begged Father to put the whole thing out of his mind. It was the end of his seventeen-year association with C. F., not from any rancor, but simply because Father was more interested in his own productions from then on. He needed at least one respected and prominent name to dignify his project. Wilton Lackaye, a distinguished character actor, agreed to join forces, and Father guaranteed him one-third of the profits.

By then, a theater was his principal grief. He sent a copy of the play to Sam Harris who, without reading it, offered him the Cohan Theater for production, but someone gave Mr. Harris the general story line of *Damaged Goods,* and he was said to have suffered a seizure in his haste to withdraw his offer. Next the Princess Theater was offered, accepted, and just as hastily withdrawn. The same was true of Winthrop Ames, who feared the effect on his public and refused to lease the Little Theater. But Father was a cultivator of perversity. Thriving on the opposition, he came up with the idea of producing the play in a hotel, and engaged a dining hall at the Waldorf-Astoria. A few days later the management suddenly declined to permit a drama of such controversial nature to be seen within its walls. Publicly, Father called them all "a bunch of damned cowards!"

A curious coincidence filled the need of a theater. Henry B. Harris, the director of the 1906 London production of *The Lion and the Mouse,* was the son of William Harris, a prominent New York producer. Henry had read *Damaged Goods* just before his departure for Europe in 1912. He'd spoken to his father about producing it on his return, but he died on *The Titanic* when it sank off Newfoundland on April 14. Father was unaware of his interest in the play until he approached William Harris after his son's death for permission to use the Fulton Theater. William granted it and for his gesture, Father gave him one-third interest, making Harris an equal partner with Wilton Lackaye.

News of the crusade began to appear in the New York newspapers beyond the theater pages. The editor of *The Medical Review of Reviews,* a respected medical journal, read the items and offered the cooperation of his publication, and about the same time, Father received a pledge of endorsement from The American Federation of Sex Hygiene and The American Vigilance Association. In turn, they organized a committee that was joined by John D. Rockefeller, Jr., well known for his crusades against related social problems. Backed by such formidable support, Father was ready to fire on the enemy and leased the Fulton Theater for a single trial matinee performance to be attended by invitation only.

There remained only the problem of casting the play. Father and Wilton Lackaye were already set in the principal roles, but they needed nine other members to fill out the cast. Twenty-five actors were engaged and, as promptly, disengaged themselves from the production. Many of them were game personally, but were warned by others that to identify themselves with such a play could damn them to professional suicide. However, at last every part was filled but one, the small and difficult role of the prostitute, Laura, who had some of the frankest, most revealing lines in the play. Most actresses found the part objectionable, and those few who accepted it were unacceptable to Father's idea of the role. Six actresses were rehearsed, and all six vanished. That final casting problem held up production, and the search for a suitable actress continued.

Mother hadn't been altogether supportive of Father in his determination to produce *Damaged Goods* for the single personal reason that his obsession was tearing him apart. But since the unfilled role of Laura seemed to be the final obstacle in the long, painful struggle, she went to him quietly and offered to play it herself. For once, Father was glad he'd married an actress and he accepted her gratefully. Finally the play went into full-time rehearsals, with Father directing and playing the principal role of George Dupont.

The first American performance of *Damaged Goods* was seen at the Fulton Theater in New York City, March 14, 1913, under the auspices of *The Medical Review of Reviews* and its Sociological Fund, and the spectators included city officials, social workers, state legislators, doctors and ministers. The effect of that single matinee performance was like a thunderbolt. The "conspiracy of silence" surrounding an objectionable subject had been lifted at last.

The next performance was played in Washington, D.C.'s National Theater at a special Sunday matinee, the first Sunday theatrical performance in the District's history. Invitations were restricted to members of Congress and their wives, cabinet officers, members of the diplomatic corps, district government officials, foreign diplomats, ministers and social workers. Four thousand applications for tickets were received for the National Theater's seventeen hundred seats. The indications were clear. *Damaged Goods* returned, full time, to the Fulton Theater in New York and from then on the box office was besieged.

For the entire New York run it played to standing room only. No production within a dozen seasons aroused such widespread discussion. It was denounced or defended in newspapers from coast to coast. For twenty-two months, in New York and later on tour, it incited people to violent opinions. Some thundered against it and branded it as corrupt and unfit for public view; others applauded the courage that had brought into the open a social problem hidden too long by moral hypocrisy. Some religious and social groups tried to suppress the play altogether, and others bought whole blocks of tickets.

When the play reopened at the Fulton in the fall of 1913 after the summer break, Father began plans for an extended road tour. Since the advance bookings would mean forty-two weeks away from home, Mother and Father included Constance, Barbara and me, and we toured with them for much of that period.

On tour the play broke records in every city, and in each one the controversies were continued. In Boston the mayor tried to ban performances but the police commissioner outvoted him on the Board of Censors. In Louisville, a fight started in the balcony and Father quelled it with a lecture and brought down the curtain until order was restored. In Cincinnati a Board of Censorship, the first in the city's history, was formed by the Department of Public Safety to determine whether the play should be allowed to finish its week's run. Its judgment was that *Damaged Goods* should not only be allowed to continue, but the public should be urged to attend. In Los Angeles a social worker petitioned the Superior Court to restrict attendance to adults. In Chicago the city's censor chief and its mayor forced some deletions in the play and refused admission to anyone under eighteen years of age. Father showed his scorn by including his three daughters in the curtain call, aged four, eight, and ten. Constance, Barbara and I sat out front in a box seat enclosed in velvet drapes, and then were whisked backstage to bow with Father at the final curtain, to prove he was an enlightened family man with three healthy children and in open defiance of the mayor's ruling on age limits. I think that's my first remembrance of being in a theater, though the effect of the play's subject matter on the three of us was negligible. Constance couldn't spell it, Barbara couldn't pronounce it and I couldn't read it.

War was declared in Chicago. The city's official attempts to shield its citizens from indelicate themes brought forth a savage attack from Father, and he began addressing his audiences in curtain speeches that were described by a 1914 Chicago newspaper as "the strongest language ever shot across the footlights." The dialogue of the play was mild compared to the monologue after the last curtain. He poured rivers of vitriol into the auditorium nightly, the press reported them gleefully each morning and the lines grew longer, if possible, at the box office. It was the beginning of a lifetime custom.

During the Chicago uprising, the stage of the Olympic Theater became a flaming rostrum for Father's fury, and how he avoided prison, slander suits and a lynch mob is beyond me. A few pungent examples follow.

This country is populated by acidulated mental virgins.

People who come to see me must be prepared to listen to my talks. I'll always tell them some things not in the play, and I'll tell them frankly and brazenly. If they're afraid to listen they can stay home. I don't need the money.

Your mayor is a sour-bellied ass who recognizes no distinction between Balzac and Laura Jean Libby!

I do not feel that I am an inspired or divine Messiah sent to reform the world, but I intend to behave as though I were. Some day, when millions owe me clean veins and clean hearts and a birthright realized, my children's children may see monuments to their ancestor, whose generation afflicted him with criticism from flat-headed ignorami, annoyance from beer-soaked censors with the mental breadth of cockroaches, and managers who value a dollar above an epoch! There is no manager big enough to manage me, there is no director able to direct me, there is no censor big enough to stop me!

After lecturing his audience on the evils of censorship and denouncing his detractors, he usually finished with a speech from the play that ended with a ringing battle cry:

. . . A respectable man will take his son and daughter to one of those grand music halls, where they will hear things of the most loathesome description, but he won't let them hear a word spoken seriously on the subject of the great act of love. No, no! Not a word about that without blushing; only as many barrack room jokes, as many of the foulest music hall suggestions as you like. Pornography as much as you please—science, never!

The last line always brought down the house and, in Father's estimation, was no less stirring than "Damn the torpedoes, full speed ahead!" or "Remember the Alamo!"

He enjoyed himself hugely in those exchanges and his audiences enjoyed them as much as he. The more he talked, the more they multiplied. Though he wasn't above stirring up the controversy from in back of the footlights, never at any time did he allow sensational advertising for the play. He bought space in the daily newspapers of each city, but the ads on the theater pages only informed the public of the title, the time and the place.

The deep honesty of his convictions was totally unassailable, and he worked tirelessly to enlighten the public off-stage as well as on. As Brieux's apostle, he wrote newspaper columns, spoke at service club luncheons, and often was invited by the more liberal ministers to address church congregations from the pulpit, an opportunity he seldom refused. Often *Damaged Goods* was played for university students, beginning with a performance early in 1914 before an overflowing crowd at The University of Pennsylvania. Once, he was approached by a young Dartmouth College student named Walter Wanger, for permission to produce the play on the Dartmouth campus.

In some cities, the production was given under the auspices of service organizations, legislative leagues, church groups or medical societies, and Father was always delighted to have official endorsement. But he wasn't always welcome. Once he met refusal from Josephus Daniels, Secretary of the Navy under Woodrow Wilson, when he offered to take the play to Annapolis for one performance, gratis. Secretary Daniels would permit no such thing, since it would tend to put amorous thoughts into the heads of the young naval cadets, from which point there was a possibility of morally contaminating the entire United States Navy. Asked during that period by a politician if he didn't think he was working at a crusade that was ungodly, Father replied, "I have my own God, a splendid God, a kind God. He is not a political chiseler guided by hypocrisy and greed. Why I know ten actors, three philosophers, and one keeper of a brothel who are far more godly than any one politician in or out of Christendom!"

While the Bennett powerhouse was generating at full capacity, Mother quietly went about the business of coping with three small girls on a tour of the country. It couldn't have been easy to keep us amused and occupied, though Constance was seldom at a loss and I have one vague recollection of her lowering a puppy out of a hotel window in a basket to expedite its needs. In the larger cities, the company played for several weeks at a time, but often we stayed in one place only for a few days and then moved on to a new town, a new hotel, a new theater. Each time it meant packing up what amounted to a whole household with children, pets, luggage, governess, toys, all transported in Father's big touring car.

It was late in the first year of *Damaged Goods* that Mother changed her professional name. In that year of 1913 there were no less than three Mabel Morrisons in the theater and the resulting confusion of mistaken identities and missent mail was trying to all three. She'd always wanted to use her middle name anyway, and the surfeit of Mabel Morrisons gave her a good excuse. From then on, she was known in the profession as Adrienne Morrison.

By the end of 1914, Eugene Brieux's play had run its

course, and in the interim Father had shaken the foundation of some of the social pretenses in the country and wreaked havoc on his puritanical opposition. But the warfare had been worth it, for it brought a reevaluation of the legislative blocs in some areas and enlightenment to the general public. In spite of those strides, however, the Wasserman Test wasn't adopted as a prerequisite for a marriage license until 1926, and then only by a few states. New York was one of the first, though even today no test is required in Washington, D.C., Maryland, Nevada, South Carolina or Washington. Nevertheless, many people in legislative, sociological and medical circles felt that it was Richard Bennett who'd fired the first big guns.

From the time he first read *Damaged Goods* to its final performance almost four years later, he'd waged a ceaseless battle, fraught with fanaticism born of his conviction. By the time it was over he was forty-two years old, he was tired, his nervous system was frayed, his hair had turned gray, but he would recall it later as "one of the few wonderful times in life when you stand with the gods and, like them, are young and powerful and invulnerable."


For someone who loved his children and everyone else's so much, my father certainly was interested in birth control and legalized abortion. He was quite adamant in his view that the world would be a lot better off if there wasn't so much indiscriminate breeding going on. "Let a Margaret Sanger be placed on top of every steeple in the world to preach the gospel of birth control," he declared. "Then and only then can we expect to do away with rotten tenement districts, childhood sweatshops and all their kind!"

The play *Maternity*, also by Eugene Brieux, was a reflection of his strong views on legalized abortion and to him at least, a worthy successor to *Damaged Goods*. The plot flitted from the sins of an alcoholic father, visited on his children, to the sins of a state that ignored the children it already possessed, to the crimes of irresponsible paternity and the social hypocrisy that sometimes makes motherhood a tragedy. The day after the opening on January 6, 1915, Burns Mantle wrote that *Maternity* was "a play of sociological shreds and patches." He thought Richard Bennett fine as the brutal and pompous Brignac, and Adrienne Morrison "movingly effective" as his wife, but good performances were not enough. Wordy, rambling and less a theatrical piece than its predecessor, it lacked the power to hold an audience in spite of its debatable theme. *Maternity* was kept running by a few interested groups composed of feminists, settlement workers, lawmakers and a generous sprinkling of social anarchists, but not for long. Within a few weeks it died of box-office indifference, and Father declared, "In spite of the desperate need, I am dropping the idea of educating the masses. Hereafter, I shall amuse only!"

Shortly after *Maternity* closed, our house in Palisades, New Jersey, burned down, though I don't see any particular connection, and we moved into the Ansonia Hotel in Manhattan until Mother and Father could find a suitable replacement. Not very much of importance happened at the Ansonia, except for Constance's liberal use of the hotel stationery. Father called her "the high priestess of destruction," though from time to time he wished Barbara and I had a little more of her assertiveness. All in good time.

Sometime in the spring of that year, Father received an offer from the American-Mutual Film Company to make *Damaged Goods* into a movie with the original Broadway cast. Like many stage people then, he regarded the business of film-making as on a par with treason, dope peddling and matricide, and once told his stage manager, "Whenever you think there are movie scouts out front, let me know and I'll stay home sick."

However, it was no longer possible to ignore the growing

business of silent movie-making. Although he had complete control of the highly successful movie version, since he wrote the script, directed the film and recreated the role of Brignac, it began a lifelong disaffection with the industry. Eventually he made many films, and finally, when pictures went to Hollywood and began to talk, he enjoyed them somewhat more, but neither he nor Mother ever regarded them with anything but polite tolerance and contempt. In fact, Father's views were sometimes very impolite and always vocal. "Hollywood is a shooting gallery! I am a stage-struck actor, born with a lust for the theater!" And often he repeated the grim warning on the dangers of working in Hollywood. "A person comes out here for quiet, health, success, money and enough sleep, and then suddenly begins to die of them all." Years later he wrote to me in a letter,

> I have tried to rise to the top in all I've undertaken except in pictures, but after all, that is much like being the champion privy cleaner of Crown Point, Indiana. . . . Aristotle kept me up until 3:00 last night. What a pity he couldn't have lived to have his mind enriched by a few sallies from Jack Warner or L. B. Mayer. What then would he have given to the world's literature?!

After the film version of *Damaged Goods* in 1915, Father directed and acted in another film called *The Valley of Decision,* which he adapted from a story by Clifford Howard. It was filmed in Santa Barbara, California, again for American-Mutual. Perversely, he'd chosen it because it was a powerful preachment against birth control, and proclaimed the undisputed fact that the highest good in life was parenthood. *The Valley of Decision* was composed of a whole covey of Bennetts, including Mother and Father, my sisters and me, and Father's sister, Blanche, who'd come to visit us. There we all were in Santa Barbara with an allegory on our hands. In a prelude to the film entitled *The Shadowland of Souls Unborn,* Constance, Barbara and I appeared as three "unborn souls," in Grecian dresses, headbands and a hideous makeup, and danced around looking like refugees from a number three company of Isadora Duncan's. Films were entirely dependent on sunlight in those days, and I remember one whole side of the studio stage was made of glass to catch the light.

After the house in Palisades burned in 1915, Father developed a yen for the wider spaces of the open countryside, and we moved to a home in Park Hill near Yonkers, New York. He loved each hearth he owned and proceeded to "Bennettize" the new house after moving bag and baggage, dollhouses, theater memorabilia, family, household help and assorted cats, dogs, goldfish and canaries. Between performances, he messed around in the flower beds, the green sloping lawns and a vegetable patch where he raised Ponderosa tomatoes. He loved the earth and growing things and whenever time permitted, he dug, potted, fertilized and transplanted with a great show of exertion and bragged of his green thumb. After orgies of antique buying for the house, he'd drag the furniture in and out, up and down, and then put it all back again. He had a beautiful time when he could stain, paint, sandpaper and wax anything in sight. If it didn't move, he'd paint it. Father at home was Father at his very best.

Mother was wonderfully talented at decorating, as well as being a fine amateur painter and sculptress, and much of the interior beauty of the house was due to her skillful hand. In fact, she even helped a friend in a professional interior decorating studio for a time, and that probably was an influence on me since at the age of twelve I decided on a career as a decorator. At Park Hill Mother arranged an attractive wall treatment of her theatrical ancestors, pictures of Woods and Morrisons by the score. She'd always been extremely proud of her family's long theatrical tradition and saw no reason not to express it. Father, to defend his domestic and professional superiority, promptly framed his best press clippings and hung them on the adjoining wall.

I remember I loved that house in Park Hill. I was going on six years old, and because I knew a great deal about a lot of things by then, was among the first to urge Father to buy it. I was especially pleased to find that one of the bedrooms had an enormous closet with a peaked ceiling pitched so low it couldn't have been used for anything but a child's wardrobe. To me, however, it was perfectly clear it wasn't a closet at all, but an indoor doll's house, and had never been intended for anything else. The whole thing met with my approval.

Father was particularly busy for the next few years after we moved, and between films on the West Coast and several plays a year in New York or on tour, he was in and out of our lives a great deal during that period. When he was home, Park Hill was more like Bunker Hill. For a time, he played the Mad Scientist. Aunt Rosabel's son, Lewis Morrison, lived in nearby Lincoln Heights, was an expert chemist and at the time, worked on a substitute for gasoline in the laboratory of his home. Father often visited Lewis to "assist" in the experiments and Mother shuddered at the thought. He smoked a lot.

In 1917, the theater reflected the war in a rash of war plays, soldier revues and all-star benefits, and Father threw himself into all kinds of activities for the war effort. I remember that summer we did a benefit performance of *A Midsummer Night's Dream* on the grounds of the Park Hill house. Aged seven, eleven and thirteen, respectively, I played Peaseblossom, Barbara was Mustard Seed and Constance played Titania. Whatever our merits as child Shakespearean actresses, the greatest impact of the evening on us was the excitement caused by the presence of Florenz Ziegfeld and Billie Burke, right in our own backyard. I remember, too, that even our tickets had an Elizabethan flair, and in case of bad weather, the back of each ticket noted:

> If our fete by rain is reaved,
> Kindly come on this day week
> July Fourteenth, I bespeak.

Father was proud, even if the iambic pentameter was a little off.

I had to remember things like that. I certainly couldn't read them, for it was along in there they discovered I was nearsighted. I had to wear glasses, which I hated because I thought they made me look ugly, but without them, if an elephant had strolled by, I'd have missed it. I've been fumbling my way through life ever since.

Classic theater was very big with the Bennetts during the war years. At an experimental theater in Greenwich Village, Mother and Constance appeared together in the sixteenth-century morality play, *Everyman*. Pedro de Cordoba played Death, courtesy of David Belasco; Adrienne Morrison was Good Deeds, courtesy of Anderson and Weber; and that hellion, Constance Bennett, was the White Angel, courtesy of Mother and Father. Father declared she played it like a Roman senator, but she looked beautiful, and he was "damn proud."

Pedro de Cordoba was a fine and prominent actor of the time, and later had a long, distinguished career in films. His wife, Antoinette Glover, also appeared with him, Mother and Constance in *Everyman*. Great friends of the family, it was an interesting coincidence that Pedro's grandfather had lived on the neighboring plantation in Jamaica when my grandfather Morrison was a little boy. Barbara was completely devoted to Pedro's wife and when Antoinette died four years later, she was inconsolable. Emotionally overwrought, she wouldn't eat, turned alarmingly thin, and withdrew into her own private shell. Because the de Cordobas were devout Catholics, Barbara embraced Catholicism with a passion, and declared she would become a nun. I remember I used to sit in St. Ignatius Church, doing my lessons while I waited for her to finish interminable Stations of the Cross. Father ranted and made a great fuss about Barbara's religious leaning, a reaction that may have been cause for future problems when he might have let well enough alone, and allowed her to work out her own spiritual decisions. But it worried Mother, who thought her grief over Antoinette's death was overly prolonged for a fifteen-year-old, and she asked Rudolph Valentino to convince Barbara that there were more fulfilling pleasures in life for a young and beautiful girl. Mother, of course, had chosen the most persuasive and attractive symbol of masculinity in the world, and Valentino must have made an eloquent plea, for Barbara was finally dissuaded from the cloistered life.

Father's activities for the war effort rewarded him with a moment of sweet triumph when in September of 1917, he received a request from the United States War Department to release his film of *Damaged Goods* for the enlightenment of the million and a quarter men in America's military forces. Both Secretary of War Baker and Secretary of the Navy Joseph Daniels combined their efforts to show the film in army, navy and marine training camps throughout the country. It was four years before that Secretary Daniels had refused Father's offer to present the stage play at Annapolis. The film was shown under the auspices of the District War Service Commission in Washington, D.C., to kick off an educational campaign designed to insure the health of the nation's military youth, and Father appeared at the first showing to give the opening lecture.

My father was a man of many facets. Beyond the theater, there was little in life that didn't invite his radical interest or devoted attention at one time or another. In addition to his passion for his children, Mab, prize bulldogs and airedales, beautiful women, horses, polo, legalized abortion, books, liquor, high-powered automobiles, poetry in general, his own poetry in particular, birth control, eugenics, chemical experiments, politics and gardening, he was also an ardent feminist. In spite of certain mid-Victorian views, he was a strong believer in the emancipation of women, especially their suffrage movement. Above all things he hated inequities or injustices of any kind, and on principle, jumped into the middle of whatever they happened to be at the moment.

Several months after the film version of *Damaged Goods* was released for the War Department's use, he was offered a commission in the United States Army to accompany the film on a lecture tour of military installations in France and England. His answer was sent to Secretary of War Baker in a telegram.

I HAVE BEEN ASKED TO GO TO FRANCE PERSONALLY WITH THE FILM OF DAMAGED GOODS AS HEAD OF A LECTURE CORPS IN THE AMERICAN ARMY. ON RELIABLE AUTHORITY I AM TOLD THAT AMERICAN WOMEN, BECAUSE THEY HAVE DARED DEMAND THEIR POLITICAL FREEDOM, ARE HELD IN VILE CONDITION IN A WORKHOUSE IN WASHINGTON, ARE COMPELLED TO DO DEGRAD-ING WORK FOR EIGHT HOURS A DAY, ARE DENIED DECENT FOOD AND DENIED COMMUNICATION WITH COUNSEL. WHY SHOULD I WORK FOR DEMOCRACY IN EUROPE WHEN OUR AMERICAN WOMEN ARE DENIED DEMOCRACY AT HOME? IF I AM TO FIGHT FOR SOCIAL HYGIENE IN FRANCE WHY NOT BEGIN AT THE OCCOQUAM WORKHOUSE?

1918 was the year of my theatrical triumph in Los Gatos, California. As usual in the summer, Father played stock in Los Angeles and San Francisco, and that year we went to Los Gatos in northern California to visit an old family friend, Ruth Comfort Mitchell, a writer and wife of one of the state's political leaders. By then I was eight years old and decided I'd wasted enough time, so I produced a play written, acted and directed by me, called *Timid Agnes and the Mouse*. Naturally I played Timid Agnes, which may have had some significance, and I wrote a great switch for the surprise end-ing; the mouse turned into a prince. It seems a shame that I've lost the original manuscript since it might have made a great musical. In any case, I charged friends my own age a nickel to watch me emote as Timid Agnes, and brazenly set the admission at a dollar for adults. I remember I was very big in Los Gatos for a time.

After four years in the Park Hill, New York, house we moved back to Manhattan. Mother had endured the semi-isolation of the country and the inconvenience of commuting to satisfy Father's yen to be a gentleman farmer while he frolicked in virtual freedom in the glittering environs of Broadway. She was quite aware, too, of the various temptations that crossed his path, particularly on matinee days, and of the subtle evidences of his amorous acrobatics. Those little recreational exercises often resulted in scenes worthy of a second act curtain, and I remember once I came tearing down the stairs thinking it was the Battle of Armageddon, only to be told it was the shutters banging.

Mother put on the pressure and in the late spring of 1918 we moved to a house at 22 West Eighth Street in the Washington Square area of Greenwich Village. Although the Village was considered something of a Bohemian atmosphere even then, it had none of the squalid air it has today. Washington Square was a lovely patch of shaded green park at the base of Fifth Avenue where families strolled casually on Sundays, and children played in freedom around an organ-grinder.

I remember that the house was four-storied and its back windows looked out on the artists' studios of MacDougal Alley. It was an older house with large rooms and high ceilings, wooden-pegged floors and heavy mahogany doors with shiny brass knobs, things reminiscent of a more gracious age when the pace of life was more leisurely. At first I was horrified to find that the kitchen was below street level, which, for some reason, was very distasteful. In one of my more endearing moments, I asked Mother and Father if we were really going to live in that tenement. But, eventually, I came to recognize and love the beauties of that gracious house, even the basement kitchen.

With his customary zeal, Father went to work on the renovation while Mother tastefully decorated around him and added some furniture that had been used in his stage productions. I can remember a big kidney-shaped desk of dark carved wood, and two brocaded chairs that had trouped all over the country with him.

The next couple of years were eventful ones for the Bennetts on West Eighth Street. Barbara and I followed Constance into Miss Chandor's Day School at a time when, either by invitation or choice, she moved to Miss Merrill's Boarding School on Long Island. Father, on tour with the smash hit, *The Unknown Purple,* gave Kansas City hell for closing the theater as "non-essential" during a fuel shortage. Mother and Father toured together in *For the Defense,* a successful courtroom drama by a rising young playwright, Elmer Rice. Father rewrote the manuscript and incurred extreme displeasure from several quarters, particularly the author's.

We christened our home in Greenwich Village with a seething family melodrama, one of our best as I remember it from an eight-year-old's standpoint, and it's vivid still. I remember that Barbara and I were sound asleep in an upstairs bedroom we shared when suddenly we were awakened by a great commotion. We both ran out to peer over the top of the stairs and found Father reading the riot act flanked, on either side, by Constance and Mother. In full chorus Father was roaring, Mother trying to placate him, and Constance trying to top it all with an explanation.

Apparently, she'd broken a household rule by coming in late. At any rate, by the time Barbara and I stood gaping at the head of the stairs, the argument was white-hot and loud enough to turn heads in a graveyard. Then all three started toward us up the stairs and Barbara, wanting none of it, promptly started a nosebleed and ran back to bed. I wasn't about to be left out in the open under fire so I joined her immediately and was followed by Constance, who came charging in and got under one of the beds. Mother and Father followed almost at once. Father had reached new dramatic heights and was brandishing a gun, or what looked like a cannon to me. He ordered us out of bed, we lined up at attention, and in a magnificent Madison Square Garden voice, he roared, "I'm going to run this family the way I want it run, or there isn't going to be any family!" By then the thought was not wholly unattractive. Mother finally calmed him down and he burst into tears, while Barbara still had her nosebleed, Constance shivered in stony silence for once, and all I could do was stand there in stark, bug-eyed terror. After threatening to exterminate the lot, then weeping copious tears, Father finished off the thriller with a great exit line as Mother led him away. "I want my baby Joan!" which succeeded in terrifying me even more, since my only wish was to put as much distance between us as possible.

For all of his own unconventional behavior, Father was quite puritanical about the women of his own household. I remember he was scandalized when Mother bobbed her hair in the fashion of the twenties, and he acted like a prim maiden aunt when she started to smoke. Mother was more permissive with us, but Father was quite a strict disciplinarian who laid down some hard and fast rules and expected them to be followed. I admit, he didn't always get his wish.

Sternly mid-Victorian, he often tried playing the heavy-handed father. He was absolutely obssessed about time and punctuality. A minute beyond the designated hour, he'd begin to froth and threaten harrowing consequences. I remember once when Mother was on tour, Father was in a New York production and supervising the household himself. At the time, I had a big crush on Rudolph Valentino whose film, *The Sheik,* was playing at the Plaza Theater. I went to see it one afternoon with a friend from school and we were so devastated by the Valentino charms, that we stayed to see the second show. I'd been instructed to be in by six o'clock, but was an hour late by the time I got home. With a great show of disapproval, Father locked me in my room and told me he'd station his valet downstairs to keep me from leaving the house. I don't know how he thought I could have left the house, unless I jumped out the window.

Constance, of course, would have jumped out the window. As a feminine image of Father, she'd thwart his discipline, stand up to be counted and freely speak her mind. Not I! I'd have collapsed on the floor before I could answer him back. I looked on him with mute idolatry but he scared me witless. Come to think of it, I guess I was only slightly less in awe of Constance. She used to help herself to Mother's things, and once I caught her taking a beautiful decorative pin, one of Mother's favorites, shaped like a pond lily. She put it down immediately, and as Mother's little helper, I snatched it up and ran into my room. But she ran right after me, and said, "If you don't give that to me this minute, I'm going to lock you in your room!" So I gave it to her. In retrospect, somebody in that family was always locking me in my room.

Sometimes Father pontificated on the weighty problems of parenthood, and the grave responsibilities of being the father of three impossible daughters. Asked if he thought girls were too pampered ordinarily, he replied, "Certainly, by fathers. It's possible that mothers handle them better and have fewer problems as a parent, because they know the chicanery of their own sex." Years later, a reporter asked if he was proud of his daughters, and he said, "No, but I am satisfied with them." Despite his phony displays of disapproval he loved us all dearly, though he went to great lengths to keep from being thought soft or pliable, and frequently he indulged us when Mother wasn't looking.

Once, he took me to Hot Springs, Virginia, when I was recovering from an operation. I was about twelve and I remember that Mother saw to it that I was always dressed in very simple, childish clothes, which I thought were simply babyish. It seemed perfectly obvious that I was far too grown up for that sort of thing. The first night we were in Hot Springs, I dressed for dinner in one of my "baby" frocks, and right away Father saw how I felt about it. He went out and returned a short time later with a bunch of artificial flowers and bits of ribbon, and then he sat down and sewed them on my dress himself. We went to dinner, as I remember we even danced, and I felt chic and splendidly mature.

As a child I was aware, of course, that my father was a famous actor, but that knowledge made me more self-conscious than anything else. Later when I came into the city from boarding school in Connecticut, if Father was playing in New York, I frequently went to the theater first to see him. Invariably, he asked what I wanted to do that day, and invariably I answered that I'd like to go to the theater. "Then just go to the box office," he'd say, "and ask for a ticket. Tell them you're Richard Bennett's daughter." I'd finally work up enough courage, but I hated the embarrassment it always brought.

Another thing I remember about our childhood; I was an awful snitch. Constance had developed a great system for hoodwinking Father. Obediently, she'd come in at the appointed hour, go to her room which was across the hall from Barbara's and mine, noisily demonstrate that she was present in the house, then she'd sneak right out again. I'd run to tell Mother, who, in turn, would get Father up because she was worried about Constance. That, of course, incurred his wrath, and the Bennetts were at it again.

# 4

By 1920 there were a number of producers in the theater who were leading a revolt against the ponderous traditions, the spectacles and tinkling comedies that had been the trademark of men like David Belasco, Charles Frohman and William Harris. Among them was John D. Williams. Williams, an erudite man who'd been Frohman's business manager, was more interested in producing plays of substance and literary value than the old blood-and-thunder melodramas. Having successfully produced John Galsworthy's *Justice*, which starred John Barrymore, and Elmer Rice's *For the Defense*, with Father in the leading role, he'd begun to build a reputation in the profession for producing plays of quality. At the suggestion of George Jean Nathan, he optioned Eugene O'Neill's first three-act play, *Beyond the Horizon*. At a time when Eugene was still known as "James O'Neill's son," Williams paid five hundred dollars for the option, but his attention wandered to other productions and he set it aside, while its author chafed with impatience. One day in 1919 during the run of *For the Defense*, Father paid a visit to Williams's office, pulled the manuscript out of a nearby pile and began to read it. He was moved by the play, and although he had some strong reservations about its length and awkwardness, he asked Williams to give it a full production and offered himself for the principal role of Robert Mayo. There was a shortage of theaters in New York at the time and the producer raised that as an objection, but once bitten by a desire, Father wouldn't rest.

In November he went on a brief tour of the Midwest, took the manuscript with him, and began to make cuts in the play. He wrote to a friend, Felton Elkins,

> . . . I started to blue pencil day before yesterday and, God knows, it needs blue penciling. As I read it now, it seems terribly stretched out, and a lot of words with little active material. But having done so much with the rotten subjects I've been getting, I myself think that with the acquiescence of the author, a great play can be made out of *Beyond the Horizon.*

When Father returned to New York to reopen *For the Defense,* he discovered that John D. Williams, too, had been making judicious cuts. They tried presenting them to the author, with abrasive results. O'Neill refused to cut a line from a play that was nearly an hour too long, and Father wrote later, "Of course, O'Neill went off his head!" Eugene confronted his tormentor at the stage door of the Morosco Theater one evening with tears in his eyes. Father suddenly got the brilliant idea of resolving the whole thing by satisfying Eugene's inordinate affection for absinthe, took him home to West Eighth Street, opened a bottle of Pernod and filled him to the brim, without excluding himself altogether. By morning, O'Neill had not only okayed the deletions, but had somehow managed to initial every cut in the manuscript's margins. Father had a hangover, but he also had one of the greatest plays of the decade and he forged ahead with the production.

He planned a series of matinees at the Morosco, played in between performances of the current play, recruited three cast members from *For the Defense,* Louise Closser Hale, George Riddell, and Mary Jeffrey, and included two actors from *The Storm,* Helen MacKellar and Edward Arnold. The idea was to play matinees on Monday, Tuesday, Wednesday and Friday, until a theater was available for a regular run. It was a grueling schedule, since it meant rehearsing daytimes and performing the Elmer Rice play on a regular routine of six evening performances and a Thursday and Saturday matinee. But Father's wholehearted enthusiasm fired the entire company, if not the author's, and for the actors it became a labor of love. John D. Williams, considering the risks of presenting a contemporary American tragedy by an unseasoned playwright, was delighted with the scheme. It meant only a small investment in scenery and, for a time, met the problem of the theater shortage.

The first performance on Broadway of a three-act play by Eugene O'Neill was presented February 3, 1920, at a Tuesday matinee. Eugene brooded at the back of the Morosco as the audience filed in, an audience that included the first-string critics despite the 2:15 curtain time, and also his parents, James and Ella O'Neill. In this tragic tale of the struggle between two brothers, the audience witnessed the creeping decay of an entire doomed family, and as the chaotic story unfolded with relentless realism, the spectators sat in stunned silence. The seventy-four-year-old James O'Neill watched, rigid in his seat, weeping.

The critics liked the play but they were not rhapsodic. Most of them were impressed with the writing, though they found fault with its occasional awkwardness, a muddled ending and the length, but all were unanimous in their praise of an uncommonly fine cast. Father's performance, thought by many to have been one of the most brilliant of his career, was a heartbreaking portrayal of a man dying of consumption and pitilessly haunted by his failures in life. His death scene was alarmingly realistic and when his sister, Blanche, saw a performance she was inconsolable until she saw him backstage, alive and healthy. *Beyond the Horizon* is the first full remembrance I have of seeing my father onstage.

In late March, Father wrote again to his friend, Felton Elkins, to share his impressions and the events after opening.

Of course, you have learned by this time that O'Neill's play is one of the season's sensations, and strange as it may seem, we are playing to really splendid houses. Now we are in a regular theater, The Little. I closed *For the Defense* to big business in order to keep *Beyond the Horizon* in New York and we are growing every day in advance. I shouldn't be surprised if we stayed here until July. . . . It's glorious to have done it, Felton. Very few besides Williams believed in it and even he got cold feet. I had to do it all, cast it, cut it, and produce it. Still I owe the finding of it to him. I've lost many pounds and am very tired, but what matters that?

The first of his four Pulitzer Play Awards was given to Eugene O'Neill for *Beyond the Horizon* in the 1920–21 season.

Early in the fall, after a summer of stock, Father took *Beyond the Horizon* on a road tour. It was a failure. He couldn't understand it. With all its deficiencies, it had played a full season in New York, had been acclaimed the best play in a decade, won a Pulitzer Prize, and above all, he believed in it passionately. On the road, too, the press had been enthusiastic in its praise, though he didn't know whether to be pleased or annoyed when one critic said he was "like a man who had unduly mixed his metaphors, by having one play under the feet of the average audience and another play over its head." But as Father said, "There is simply a lack of patronage." To say that he overreacted is putting it gently. He flayed them alive, and gave scathing interviews to newspapers and harangued audiences from the footlights in blazing curtain speeches.

Since *Damaged Goods,* seven years before, he'd by no means given up addressing his audiences when the spirit moved him. If anything, his rabid speeches had increased in number and the stage became a platform from which he issued statements like papal bulls from the Vatican. He'd become a self-appointed messiah for the profession, but he was deeply sincere in the feeling that his position and the weight of his talents also carried the responsibility of raising its levels if at all possible. Admittedly, he didn't always meet those standards himself, but if he seemed opinionated, and he was, it was because he cared deeply about the state of things and rage was a by-product of his concern. Furthermore, he thought everyone else should be as passionately engaged as he, and he went about the job of educating audiences with huge energy and relish. "The only thing wrong with the taste of the public," he said, "is the taste of the public."

For minutes he'd regale and attack his viewers while they sat in rapt attention.

> The theater invites the lowest form of literature because it appeals so directly to your basest emotions. The fault is mine. I bring you great plays when you would much prefer *The Student Prince,* The Dolly Sisters, or Fink's Mules. As for the general run of plays nowadays, they're stereotyped. The theater has become one big syndicate for a certain kind of play and managers and writers don't dare to experiment because they have one eye on the box office and the other on motion pictures. And motion pictures have an even lower form of literature. As a matter of fact, they have no form at all!

At first his audiences were shocked and dumbfounded, but as time went by, they began not only to enjoy his lectures, but to expect them.

Quite often his subject was the audience's behavior during a performance and he gave them strict lessons in deportment. "My God," he said, "is Omaha one seething mass of bacteria? You coughed like a bunch of trained seals out there tonight and you spent the entire play taking off and putting on your galoshes. How do you expect creative artists to give you their very best with such distractions going on out front?"

Writing about impolite spectators in 1936, his views might just as well apply to 1970.

People come to the theater to be entertained, interested, amused and informed, or at least that is most people's excuse. But all too frequently they are annoyed by some nitwit who laughs inordinately in the wrong places or explains to a lady friend, in a voice loud enough to be heard in the next street, some quite obvious point that a child of six might understand. All this, to display his own perspicacity to everyone within earshot; rattling his program to find the name of a new character that has just come on the stage, yawning brazenly when some philosophical passage is being uttered in the play that does not smack of pruriency. Returning five minutes after the curtain has gone up on the second act, he jabbers down the aisle and steps on everyone's feet without so much as a by-your-leave, as he finds his seat and crashes into it. He spends the next few moments opening a fresh box of chocolates, munching them with smacking lips and observations on the relative merits of Schrafft's over Whitman's Sampler. That is the type of auditor who creates a mass homicidal tendency in the audience. At an expense of three dollars to himself, he has destroyed fifteen hundred dollars' worth of pleasure for other people, and called down upon his vapid self a million dollars' worth of aversion.

His colorful outbursts earned him the label of being headstrong and temperamental, for which he always had a ready answer. "Temperament they call it! I call it a lesson in deportment from a person with sensitivity to persons with none. No one knows but those on our side of the footlights the torture of the giggling, coughing, sneezing, foot-scuffling audience. We work like galley slaves for weeks, giving all that's in us, only to have our work destroyed by selfishness and stupidity. If we occasionally break loose under the strain, they call it temperament."

Father's impromptu curtain speeches lingered in the memory of many a theatergoer who was treated to his unscheduled harangues on whatever prejudice happened to bother him at the moment. He had a special horror of latecomers, and in his production of *Damaged Goods,* was the first to institute the rule of not seating patrons while the play was in progress. His particular loathing was reserved for opening night audiences who came more to be seen than to concentrate on the offering before them, and he once suggested to a reporter that a school should be founded to train people for those occasions.

> First-nighters, those simian varieties who are noisy, come in late, climb over one another on the way to their seats after the curtain is up, the chatterers who rustle their programs, those who point out celebrities, lead me to suggest a way to eradicate these evils. No one should be admitted to a first night who has not attended a preparatory school designed to educate him in the social science of playgoing.

Theater managers were horrified at his infractions but were powerless to do much about them. But then Father was too celebrated an actor and too intractable a personality for any very effective reasoning. Later one manager hit on the idea of putting a clause in his contract that prevented him from making his inevitable curtain speeches, thereby robbing him of enormous pleasure and fun.

Newspaper reporters learned early that Richard Bennett was always good for colorful copy, and he seldom disappointed them. He wasn't at all unaware of the benefits of publicity and knew that saints didn't make particularly interesting news copy. He was a man with his own code of ethics who could never suffer fools gladly; an incorrigible who cared little for public opinion and made sure that his own was widely distributed. "Sure as all hell," he told a reporter, "I'm going to keep on making curtain speeches. The audience likes to hear them, I like to make them, and it helps business, so I shall continue to use the proscenium as a pulpit. All the Bennetts are propagandists. I'll have you know I come from a long line of preachers. Damn good ones, too!"

His curtain speeches weren't always confined to theatrical matters. Few subjects, as long as they were controversial, escaped his rhetoric. He discoursed on anything of current interest to him including public taste and morals, politics, income taxes, parental discipline, alimony, and on one occasion, the corruptions in American speech. "Not more than one-twentieth of one percent of the American public can speak the English language, and about one half of that number speak it so loudly, I wish they wouldn't."

One of his all-time favorite subjects was the Volstead Act. Prohibition went into effect in January of 1920 and Father went into paroxysms of rage. Although it did nothing to stem the flow of his own steady intake, he considered it an unjust, futile experiment and leveled a barrage against it whenever possible. "The whole damn country is suffering from one gigantic overdose of Volsteadism!" Addressing the astonished citizens of Philadelphia once, he said, "You Philadelphians talk about upholding Prohibition, then drink as much as you can. Rome wasn't as rotten, when it fell, as Philadelphia is right now!" And he advised the good people of Kansas City, "If you can't stop your children from drinking, take them out and teach them how to drink."

Asked to address a radio audience on the general conditions of the theater, he launched instead into an attack on the Volstead law.

The average citizen is a harmless, fun-loving human being who can take his liquor or leave it alone. And what has happened? We have a law which makes it prohibitive for him to drink. And what drink! The truth, oh supreme heads of government, is that your average citizen doesn't want the Volstead law. He doesn't want to hide in shadowy places, to pay excessive prices to aliens whose paunches have swelled on their dollars. He doesn't want to drink liquor so vile that it causes strong eyes to fail and good health to fall to pieces.

I'm somewhat fed up with a system of government that permits the theater to lose many of its theatergoers. To be specific, if matters continue the way they are, it will be only a question of time before actors lose all their usefulness. They will be discarded like Mah-jong games and crossword puzzles. Under the present system of law and order, we have our citizens seeking hidden dives to find a substance to quench normal thirst. They are served such putrid hooch that they leave wearing coffins as overcoats. Why, some of my best friends have died of bootleg whiskey, with the result that many of my admirers are missing in my favorite towns!

Father certainly took no chances with the lethal bootleg poison he described. He made his own "bathtub" gin at home, rigged up an intricate "Rube Goldberg" system of copper kettles, tubing and funnels, and merrily distilled his way through nearly fourteen years of Prohibition.

Sometimes he trained his big cannons on geographical locations and one of his most treasured targets was Boston. He detonated when asked by journalist Ward Morehouse if he was planning to play Boston in his current production. "Never! Why, I wouldn't play that damned town if they gave me Bunker Hill Monument, threw in the Copley Plaza and called out the National Guard to meet me at Back Bay station. Whenever I hit that place I lose all desire for everything on God's green earth, except a desire to leave. It's the most lascivious, interfering, the most mendacious, bigoted and immoral place you'll find in a lifetime of trouping!" He swore he'd once seen a sign over a tunnel in Boston Common that read, "No Flirting!"

Frequently he was invited to address luncheon clubs, and he found them convenient forums in which to air his views. Addressing The Drama League of Detroit, he was fired to new heights of eloquence. "Detroit is a city of lowbrows unable to appreciate anything but musical comedies and motion pictures. You should go to the theater to see style, to hear good diction and to use your mind, if you have one. I love any of you who have brains, but I despise your provincial ignorami. I have been greatly criticized of late for daring to tell the truth in the provinces. I daresay I am a propagandist, but I believe the theater was put here for a purpose other than entertainment. For the last fifty years, your minds have been atrophied with trash. Now, you must go to the theater with an open mind and the heart of a child. I will entertain you that way. Otherwise, I shall only baffle you and God knows, I don't want to do that. I am baffled enough myself. Goodbye; I am not coming back to play to empty seats. I mean GOODBYE!" Mr. Bennett, it was reported, fairly flung himself out of the room.

Next to addressing audiences, Father's favorite exercise was attacking drama critics, though he grudgingly admitted that there might be a few poor benighted souls who were equipped to practice their profession. "The difference between a critic and a reporter is standards. One has them, the other does not. A hold-over from the old guard is Burns Mantle; he is a critic. And Kenneth Macgowan is not only a critic but a gentleman, a very rare bird nowadays. Then there is Smart-Alex Woolcott; he is a plumber." Father had a particularly fond hatred for George Jean Nathan, and reserved his choicest invective for one of the most widely syndicated journalists in the country. "George Jean Nathan is as insidious a virus as ever skulked through a stage door!" Years later, when occasionally I was escorted by George, in Father's eyes I couldn't have done a worse thing if I'd burned the American flag, or dated Jack the Ripper.

In spite of his contempt, however, there were times when he enjoyed their personal friendships. "Some of them are quite intelligent," he admitted grudgingly, "and they would more often prove it if it were not for their prejudices. You know, dramatic criticism is made up of people who are either aspiring to have a play produced, or who have had one produced and failed. In personal contact, I have found many theatrical critics to be adorable companions, but that was only after they lost their self-consciousness at contact with greatness."

Even when Father was handed a bouquet, he tossed it right back with a brickbat, and once sent the critic, Percy Hammond, a letter in reply to an admiring column.

My Dear Sir:

Over your signature, you recently indicated that I am the best actor in the Western Hemisphere. Since that time, I am wondering by what right you hand down your lofty decisions. Where, I have tried to find, are your credentials as a chancellor in the affairs of actors, managers, playwrights and audiences? In the vernacular of Canal Street, where do you get off to say that anyone is the greatest or the rottenest?

What feathers from the wings of God's pet angel decorate you with an arbiter's plumage? None, I dare say. And yet, you are permitted to tell the world that my interpretations are masterpieces. Is this a self-imposed, divinely inspired freedom of thought, or just a means of attracting a moron public to your point of view?

The constructive reviewing that you indulge in, especially as it concerns me, is worse than useless. I do not doubt that you think me a great actor, but I wish hereafter you would, if possible, abstain from saying so.

Yours truly,
Richard Bennett

Mr. Hammond promptly responded with a gallant reply. Undoubtedly he knew that Father was just practicing a few minor scales on a major theme with his customary relish. Sounding off was part of the fun of being Richard Bennett, and of course, he knew all along that his letter would be printed in Hammond's column.

Beneath Father's temperament and anarchy, however, was a deep, obsessive love and concern for the theater that was never far from the surface. Always expressing himself in the strongest terms, he was an articulate man who knew that the acids of sarcasm and satire were keen and deadly weapons. A passionate idealist, he thought he could incite people to action with those weapons and goad them, and himself, into being a little better than they really were.


While Father was on tour with Eugene O'Neill's *Beyond the Horizon* in 1920, Mother was no less busy with the issues of our education and upbringing. We'd moved that year from the house in Greenwich Village to Park Avenue, though now I can't remember why. In any case, Barbara and I went from Miss Chandor's Day School to Miss Hopkins's, and Constance went to Miss Merrill's. At this point, I'm wondering why girls' schools in America are never run by married people.

I do remember one thing of grave importance that happened while we were living on Park Avenue. My pet canary died. I put the bird in a Coty perfume box, buried it in Central Park, and bought a plaster madonna at the dime store for the headstone, quite a complete little burial package, I thought. Barbara was impressed with the solemnity of it all, but I don't think Constance cared very much. Later, in fact, she developed a strong phobia against birds and wouldn't have so much as a canary in the house. Anyway, Constance was too busy at that point to give much thought to my canary's demise.

She graduated from Miss Merrill's, a cause for much relief on both sides, for restrictions for the students included a chaperone at every breath, prim uniforms of navy blue, and every evening they sang "Lead Kindly Light." That fall, Mother took her to Europe to enroll her at Madame Balsam's in Paris for the final stages of her education. But there, again, restrictions were too numerous for my lively, headstrong sister, and she decided that one year of finishing school was quite enough. The school felt just as strongly; it nearly finished Madame Balsam. On her return, Mother gave her a glittering society debut in Washington, D.C., and she "came out" with several other debutantes of the season. Father choked on that one, but was too far away to do anything about it.

Constance came home in the spring of 1921, a lovely vixen of sixteen with a few ideas of her own on how to get the most fun out of life. The nineteen-twenties had roared in and Constance roared right back, trailing a long line of adoring males wherever she went. Blonde, beautiful and restless, she lit the social scenes of New York and Washington like a Fourth of July sparkler, made the rounds of seasonal parties and football games, danced until dawn, and was queen of the Ivy League college proms. She changed beaux like she changed her mind, which was frequently. During Easter Week at the University of Virginia, she met an eighteen-year-old student named Chester Moorehead, the son of a prominent Chicago dentist. Two months later, Chester "dared" Constance to marry him, they eloped on June 6, 1921, and were married in Greenwich, Connecticut, by a Justice of the Peace. Fortunately, Father was in Los Angeles.

My, it was a stirring time. Mother went speeding and weeping all the way to Greenwich accompanied by my cousin, Lewis Morrison, and they brought the bride home without a honeymoon. Father roared his indignation from out of the West, cleaned his gun, swore vengeance and called down the wrath of God, though on whom was not exactly clear. The Mooreheads weren't any more delighted than the Bennetts, though they were less vocal about it, and there was only a discreet silence from Chicago.

The unkissed bride was sent off to Europe as a diversion from "the recent unpleasantness," but it was no longer so easy to divert her. She grew ever more restless, driven by a relentless energy. She wrote charming poetry, which Father said was cribbed from him, and tried her hand at sketching, but none of those efforts satisfied her for long, and she returned home to the breezy social rounds. In the midst of those pleasant pursuits, Constance met Philip Plant at a football game, the handsome twenty-one-year-old heir to a steamship and railroad fortune. He was attractive, fun-loving, and drank too much, but he offered her the excitement and variety she craved. They promptly fell in love, and, just as promptly, fought like mad. Hide and Seek became the favorite sport. They advanced and retreated from each other, and each spent a good deal of time in trying to spite the other.

When Constance and Father merged in New York after her first matrimonial adventures, he tried to interest her in an acting career and got her a job playing small parts in a few movies produced by Lewis Selznick. She did *Reckless Youth, Evidence* and *What's Wrong with the Women?*, the last for an independent company, with Wilton Lackaye and Hedda Hopper. Constance played a hell-raising flapper, and got her first recognition from a New York critic, but none of those projects interested her for very long. They were fun, nothing more. Anyway, she was too busy testing Philip Plant with daily acceptance or rejection of his marriage proposals. Phil strongly disapproved of her movie acting, and it was a convenient threat to hang over his head.

After that, things settled into a more tranquil disorder. Father did a couple of undistinguished plays in New York; then he rewrote and played in an antiwar drama called *The Hero*, which was acclaimed by critics and damned by the American Legion. That one didn't last long either and having nothing else to do while he was waiting for a new play, he revisited his old haunts. Among his favorites was Texas Guinan's Club on Fifty-second Street, one of the attractions being Texas's parrot, who could say two things: "telephone" and "go to hell."

That period produced one of the most widely repeated stories of the many incidents in Father's checkered night life. In search of what he called "a little innocent merriment," he went to Texas Guinan's to observe the furtive evils of Prohibition. The club was filled to capacity, as were most of the guests, and finally the frivolity reached a rowdy high point which Father thought should be subdued. Tex didn't know it, but salvation was at hand. At the height of the din, he rose, addressed a few words to the congregation on the wages of sin, then whipped out a pocket Bible and began to read from one of his favorite chapters. Reverberating off the walls, the golden voice read on until, one by one, his marinated flock was silenced and spellbound. Except for those who'd passed out, there wasn't a dry eye in the house. He recalled it later as a genuine triumph. "I believe it was one of the most dramatic moments I have ever known in my life. When I read the finish—'and the greatest of these is Charity'—the effect was overwhelming!" I can well believe it.

It's unlikely that Father's sermon had any lasting effect on Texas Guinan's cover charges, but coming from a long line of lay preachers, he was merely upholding the Bennett traditions. I'm wondering now who held him up. There were times when his capacity was formidable, and his intake would have endeared him to the distilling industry.

His nocturnal frolics produced some interesting moments at home, too. I can remember bounding down the stairs one morning on my way to school, and being suddenly confronted by an apparition fully dressed in evening clothes, complete with cape, top hat and cane. He was sitting upright in a chair sound asleep and, to me, looked like some monstrous giant in a black shroud. I fled in terror and I'm sure Timid Agnes was early for the school bus that morning.

Late in 1921, the newly formed New York Theater Guild sent Father the play he'd been waiting for. *He Who Gets Slapped* by the Russian playwright, Leonid Andreyev, was a bittersweet tragedy, the story of an anguished man in the agony of a personal grief who turns to the life of a painted clown. Rehearsals were lively. Theresa Helburn and Lawrence Langner of the Theater Guild thought it should be done as a bitter, sardonic Russian tragedy, while Father saw it instead as a fantasy focused on the noble suffering of the clown, and he gave the character a touch of spirituality to overlay the gentle humor. Recalling the time in her auto-biography,* Miss Helburn wrote:

It is beautiful as you have done it, we admitted, but this is a play about Faust and not about Christ. Dick insisted on playing it like Christ. That was the way he saw it. Of course, given half a chance, any actor will leap at the chance to play Christ. And, as a rule, when he does so you are lost. . . . His interpretation, though it completely altered the intention of the play, making the theme one of suffering instead of bitterness—a play about the cruelty of the world transformed into a play about one unhappy human being—made it much more successful than it had any right to be. In this case, it was the actor more than the director who set the mood of the play.

*He Who Gets Slapped* opened January 9, 1922, at the Garrick Theater. It was an unqualified success and the critics poured out enthusiasm in waves. Responding to the applause on the second night, Father came forward to make a little speech of acknowledgment, thanked his audience and said, "Now, ladies and gentlemen, don't let anyone tell you that you have to be an intellectual to enjoy this play. My eleven-year-old daughter, Joan, was here last night and she loved it!"

At that time, actors still took curtain calls at the end of each act but after *He* opened, the Theater Guild decided to do away with the custom. Rather than break the mood of the play between acts, they invoked the rule of taking bows only after the final curtain. The idea enraged Father and at intermissions, in full makeup and costume, he ran up the fire escape that led from his dressing room to the Garrick's balcony, and made his bows to the crowd up there. For weeks, no one could figure out why there was a sudden burst of applause from the balcony between acts.

From a critical standpoint, I think that *He Who Gets Slapped* was the summit of Father's acting career. He created

* *A Wayward Quest* (Boston: Little, Brown and Company, 1960).

many brilliant portrayals after that, but in the Andreyev play he reached a kind of winged victory over himself, that of total submersion in the dream world of the character. Sometime during the run, Constantin Stanislavsky, the messiah of Method acting, came to the United States with the Moscow Art Theater and after witnessing a performance of *He,* immediately dubbed Richard Bennett America's greatest actor and the foremost exponent of the Method's art in this country. The night of his visit to the Garrick, Stanislavsky went backstage to meet Father, and, emotionally overwrought by the performance, he threw his arms around him and kissed him. "My God!" Father said later, "I thought he was a Russian fairy!"

Except for the little he'd heard, Father knew nothing about the Russian techniques of acting, "sense memory," or any of the other mysterious, intellectual exercises of the cult. The Moscow Art Theater made brief appearances in the United States in 1922 and 1924, but The Group Theater, which spearheaded the message in America, wasn't established until 1930, and Stanislavsky's writings had no wide distribution until after his death in 1938. As an actor, Father relied on instinct, intuition and his own supreme imagination.

If asked what his greatest creative aspiration was, he always answered, "Versatility! There have been many fine actors spoiled by playing the same character year after year. To keep keen, to keep alive, to keep abreast of the times, one must work and study constantly. In the long run, the man in the theater who wins is the man who gives up the glory of the moment to gain the fine stability which versatility brings with it."

In certain ways, he used some of the Method's devices without realizing it, though he'd have been horrified to find the art of acting cataloged, labeled and diagramed. At rehearsals, like Method actors later on, he avoided straight memorization of a part and ad-libbed or improvised his lines for the first week or two. He said it kept him from consciously waiting for a cue, preparing a posture in advance, or mechanically arranging his voice before he spoke. Then, very quickly, he learned the lines as they were written, and at that point, relied on his photographic memory. Asked to explain the process of creating a part, he answered, "Acting is the nearest approach to the occult I know. I guess the only way to explain it, is not to explain it."

During the summer break of *He,* Father made his annual trip to the West Coast and got into another controversy, this time with Channing Pollock's *The Fool.* For ten years, Pollock's play had been industriously rejected by producers on both coasts, until Father read it and agreed to do a production at the Majestic Theater in Los Angeles. He made his usual unwelcome literary contribution and rewrote the ending, after sending the unsuspecting author off on a fishing trip. It was a four-act drama depicting what might happen to a man if he tried to live in modern times as Christ had lived in his. Few plays have ever survived the open hostility that greeted *The Fool,* a condition that was tailor-made for its star.

Despite the poisonous newspaper criticism, however, box-office receipts at the Majestic were excellent, and, when Father returned to the East in the fall, he talked Arch Selwyn into a New York production. Since Father was due to reopen *He Who Gets Slapped,* Selwyn cast James Kirkwood in his role and the cast included Mother, Henry Stephenson, a young juvenile named Robert Cummings, and Sara Southern, Elizabeth Taylor's mother. *The Fool* was given a few preliminary performances in a movie theater in White Plains, New York, and opened on Broadway at the Times Square Theater on October 23, 1922. Again the reviews were venomous, but little by little the tide turned, receipts jumped and from the fourth week on, the company played to standing room.

While Mother was enjoying a new hit, Father took *He*

*Who Gets Slapped* on the road. Once more his reviews rang with ecstatic praise, but business was only sporadic. In some cities he played to packed houses, in others the theaters were only half-filled, and again, he proceeded to take matters into his own hands to elevate the public's taste. In Dayton, Ohio, he placed an advertisement in the local newspaper, which was heavily outlined in black borders as his expression of mourning.

To the
Theater Goers
of Dayton
    I Continuously Hear
    the Cry That You Have
    QUIT GOING TO THE
    THEATER
        BECAUSE
    You Get Nothing Good
        WELL. . . .
I'm bringing you something to test your intelligence. Your sense of the beautiful. "HE WHO GETS SLAPPED" is a test of anyone's mentality, and your only excuse of absence from the Victory Theater tonight and tomorrow is sickness, previous engagement, poverty or the apathy of your own atrophied soul.

RICHARD BENNETT

In Cincinnati, however, Father waxed positively lyric, and praise from Caesar was praise, indeed. "Among Cincinnati theatergoers are people of rare discernment. I felt the understanding of my audience at once; a sort of mutual understanding that the experienced actor is quick to sense. *He Who Gets Slapped* is not a play whose meaning is obscure or difficult to comprehend, but its fullest charm is disclosed only to people of perception and delicacy. Such an audience I have found in Cincinnati!" In that city, of course, he never played to an empty seat.

When he reached the West Coast, due to the poor box-office in San Francisco, the run was cut short by two weeks and Father closed his beloved play, but not before a parting shot. Stepping before the curtains on the closing night, still clad in his clown costume and makeup, he addressed his audience with a dazzling smile, pointed out a small boy in one of the front rows, and said, "Do you see that little boy down there? His mother thought she was bringing him to the circus. Well, ladies and gentlemen, that little boy is going to have a beard down to his navel before I play this God damned town again!"

# 5

When Father returned from the tour of *He Who Gets Slapped*, the family faced the serious domestic crisis of Mother's and Father's separation and the establishment of separate residences in the fall of 1923. Occasionally, Father merged his personal life with his professional one, and he was seldom shy about sharing his domestic troubles with anyone who would listen.

His next play was *The Dancers* by Gerald du Maurier, a huge success in London, with the author and Tallulah Bankhead in the leading roles, and transported to New York's Broadhurst Theater on October 17, with Father and Florence Eldridge. Projecting himself as the hero, it provided him with a chance to express something of his domestic martyrdom. "A play is not worth producing," he said, "unless it exemplifies some vitally significant human trait. *The Dancers* has the world's most sympathetic theme: a true heart rejected. Its central theme lies in the hunger for romance that's in the soul of every man in the sense of hunting the wide world over for an ideal loved one. The love scenes are so written as to make each woman in the audience wish she were playing them with me." Privately, he told a friend, "I wish to hell Mab would come to see every performance."

There was a small role of a dance-hall girl in the play, and Father thought it would be a good opportunity for Constance. She half accepted his offer; then she realized it would demand a run-of-the-play contract and the subsequent tour and refused, because she said she didn't want to be bound by anything. The part went to Barbara instead.

For more than a month all was serene and polite, and seemingly things worked in perfect harmony for the Bennetts, despite their separate residences. Nightly, Father and Barbara appeared together in *The Dancers*—he, puffed with pleasure that one of his offspring had been introduced to the footlights of Broadway, a fact particularly noted in his opening night curtain speech. Seventeen-year-old Barbara quietly went about her work and managed to thwart his discipline in a number of adroit ways. The results were often cataclysmic.

For Barbara, life with Father was something akin to that of the Barretts of Wimpole Street. One of the regulations laid down for her conduct under his roof was a twelve-o'clock curfew, and he was rigid about it unless she told him in advance where she was going and with whom. On a night late in November, Barbara accepted an invitation to a post-performance party from Pat Somerset, a young actor in *The Dancers*. She left Father a note, which seemed to have escaped his notice, and by four o'clock in the morning he'd worked himself into a lather of old-fashioned Father Bennett rage, breathing brandy and disapproval from every pore. He called Mother, who joined him in the vigil, and they waited together until dawn, when Barbara finally drove up with Pat Somerset in tow.

Armed with a stout walking cane, Father greeted the guilty pair with a running stream of violent abuse and made a dash for Barbara. Mother interfered and he turned his wrath on Pat Somerset instead. The very sight of the young actor was equivalent to waving a cape at a wild bull, and Father charged right in and gave him what he later described as "a damn good caning!" while Mother and Barbara watched and wept from ringside. At that point a policeman appeared, but Father was so fired with victory he invited the officer to mind his own damn business and accompanied the invitation with a poorly aimed blow. That was a tactical blunder. The policeman apparently misunderstood the noble motives of an outraged parent, belted him right in the eye, and dragged him off to the West Forty-seventh Street Police Station. They were followed by a tearful wife and daughter, while Pat Somerset fled into the dawn to a safer, saner climate.

At the police station Mother was urged to press charges, which she declined. The desk sergeant must have been a family man because "The Indiana Mauler" was sent home with only a reprimand, a somewhat discolored eye, and the comforting thought that the family honor remained un-sullied. Barbara refused to return to life under Father's roof and moved in with Mother and Constance, all of which received a good deal of attention in the newspapers. It was not our finest hour.

That fall Father took Constance to the annual Actor's Equity ball in New York and introduced her to Sam Goldwyn who, enchanted by her blonde beauty and poise, proposed a screen test. The test proved his hunch was right, and she was offered a part in Goldwyn-First National's *Cytherea*, a screen adaptation of Joseph Hergesheimer's popular novel, to be filmed in Hollywood. Mother was opposed to the idea of Constance going to Hollywood alone, Father saw no harm in it, and it produced another donnybrook. Constance pulled a Dick Bennett and wept, stormed, cajoled and threatened. Confronted by both Father and his feminine counterpart, Mother had no choice but to relent.

Constance negotiated her own contract and Father, celebrated for his own shrewd bargaining, beamed with pride when she demanded that Goldwyn pay her round-trip transportation from New York, in advance. When Phil Plant found out the film was to be made in Hollywood, he forbade her to leave, which was all she needed to cement the deal. After breaking their engagement again, she left in a huff in the early months of 1924 to make her first Hollywood film, while Phil bombarded her with long-distance phone calls and apologies. The romance was on again, for at least twenty-four hours.

In *Cytherea*, directed by Father's old friend, George Fitzmaurice, Constance played a beautiful film actress, a role reputedly patterned after Lillian Gish in the Hergesheimer novel. In a cast that included Irene Rich, Lewis Stone and Alma Rubens, her brief but sparkling performance did not go unnoticed. By the time *Cytherea* was released in 1924, and Sam Goldwyn gave a thought to putting Constance under contract, she'd returned to New York and, for Pathe, was playing the Long Island society girl kidnapped by an international crime ring in a ten-chapter Perils-of-Pauline type of serial called *Into the Net*. None of the ten chapters pleased Philip Plant.

Meanwhile, Father and Barbara maintained a truce for the rest of the run and a brief tour of *The Dancers,* and when it closed, she went into a production of Victor Herbert's operetta, *Dream Girl,* along with Fay Bainter and Elsa Heifetz, Jascha's sister. Father was delighted that his two older daughters had embarked on theatrical careers, though he was somewhat put out that their ambitions lacked any real drive. Constance pursued a career in films only because it was fun and it irritated Phil Plant, which was even more fun, and Barbara continued in the business because she danced divinely, looked beautiful and opportunities presented themselves easily.

I was equally determined to have nothing to do with the profession, though I did relent my sophomore year at St. Margaret's and put together a revue, directed by me, with material lifted bodily from *Charlot's Revue,* a current Broadway hit starring Gertrude Lawrence and Bea Lillie and produced by Andre Charlot and Walter Wanger. My out-and-out plagiarism didn't bother me at all, but retribution was swift when I wrote the lyrics of a song on a blackboard so the girls in the cast could learn it during rehearsals. I guess the song was pretty hot stuff, at least for St. Margaret's. It began with "Virginia, Virginia, the devil is in ya" (not from *Charlot's Revue*), and the school authorities made me erase it from the blackboard because they thought it was too "racy."

In the fall of 1924, Father began rehearsals for a new play produced by the New York Theater Guild which would net him fresh laurels and new controversies. It was *They Knew What They Wanted* by Sidney Howard, with a cast headed by Father, Pauline Lord and Glenn Anders. He loved the role of Tony, an elderly Italian grape grower in California's Napa Valley, and attacked the role with customary relish.

When the play opened at the Garrick Theater November 25, 1924, critics hailed it as the best American offering of the year. Later that season, author Sidney Howard was awarded the Pulitzer Prize for Dramatic Literature. The acting company also received its share of superlatives, and the Theater Guild had another hit on its hands. With Richard Bennett in the cast, its hands were full.

Father continued his practice of addressing audiences, and although his speeches usually occurred after the final curtain, he occasionally stepped out of character when distracted or otherwise annoyed. A few minutes after the play began one night, the steam pipes at the Garrick set up a great hammering racket, and Father signaled the stage manager to ring down the curtain. Then he stepped down to the footlights and said, "I am assuming that you ladies and gentlemen have come to hear a play, not the heating equipment. It is impossible for the human voice, even mine, to drown out the sounds you are now hearing from the rear. When the engineer has finished his pinochle game backstage and attends to his business with the machinery, the play will resume." For a few minutes there was a hushed silence, during which even the steam pipes cooperated, then the curtain went up and the company played the first five minutes of the show over again.

Much of his temperamental behavior during the run of *They Knew What They Wanted* stemmed, I know, from his unhappiness over the break with Mother and the dissolution of his household. Essentially he was a family man, and deprived of a family atmosphere, his irascibility and tempestuousness multiplied. He drank more than usual during that period and for the first time his performances began to suffer. It was the beginning of his diminishing powers.

Once during a long and difficult speech of Pauline Lord's, she discovered that Father was dozing through it all, even giving out little snores from time to time. Miss Lord struggled through in valiant style, finished the speech, and said, "Poor old Bennett, he's dead at last!" Then she turned and swept offstage. Father woke with a start, jumped to his feet and shouted after her, "Polly, come back, I'm sorry! Please come back!" Since he was supposed to be an invalid confined to his wheelchair, no doubt it gave the audience pause.

His troubles were compounded in the middle of the run when, in the spring of 1925, Mother instituted divorce proceedings after almost two years of separation. Father tried to win her again with promises of good behavior, his great remorse and contrition, and the family needs of their three daughters. Each time, he destroyed the idyllic images by seeking the company of any number of other ladies in his collection, and rumors of his escapades would reach her again. Mother was then appearing with Lionel Barrymore in *Three Knaves and a Knight,* and Father mailed love poems to her dressing room daily. But his poetic attempts to make amends were of little use, for he mailed them on his way to other pleasures. With the deepest kind of regret, Mother had no choice but to make their separation final, and she filed for divorce, charging him with "misconduct."

When it was announced in the newspapers, the headmistress at St. Margaret's called me into her office and told me not to discuss my parents' divorce with any of the girls. Even then it seemed a cruel and unnecessary warning. I was too unhappy over it myself to discuss it with anyone but Mother. I'd begged her not to divorce him. Even though Father still frightened me a little, I loved them both and certainly was against any final break between them.

I clearly remember the day in April of 1925 when Mother went to court to receive her final decree. It was a few weeks after my fifteenth birthday, and I'd been invited to a spring house party at Princeton. What should have been a gay and delightful time turned out to be sheer misery. All I could think of was that my family was disintegrating, that life would never be quite the same again. And it wasn't. I suffered painfully from shyness and was terribly aware of my nearsightedness. Yes, I thought, there's no doubt about it, I'm definitely the "mess" of the family. Now, if I were only as beautiful as Constance, things wouldn't be so dismal. I've always thought her the most beautiful Bennett, anyway, and so vital that her aliveness came up and hit you like a golden fist. She'd preceded me everywhere in my young social world and left behind her a trail of beaux, flatteries and conquests. I was terribly proud of her, but following in her wake made me feel more shy than ever. Father called her "The Terrible Swede," I suppose because she looked like a blonde Scandinavian, and she was a terror. I wondered why I hadn't been blessed with a little more of the dynamism she had in such abundance.

A few days after the final divorce decree, Mother and Father were photographed together, smiling mightily in the company of Barbara and Maurice Mouvet, the internationally famous dancing star. Shortly before, Barbara had been chosen Maurice's dancing partner, a post first offered to Constance, and was on her way to Europe to begin rehearsals for their opening at the Jardin De Ma Soeur in Paris. It was a great opportunity for Barbara, for Maurice was one of the most celebrated exhibition dancers of his time and he had danced his way into the presence of every crowned head in Europe. In any case, there they were on board *The Acquitania* at the sailing: Mother, Father, Barbara and Maurice, smiling for the cameras with their arms linked, as if nothing at all had occurred.

After that, Father tried to find solace in his work, but for once it wasn't enough and he looked for peace of some kind in other areas. In mid-June, one Saturday evening performance of *They Knew What They Wanted* was so speeded up that the curtain fell a half hour earlier than usual. Immediately after the performance he took a train to Montreal and simply didn't return for the Monday performance, wiring the Theater Guild in the meantime that he was in need of a few days' rest. For Monday's performance and the balance of the week, the Guild substituted his understudy, then announced that Leo Carillo would replace Richard Bennett permanently the following week. When he returned a few days later, Father was outraged at the replacement and protested on the grounds that he was ill, needed a rest and had been plagued by monumental personal problems. There was no doubt that he was tired and needed a rest, but he'd gone to Montreal for a little merriment, which combined the consumption of large amounts of alcohol with more athletic pastimes.

For some time it had been known along Broadway that Mr. Bennett and the New York Theater Guild were not on the best of terms. The Guild complained that he'd been introducing extemporaneous lines into the play, that on a number of occasions he'd addressed private remarks to the audience, and accused him of suffering from the actor's occupational disease of arrogance and temperament. Father's chief complaint was his inability to secure even a brief respite from a play that had involved him for eight months, so he simply took an unauthorized vacation. Although he was famous for his capricious behavior and disputes with management, he'd never before put an entire company in jeopardy. He'd always taken pride in his professional ethics and integrity. It was a sad lapse and the forerunner of others.

Father played the injured victim of a scurrilous injustice, and putting his enemies on the defensive, he laid a claim against the Theater Guild, contending that he still held a run-of-the-play contract which also entitled him to the road rights. The Guild countered by claiming that he had forfeited his contract and, therefore, had no rights whatever over the proposed road tour. That's where the matter stood for months, in litigation at Actor's Equity Association. It was never really resolved, and eventually, both parties preferred to forget the whole thing.

When Father returned to discover he'd been dismissed from *They Knew What They Wanted,* he went into a sanatorium in New Jersey for a week of complete rest. "On my doctor's recommendation," he insisted, but more specifically to dry out from a monumental hangover induced by his frolics in Montreal. When he emerged, he was quite ready to tackle an offer to play the Orpheum vaudeville circuit beginning in the late spring of 1925. Vaudeville then was in such public favor that managers had a difficult time engaging enough variety talent and turned to the legitimate theater for headliners, some of whom had included Mrs. Fiske, Ethel Barrymore, Sarah Bernhardt, Henry Miller and Rose Coghlan.

A one-act play, *A Common Man,* was written for Father by Tom Barry, and he started out joyous at the thought of a leisurely, lucrative job with nothing to do but go to the theater each night for thirty minutes. But his six-month tour on the Orpheum Time was anything but relaxing. Bookings were changed at a day's notice and he was buffeted to all corners of the country: San Francisco to Denver, Minneapolis to New Orleans, Louisiana to Chicago. Despite the frantic pace, he later wrote happily of his first and last fling at vaudeville. "One met such a variety of people. Tumblers, bar acts, adagio teams, hoofers, dog acts, ventriloquists, seal and horse acts, chimpanzee dramatic actors and midgets. They were all most affable artists!"

While Father was preparing for his vaudeville tour in April, ominous signals came from Switzerland, where Barbara was rehearsing for her debut with Maurice. She was unhappy and wanted to come home. The fitful rumors were accompanied by rash threats of suicide unless she was rescued from the grind of rehearsals and Maurice's tyranny. Apparently he was a tough taskmaster, and they'd worked mercilessly around the clock in preparation for the opening in Paris on June 5. Mother gave soothing statements to the newspapers, pronounced the stories pure invention and sailed at once for Davosplatz, Switzerland, where she found Barbara in a highly emotional state, worn out from rehearsals and worried about her approaching debut with one of the world's most renowned performers. But all she needed was Mother's reassuring presence, and by the time they opened at the Jardin De Ma Soeur, she was all enthusiasm again.

The reviews for Barbara and Maurice were lyric. Father included them in his curtain speeches on the vaudeville tour whenever possible, followed by an unabashed pitch on Constance's film career. His youngest daughter, Joan, he told a Chicago audience, was still in school and too young to try her theatrical wings, but he was sure all the girls would come to the stage eventually. The theater was in their blood, why should they want to be milliners or designers, or anything save actresses? Then, warmed by his subject, he finished off with a few modest remarks concerning our potentialities, and the closing declaration, "My God, the day may come when I'll be known as the father of the Bennett girls. It would damn well serve me right!"

In retrospect, the year 1925 was one of complete distraction for Mother. She could scarcely pick up a newspaper without reading something about one of the Bennetts, from her own divorce in April, to Barbara's discontent and subsequent triumphs in June, and Father's battles with the Theater Guild. But somehow during that year she managed to find time to appear in a limited run in New York of Congreve's Restoration Comedy, *Love for Love,* in which she scored a great personal success as Mistress Frail.

By then, however, she was working less and less in the theater, and it seems curious now that the very thing Father had demanded of her for so many years began to take place only after they were separated. Her acting career had been successful and distinguished and might have been even more so had her efforts not been dissipated by domestic crises and demands. But she was no longer ambitious for herself as she once had been.

Once Barbara had been launched successfully on her new dancing career, Mother went to London to visit friends. She didn't know it then, nor did I, but I was about to give the family a run for its controversies. Until then, I'd been more or less dutiful and obedient, probably because I was too shy and too young to be anything else. Except for my display of "racy" lyrics on a blackboard and the temporary lapse of sporting red nail polish, I think I could be rated a model student. But by the end of my second year at St. Margaret's, I'd begun to protest, and as time went by, it became more vocal.

There were several reasons for my growing unhappiness at school. First of all, my two best friends had left after our freshman term and I'd found no satisfactory substitutes. Then, too, Miss Chandler, the English teacher, had told me that I'd never have enough points to graduate anyway at the rate I was going. With that engaging remark ringing in my ears, I begged Mother to let me leave St. Margaret's and finish my education elsewhere. She relented and, on her arrival in Paris, made arrangements for my entrance into Le Lierre, a finishing school in the Bois de Boulogne.

Even then, I'd quite made up my mind that when I finished my education, I'd either get married and raise a family or strike out on a career as an interior decorator. Above all, I would have nothing to do with the theater or any other part of the entertainment world, that much was certain. In any case, how could I go into the theater with an inferiority complex as big as mine? And I was much too plain, I knew that. Besides, the theater was thoroughly invested with Bennetts and the competition was formidable. I adored my family, even though they frightened me a little, but I felt overshadowed by my beautiful sisters, who'd already embarked on successful careers, and by my celebrated, tempestuous parents.

No, I preferred to blend into the background of that brilliant, gifted breed and more than anything, I wanted a stable life of my own away from the intrusions of headlines and gossip. I knew that my family would have been distressed at my feelings of inadequacy, so I said nothing to anyone, but thought it out by myself once and for all. Father's predictions that I, too, would follow the family profession would simply prove to be false. Another couple of years in school and I'd be quite prepared to face life in other directions. At any rate, that's how I thought of myself at the time and, as I look back on my fifteen-year-old wisdom, I guess I was more nearsighted than I realized, not only optically.

Chaperoned by Mother's friend, Countess Ina Bubna, I boarded *The Homeric* in mid-June, bound for the final stages of my education at Le Lierre. Years later I discovered that one of the visitors on board that day of the sailing was Walter Wanger, who noticed me in the crowd and asked his friend, Gilbert Miller, who I was.

"That's Richard Bennett's youngest daughter," Gilbert told him. "Forget it, Walter, she's much too young!"

Constance, in New York for a brief stay and a few brisk rounds with Philip Plant, came to see me off at the sailing. Among the passengers, she recognized John Fox, a young man she knew, and brought him over to be introduced. None of us realized at that moment that Constance's casual introduction would mean the beginning of the end of my childhood and bring about the next vast change in my life.

I thought he was the handsomest man I'd ever met. He was also about ten years older than I, and the thought of an Atlantic sailing in the company of such extreme sophistication was a delightful prospect. Until then I'd only dated college boys, football players and other youthful types, all so terribly callow compared to a mature man like John Marion Fox. He began to pay me a great deal of attention. I was very impressed. I knew that one of his big romances had been Norma Shearer, and I was greatly flattered to be considered in the same league.

Obviously, he was a man of the world. The son of an affluent and socially minded family, he was handsome, amusing and well-educated. But Jack wanted nothing so prosaic as the business world, he wanted to produce plays. His father was a Seattle lumberman, and from time to time, Mr. Fox had put up the money to finance his occasional attempts at theatrical production. In fact, that was the reason for his trip to London at the time, to produce a musical comedy written by Fred Jackson. There, at least, I was on common and familiar ground and could be sympathetic and understanding of his theatrical ambitions.

What started out as a casual shipboard meeting developed into a courtship in no time at all, and as I look back, everything conspired to aid us. In addition to my own starry-eyed infatuation, the shipboard setting was irresistible. There was further though unintentional cooperation from my chaperone, the Countess Bubna, for once we'd passed the Statute of Liberty, she was confined to her stateroom with a splendid case of seasickness.

There was just the tiniest flaw in that whole blossoming time. It occurred to me, fleetingly, that Jack did drink rather a good deal, but then I thought perhaps it was just a sign of his worldliness.

By the time *The Homeric* arrived in Cherbourg, I was

smitten, and apparently he was no less so. Instead of getting off the ship and continuing on to Paris, I stayed aboard and went right to London with Jack. Mother was still in London at that point, and I stayed a month with her. She didn't approve at all of my relationship with Jack Fox, and undoubtedly, she breathed more easily when I left for Paris in late August to enroll at Le Lierre.

From the moment I arrived, I didn't like that place. To me there was something cold and forbidding about it, and it seemed even more so because it was almost deserted. Since I'd arrived before the term started, there was no one at school except for a few staff members and two girls my own age, neither of whom spoke English. I spoke French only well enough to make myself misunderstood. I felt like a complete outsider. Here I am in Paris, I thought, the gayest most wicked city in the world, and I'm living in a tomb. I was, after all, a mature young woman. That should have been obvious to anyone, and if all that bright life was going on out there in the world, I thought I should be experiencing some of it myself. And surely it would add to my own image as a sophisticate to be escorted by a wicked Parisian or two. There was no sense in waiting for things to happen behind the gloomy walls of Le Lierre, so I decided to make them happen myself.

Jack came over from London on weekends, a fact that did not delight the school authorities in the least; but despite the pinched frowns of disapproval, I managed to see quite a bit of the nocturnal life of the city. Zelli's, The 400 Club and The Ritz Bar all contributed to my worldly education. Barbara was still in Paris, too, dancing with Maurice, and I went to see her on several occasions. I thought it all very lively and exciting, and indeed, it was a period in the mid-twenties which seemed the very peak of glittering high life.

But Le Lierre grew more oppressive and the time came when I felt I'd had enough of prison life. One night I crept out of the building with only a handbag and the clothes I was wearing. It was dark as a cave and I took a box of matches with me, but the matchbox held a number of safety pins, a tribute to my sense of the practical, and only two or three matches. Somehow I groped my way outside, climbed over the wall and ran to the nearest subway entrance with the idea of finding Katherine Klein, a friend who'd been one of my classmates at St. Margaret's. I'd never ridden the Paris Metro before, had no idea of direction and spoke little French, so I guess it was only luck that finally led me to the Klein address. Katherine's family was horrified to find me running around Paris alone, a cheeky teen-ager who was "over the hill" from school, and they greeted me with such distaste that I left at once and checked into a nearby hotel.

Hell time. The school cabled Mother, who had returned to New York by then, and predictably, she was furious. But the idea of anarchy grew more appealing, and I stayed at the hotel for a few days, then called Jack to come and get me. He was in a slight state of shock, too, but he did rescue me and we returned to London where I stayed for several weeks with Lady Sharp, a friend of the Fox's. Poor Mother was distraught over my deepening relationship with Jack to begin with, but was even more so when the school expelled me without much ado. Being kicked out of Le Lierre couldn't have pleased me more, but it left the problem of what to do about my education, and Mother had to make long-distance arrangements from New York for me to attend another finishing school, L'Hermitage at Versailles. It was a happy choice. I loved it from the first day I entered. We were allowed more freedom and were treated as adults, and since I considered myself a member of that select group, it suited me perfectly. My memories of L'Hermitage are very happy ones and during the period of my stay there, I made a number of good friends with whom I've never lost contact.

Certainly, Versailles was no place to forget about love. Against that enchanted background, I read Jack's ardent letters and sent my own in return. I don't think L'Hermitage approved very much either, but frequently during the year he came to see me on weekends.

For once, Father was oddly permissive of my independent behavior and wrote me his views in a bittersweet letter that I still treasure.

> How could I, who have so much in sweet memory of you possibly forget you. I exist in memory—that is the toll of age. You, in hope and anticipation which, however, demands its tithing in disappointment because of the flatness of realization. Make the most of your now so your future may have no regrets for shirked opportunities. I shall not bore you with reports that have come to me of your conduct. No censure of mine will efface or reduce your regrets. Just this, my dear, I love you. You are my privileged pride.

About the same time Father stirred a new debate in newspaper and social circles by cheerfully announcing his plans to marry Thelma Morgan Converse, the dark-haired twin of Gloria Morgan Vanderbilt, much to Thelma's surprise and that of her intended husband, the British peer, Lord Furness. It was regarded as somewhat odd that Father should ring the joy bells instead of Mrs. Converse and, far off in France, the unsuspecting lady immediately rushed to the cable offices to tell the world that there wasn't the slightest basis for Mr. Bennett's announcement. Greatly distressed, she quickly declared her indignation and denials in the press.

Father insisted there must be some mistake, and as for Lord Furness, well, that was just too absurd to discuss. The peer of the realm was dismissed with a few modest remarks. "After all, who is Lord Furness? A nobleman, that's all. Everybody knows about noblemen, and Thelma would be very foolish to marry anybody of that type. Now, take me. I've climbed the ladder of success in the most difficult of all professions. I am the father of three extraordinarily beautiful girls; they are all happy and have a beautiful mother. Constance is a celebrated actress. Barbara became the dancing partner of the famous Maurice. Joan will enter the theater as soon as she can shake free of a finishing school in Paris. I am, as I said before, their father. Let Lord Furness, or some other Lord, approach that record if he can!"

His attitude inspired Mrs. Converse to make a statement so definite that even Father admitted perhaps things weren't quite so rose colored as his early impulsive bulletins had indicated.

Unperturbed by that small flurry, Father continued his vaudeville tour, and several times in his travels reports reached the newspapers of his impending marriage to any number of more eligible ladies, most of them in the entertainment world. The announcement of his seventh engagement was timed almost to the day with Mother's return to New York in the early fall of 1925. Asked on her arrival what she thought of his amorous antics, she replied, "My, Mr. Bennett certainly has had a busy summer."

Clearly his romantic announcements were designed to attract Mother's attention in the hope of arousing jealousy, and also to counteract the disturbing rumors that had reached him by then of a new and important relationship in her life.

Aboard ship on her way to join Barbara in Paris the previous spring, Mother had met Eric Seabrooke Pinker, an English literary agent and the son of James Brand Pinker, one of England's most distinguished author's agents. Eric had been attracted to her at once, followed her to Paris, and invited her to London. There the friendship developed into a deepening attachment. I remember meeting him that summer in London. Naturally I resented and disliked him from the beginning, and the thought of Mother replacing Father in her affections, with anyone, was inconceivable. But in addition to the resentment born of love and loyalty for my father, I thought him overbearing and pompous. In all candor, he never gave me, or any of us for that matter, reason to regard him with particular affection from then on. Eventually Eric Pinker became my stepfather, though I could never think of him except as "Mother's husband." For a while he would offer her a new life of contentment, but ultimately, it turned to deep tragedy.

But all of that was in the future. For me, it was a time of transition. There were new sights and sounds, a blooming romance with Jack Fox, and always the enchanted setting of Versailles and school at L'Hermitage.

The time also netted me a flurry in the New York press. During a visit to The 400 Club, I'd met Jack Tompson, one of the celebrated Tompson twins who entertained there. He paid me some flattering attentions, that was all, but a few days later, a headlined column in the *New York Telegraph* read: "JOAN BENNETT, 15, TO WED TOMPSON?" Since it came hard on the heels of Father's innumerable romantic attachments, and Constance's public scraps with Philip Plant, much was made of our wicked, wicked ways.

Up to that time, Constance had made seven films as a freelance player, all silents and all released in 1925: *The Goose Hangs High, Married?, My Son, Code of the West, My Wife and I, The Goose Woman* and *Sally, Irene and Mary*. In the last film she was costarred with Joan Crawford and Sally O'Neill, and played the hardhearted one of a trio of chorus girls. On the strength of that performance, Louis B. Mayer offered her a seven-year contract which she signed only after insisting on a clause allowing her to do outside film work, plus a six-week vacation every year.

She confounded Mayer by taking the first year's vacation at the beginning of her contract, at which time Phil Plant went West and they announced their engagement for the third time. When Phil learned that Constance had committed herself to MGM for the next seven years, he marched back to New York, and a few weeks later, she received an invitation to his wedding to a Miss Judith Smith. Constance fired back a wire which read: "Congratulations. What do you want for a wedding present?" Philip responded by presenting himself in person. The result was another reconciliation, and they returned to New York together where Miss Smith, I feel certain, did not welcome them with much enthusiasm.

Constance still had two films to make for another company to which she'd been committed before the Metro contract. The first was to have been made in New York, but the location was changed to Palm Beach instead. Again, Phil objected violently to her leaving and Constance finally relented, agreed to marry him and give up films forever. The company to whom she owed the two films and MGM waived their contracts as a wedding present, and Louis B. Mayer extracted the promise that if she ever returned to films, she must return to MGM exclusively.

November 3, 1925, Constance and Phil were married in Greenwich, Connecticut, by the same Justice of the Peace who had officiated at her marriage to Chester Moorehead four years before. Perversely, Philip had objected to her going to Palm Beach to make a movie, then took her there on the honeymoon.

Father was furious. He'd never approved of "that young Plant," anyway. Sometime before meeting Constance, Phil had been involved in a serious automobile accident, and as the driver of the car, was the center of an unpleasant and highly publicized court case. Commenting on Constance's marriage, Father confided to a full house in Minneapolis, "I'm a little sad tonight. I've just lost a daughter. I don't believe the bridegroom's parents like Constance any better than I like Philip Plant, but they're both twenty-one and it's none of my business. I hope they're happy." Privately, he told a friend, "Now she can surely go to hell!" But Father forgot, or wouldn't acknowledge, the large helping of Richard Bennett in Constance. She would do what she wanted to do, and the similarity in their natures was cause for a good deal of friction between them in the years that followed.

A few months later, Constance and Philip were living in Europe and had become the darlings of the continental society set, what was known then as "Café Society." For a time, she was idyllically happy in that glittering atmosphere and gave little thought to the film career she'd left behind.

By early March of the following year, it was clear that Barbara's dancing career with Maurice Mouvet was faltering and near the breaking point. A tyrant when it came to the discipline of his partners, Maurice found it impossible to suffer her caprices. An argument over a Patou gown of Barbara's led to a full-blown explosion, and without warning, she left him flat just before their New York opening at The Clover Club. Commenting on her hasty departure, Maurice said, "I know nothing of Miss Bennett's private affairs, nor the reason for her leaving. I say 'hello' and we dance, then I say 'goodbye.'" The partnership was dissolved, Barbara left for California, and Maurice returned to Paris with a new partner.

I stayed contentedly at L'Hermitage all that term, biding my time, studying, and learning that a preposition was nothing to end a sentence with. Still, I was determined to accept Jack Fox's proposal of marriage, despite the energetic opposition from both families. Mother had returned to England in April and I went to London at once after the term ended in June, to make what I knew would have to be an inflexible stand. It created another family crisis. Mother put up every resistance at her command and gave me a dozen good reasons why I shouldn't marry at that time. I was still little more than a child, he was much too old for me, and there was the unpleasant fact that he drank too much. Everyone knew that. Of course, I knew it too, and simply ignored the fact because I was so taken with him. Besides, he'd made it very clear "all he needed was me" to cure him of the habit, and I believed it with all my heart. And will there ever come a day when women stop marrying men with the idea of reforming them?

Father got into the act and called long distance from the States, somewhere on tour. First of all, it was neither right nor fitting, in his view, that I should marry before Barbara. Daughters should be married in succession, based on their ages, and as the third child I must wait until the second was launched into matrimony. That's the way it was done in the best families, according to Father and Queen Victoria. He was almost incoherent with rage, although not quite, and the next and final message which came through the transatlantic cable was quite clear.

I WILL NEVER, REPEAT, NEVER GIVE MY CONSENT!

We had a church wedding with all the trimmings. September 15, 1926, Jack and I were married at St. Luke's Church in Chelsea. I wore an ivory satin gown by Lanvin and carried white orchids. Mother gave away the bride, who was scared stiff and cried all the way down the aisle. Jack's best man was Fred Jackson, the American playwright. There was Lohengrin to begin the ceremony and Mendelssohn to end it, then a reception at 22 Carlyle Square, Jack's London residence.

For once, Father wouldn't discuss the marriage even in his curtain speeches. For a time he grumbled a bit, but finally he relented and sent us gifts and messages filled with good wishes and love.

For the honeymoon we first flew to Paris and stayed a day or two at The Ritz Hotel. One night we went to the Trocadero with Philip and Constance and both she and I spent a busy evening alternately watching Rudolph Valentino and Mae Murray on the dance floor while trying to keep an eye on the amount of liquor consumed by our respective husbands, which, incidentally, was considerable. The following evening we boarded a train for Venice and stayed a week at the Lido's Hotel Excelsior. The canals, Piazza San Marco, the Basilica, all remain clear and vivid, but today as I look at the pictures taken of us then, I see only a painfully young and solemn sixteen-year-old seated beside a handsome stranger on a beach. At the time, of course, I thought of myself as a mature woman, happily facing a life filled with wonder and new responsibilities.

We returned to London after the honeymoon and took up residence at 22 Carlyle Square, and now I think I was happier there than at any other time in our marriage. Jack drank heavily, it was true, but for a while I was oblivious to anything but the fact that I was a married woman, and therefore, an adult.

I suppose if there was such a thing as a conventional Bennett, I was it, and my desire for stability manifested itself in a number of ways. I began a pattern that was set for the rest of my life. I became a systematic, compulsive housekeeper. For a time, at least, there seemed to be enough money to allow us to live well and with the help of servants, and I took over the household duties with determined energy. From that point on, my home represented the stability I needed and felt was necessary for a well-ordered life.

But too often, my wedded life was interrupted by the intrusions of alcohol. Finally I made a stand and insisted Jack stop drinking entirely, that we return to New York, and that he get a steady, dependable job, since his theatrical ventures seemed to go nowhere. It was that or else. We returned to New York a few months after the wedding and stayed for a time with Father, who by then had quite forgiven me for upsetting his Victorian views about marriage. Jack got a job as a runner on the New York Stock Exchange, we moved to the Shoreham Hotel and life was serene and happy again.

Soon after our return from England, Father left for Los Angeles to open in a new play called *Creoles*, where once more he rattled the chains of puritanism and created a flap with a daring play that dealt with sexual passions, left little to the imagination and gave to the Los Angeles stage a new baptism of unrestrained language. *Creoles* consisted of three riotous acts: the first a riot of lust, the second a riot of passion and the third a riot of nature, complete with a full-scale hurricane. In the role of El Gato, a swashbuckling Don Juan, even Father's detractors still called him "America's leading actor," and would-be censors admitted his performance was supreme, though they regretted the "shocking vulgarities" of the dialog. Spurred by the criticism, he spat out his lewd invective with such obvious relish that one critic declared it could only have been learned at first hand in a brothel, to which Father replied, "There is greater intellectual excellence to be found in a brothel than in any newspaper office in the country!"

There was nothing new in that controversy, nor is it new today. The public was extremely upset by a wave of stage wickedness in the late eighteen-nineties, when even conservative producers like Charles Frohman imported plays from Paris, and found the "spicy" ones more agreeable to the public. The first time anyone heard "God damn" from a stage was in Clyde Fitch's play, *The City,* produced in New York in 1909. Even as late as *Gone With the Wind* in 1939, eyebrows rose when Clark Gable read the famous line, "Frankly, my dear, I don't give a damn," which somehow seemed more scandalous on film than in a live stage performance.

But manners and morals are measured by what is currently standard. Those were the gracious days of old when "camping" meant pitching a tent. *Creoles,* however, would induce nothing but yawns when measured against today's theater and films where the standards include bare bottoms, tops, fronts and backs; the casual use of four-letter euphemisms for biological functions and sexual intercourse; and frequent invitations to perform the anatomically impossible. Taste, apparently, is no longer in fashion and sexual erotica often is evoked for one reason alone: to shock. Currently, the entertainment world seems to be populated with a sizable number of performers and writers who indulge their personal psychoses and private aberrations like naked primates in a zoo, while the audience eagerly plays the role of voyeur, and expects a vote of confidence for its acceptance of the "new wave" of sexual revelation and broad-mindedness. One wonders how far the current mindless orgy will go. Admittedly, some of the censorship, particularly in Hollywood, when I was involved in the industry, was ridiculous, unnecessary and often a product of fear, but the present excesses of pornography, it seems to me, have blurred the focus and parboiled the senses into believing that there is some relationship between creative art and acres of bare behinds. Fortunately, the public is often its own censor, and no doubt sanity will return before we revert completely to the prehistoric.

While Father conducted the campaign in Los Angeles, I managed to destroy the romantic image of marital bliss in New York by coming down with a rousing case of the mumps. Jack responded to the crisis with the quickest disappearing act in show business and lost no time in fleeing to London, using the excuse of pressing theatrical duties. He suggested I go to California to stay with his family for a time, and finally well enough to travel, I left for Los Angeles to visit my in-laws. It was a disastrous move in every way; a grim, unhappy time. They didn't like me any more than I liked them, and I didn't like them at all. They seemed to me the Western distributors for Babbitry, ultraconservative types who offered no room at all for high spirits and fun. My dogs, a couple of scrappy Pekinese, were my only source of pleasure and companionship. Eventually I met some friends of Barbara's with whom I could communicate and a special friend, Marge Kelley, also helped to make life more palatable. House rules at the Fox's included a ten-o'clock curfew, and once, when I was entertained at Marge's for dinner and returned at eleven, I was delivered a stiff lecture.

Matters didn't improve much, even when Jack returned from London two months later. I was in for a shock. There was something so different about him. I seemed confronted by an utter stranger. He'd grown a moustache for one thing, he'd gained weight and seemed much older than I'd remembered. Of course, there was the same old problem of heavy drinking. I found him something less than adorable when, in a rage one night, he stuck his foot through the windshield of his mother's car. I began to suffer from a plain, old-fashioned case of disenchantment but tried to stifle my uneasiness, and we returned to London and 22 Carlyle Square.

It was shortly after our return to England that I discovered I was pregnant, and I went off expectantly to the nearest doctor to confirm my suspicions. He must have been a veterinarian and told me my symptoms were merely due to the sudden change of climate. Then I found another doctor in Harley Street who was more positive in his diagnosis; yes, it was true, I was going to have a baby. For a time, despite my growing apprehensions over domestic difficulties, my joy made me oblivious to anything else.

But the old haunt of alcohol returned, and in desperation I left Jack and went to live with a friend. He tried to make amends, and finally I decided on one more attempt. I agreed to a reconciliation, after extracting a solemn promise that he'd stay on the wagon. Then, because I wanted the baby to be born in the United States, I insisted that we return home. Prohibition was still in effect, so I chose a ship on a United States line which served no liquor during the crossing.

We arrived in Los Angeles and moved into a small, one bedroom house on Bronson Avenue in Hollywood. Jack kept his promise to stop drinking and managed to get a job. Life was a little more sane as I waited out the months before the baby's birth, but it turned out to be only a prelude of deceptive calm.

# 6

Modernized versions of Shakespeare enjoyed some vogue in the nineteen-twenties and in 1926, Mother observed her thirtieth year in the theater when she appeared in a controversial modern-dress version of *Hamlet,* produced by Horace Liveright and directed by Basil Sydney, a celebrated English actor. Sydney also played the title role, Mother appeared as Queen Gertrude, and the cast included Helen Chandler as Ophelia, Kay Francis as the Player Queen and Eugene Lockhart in the role of the First Gravedigger. Conservative reviewers lambasted Sydney's daring production, while the liberals applauded it and the public lined up at the box office to take sides.

Unfortunately, Mother's appearances were limited. Two months after the opening, she fell on a flight of steps onstage, and broke an ankle. "I always wondered," she said later, "if it was Shakespeare's revenge!" Nearly fourteen years would pass before she stepped on a stage again, and then for the last time.

Until the updated *Hamlet,* Mother had traveled a great distance in her career. There had been a multitude of stage appearances since those early days in Grandfather Morrison's company, from small-town gaslit opera houses to Broadway, cross-country tours and continually shifting hotel rooms. She'd given thirty years to the feverish life of the stage, twenty-three of them spent as the wife of a gifted, erratic genius.

Finally, if regretfully, free of her beloved tyrant, she was restless and wondering what to do with the rest of her life. Acting held fewer charms for her, the stage was all too hectic and uncertain. Tranquility and security must take its place. Inevitably, of course, the theater still claimed her interest, and she felt she must do something with her energies and knowledge, if not in front of the footlights, then in some related field.

By then her personal relationship with Eric Pinker was cemented, and it was he who offered her, at least for a time, the emotional security she needed. Eric's father, James Brand Pinker, headed one of England's most successful and distinguished literary agencies, established in London in 1897. He'd encouraged and helped to develop many of Britain's most successful authors, and his client list had included Thomas Mann, John Galsworthy, Joseph Conrad, Frank Swinnerton and Arnold Bennett. Eventually both Eric and his brother, Ralph, were introduced into their father's business.

For some years, James Pinker had hoped to establish an American branch of his operations headed by Eric, and about the time Mother appeared on the scene, plans for a New York office had moved closer to reality. She urged Mr. Pinker to include more theatrical literature in his properties, but that aspect of the business had never been an important part of his agency and he hesitated at the idea. Plays, she insisted, would continue to be written, and playwrights needed business advice and encouragement as much as writers of fiction. To prove her point, she wheedled three plays from the Pinker agency and sailed for Manhattan in a completely unfamiliar role; she was no longer playing in the theater, but selling to it.

She had no office, no experience, no prospects and very little money, but within a week after her arrival in New

York she sold one of the Pinker properties, Arnold Bennett's play, *Don Juan*, to the Shubert Brothers. A day or two later, she gave a party at the Algonquin Hotel, to which she invited producers, actors, directors, press agents and news reporters, and announced that she was now in the business as a play broker and needed clients. The next day, twenty-three plays were delivered for her perusal and within two weeks the pile mounted to nearly one hundred. She managed to read them all, found five acceptable and by then had become the victim of a nightmare that pursued her for years. She dreamed that New York's population had taken to playwriting, and each one of its seven million people sent her a play, demanding that it be read.

When Eric rejoined Mother in New York, he found her deluged with plays, new clients and willing managers. The Pinker branch office was finally established in New York City in 1927, and began professional life as the Pinker–Morrison Agency, with offices at 515 Madison Avenue. Duties were divided between them. Eric handled the fiction and nonfiction writers and all business and financial matters of the agency, while Mother handled theatrical literature exclusively. Within two years, she'd become one of the half-dozen topflight play brokers in New York and represented some of the most distinguished plays on the American stage. She turned into a subtle, hypnotic saleswoman, although she used none of the techniques usually employed in the business of agenting plays. Rather, she conducted her business with a deceptive coolness, easily and sociably, and charmed contracts from some of the most ruthless theatrical figures of the time.

Beneath the gentle exterior, her tenacity was immense. If she had faith in a play, nothing short of a natural disaster would stop her from sending it on to another producer who might consider it. She touted Rose Franken's *Another Language* for four years before it was sold. Thirty-eight producers turned it down before Arthur Beckhard accepted it and brought it to Broadway as one of the big hits of 1932.

Soon after the Pinker–Morrison Agency was established in New York, Mother and Eric were married, June 19, 1927, at Marie Sterner's art gallery on East Fifty-seventh Street. They were attended by Mr. and Mrs. Basil Rathbone, and among the guests were Jane Cowl, Violet Kemble Cooper, Blanche Yurka, Edward Knoblock and my sister, Barbara. I was in London, wondering if Mother would want to be made a grandmother when she was so recently a bride. Constance was still in Paris, and Father was sulking in Chicago.

Earlier in the year, most of Father's theatrical assignments had been centered on the West Coast. He'd signed a temporary cease-fire with the New York Theater Guild for a brief tour of *They Knew What They Wanted* and ended the run in San Francisco. It was then that he renewed his acquaintance with a society woman and theatrical dilettante named Aimee Raisch Hastings, and in no time at all added her to his growing catalog of possible fiancées. Previously she'd had a small walk-on role in his production of *Creoles*, an experience that induced in her a case of instant hero worship, but since he'd been preoccupied with other pleasures of the moment, their friendship didn't develop until he returned to San Francisco in Sidney Howard's play.

Smitten like a schoolgirl by the glamor of the theater, Aimee had appeared in a few amateur productions in San Francisco's little theater and church groups and seemed the very prototype of Father's archenemy, "the society woman determined to elevate the stage." Nonetheless, she entered his life at a time when he was "between engagements," that is to say, romantic ones. Overcome by his personal charm and his celebrity, she followed him everywhere like a dutiful shadow.

Soon, however, Father's attentions were diverted to a new production, *The Dove,* by Willard Mack. It was slated for a Los Angeles opening at the Belasco Theater only three days after the close of *They Knew What They Wanted,* and the director rehearsed the company in Los Angeles while Father worked independently on the leading role in San Francisco. On a Sunday morning he flew to Los Angeles in four and a half hours to begin rehearsals with the assembled company, and opened the following Tuesday. Today that flight is like going to the corner drugstore, but in 1927, when flying was a rarity for the general public, much was made of Father's feat as a flying actor. Aimee accompanied him and was brought down to earth when Father placed her in the crowd scenes at the Belasco.

In *The Dove*, a play with a Mexican setting, he played Don José Mario Lopez y Tostado, a swaggering, flamboyant character who described himself as "the best damn caballero in all Mexico." At one point during the run, he was forced to look for a new leading lady and, as a possible replacement, he brought a fiery young dancer from Mexico named Lupe Velez. Miss Velez's English was limited to "I'm hungry" and "please go to hell," and she was unable to cope with the extensive dialog in *The Dove*. For the first and possibly last time in his life, Father was bullied and intimidated by a member of the opposite sex, and later wrote of her, "She was born wild and she stayed wild. My God, how she carried on and led me to the belief that she would stick a knife in me at any moment. Hollywood, thank God, could never tame her and for that, she has my compliments."

He returned to San Francisco for another month as "the best damn caballero in all Mexico," and managed to evade Aimee long enough to flee to Chicago to open in *The Barker*, a play written by one of his Indiana boyhood friends, Kenyon Nicholson. In this raucous drama of carnival life, Father played a carnival pitchman and lost no time in barking back at the critics who dared to criticize the salty dialog. Charles L. Wagner, the producer, had taken the precaution of including a clause in the contract that prevented him from making his inevitable curtain speeches, one of the first to rob him of his public platform. The stipulation hurt his feelings but he finally agreed to it, and instead lobbed insults at the critics at other public gatherings and through correspondence.

One of his most ardent admirers at the time was the opera diva, Mary Garden. After witnessing a performance, Miss Garden sent a wire to producer Wagner filled with such extravagant praise that it was used thereafter in the advertisements. Such public attention from one of the world's most glamorous women drew fire from Aimee in San Francisco, and within days she arrived in Chicago to restake her claim. Meanwhile, she'd divorced her husband, a polo-playing San Franciscan named Harry Hastings, who showed his regret by immediately remarrying his first wife.

Then, news reached Father of Mother's marriage to Eric Pinker in New York. He felt it cruelly. Ever since their separation four years before, he'd secretly hoped for a reconciliation, and despite his amorous derelictions he still loved her dearly. But his pride went before reason, and determined to show his indifference, he married Aimee in Chicago July 11, 1927, less than a month after Mother's marriage to Eric. The wedding took place between a matinee and evening performance, with members of Aimee's family and the actors from *The Barker* company in attendance.

And that made two stepparents I didn't like. When I met Aimee later, I thought her the least likely person in the world for Father to have married. He, who'd always surrounded himself with beautiful and intelligent women, had chosen a rather superficial creature who strangled him with attention and hadn't the least idea of how to cope with his unrestrained impulses or his professional demands. To put it right on the line, I thought she was a horror. In her defense, however, it was like throwing a Christian to the lions, and he led the lady a merry chase for the next ten years.

From the beginning, the marriage was a disaster. Although not much given to admitting his mistakes, Father later wrote bitterly, "The only pleasure I remember during the run of *The Barker* was seeing Dempsey and Tunney in their memorable twenty-one-count bout, which was mild compared to the rounds coming up for me. The heat that summer wasn't the only thing unbearable in life. It was then that the most disastrous thing of my life occurred when I married a stage-struck society woman from San Francisco, Aimee Raisch. If, in a previous life, I had harmed anyone, I fully expiated the crime through this great folly. I suppose there is no one on earth who has not had a cross to bear, but I carried that one to a point beyond endurance." And in a rare moment of self-revelation, he added, "I trust that I may never again have the foolhardiness to feel the spleen that created that mistake."

Through the rest of the year and the early months of 1928, Jack Fox stayed within the bonds of his promise to stop drinking. That is, until two days before the baby was born. Then he disappeared and went on a forty-eight-hour binge, but my main concern was the impending arrival of the baby and I had little choice but to keep myself as free from dissension and emotional upheaval as possible. Jack returned from his frolics in time to drive me to the Good Samaritan Hospital in Los Angeles, but because it seemed we'd be kept waiting for a few hours, the doctor told him to leave and come back later. He left, but didn't return in time for the birth of our daughter on February 20, 1928, one week before my eighteenth birthday. Adrienne Ralston Fox, she was named after Mother, and also given a Fox family name. Of course, I thought her absolute perfection.

I've always thought that being a mother was the best of all possible careers. Like my own mother, I doted on babies, mine and anyone else's, and I think if I'd been born to a more conventional, nonprofessional family, I'd have doubtless grown up to be the old-fashioned one who did embroidery and minded the neighbors' babies until I had some of my own. Once I married, being anything but the mother of a family never occurred to me.

At last I had a living doll of my own, but playtime was over. I was about to face some hard realities. Apparently, Jack was overwhelmed by fatherhood and resumed his drinking on an even grander scale. Suddenly, we were in financial trouble. All of his theatrical ventures had failed and his jobs didn't seem to last very long for one mysterious reason or another. That state of affairs, combined with the drinking, aroused the disgust of his family, and they simply refused to give him any more money. They'd never approved of me, and our marriage did nothing to endear him further.

When Adrienne was born, Father paid for the hospital and Mother sent me money to engage a nurse. I remember I first found a "Dr. Holt" nurse, a trained specialist in baby care, but she turned out to be a specialized gin drinker and I had to replace her immediately with a less giddy type. I wasn't aware of it then, but Dr. Morris Slemons, who delivered Adrienne, wasn't paid until some time later when I returned to Hollywood with a film contract. He'd waited all that time, then hesitantly submitted a bill for his services.

I started managing the household on a shoestring and if I do say so, I got to be fairly efficient at budgeting. At one point, I remember saving dimes in a small savings bank. I might have saved myself the trouble, since they disappeared across the nearest bar along with a check Mother had sent me for the rent. On rare occasions, Jack's family relented and gave him money, but I never saw that for household expenses, and there was seldom anything to show for it except my husband's considerable hangovers.

It was a time of sheer misery. My only moral support was my friend, Marge Kelley, who lived nearby and whose husband, Billy, was also wrestling with a drinking problem. Mr. Kelley and Mr. Fox were thick companions. Once they went on a wild spree in one of the Mexican border towns and, judging from their condition when they returned, we were lucky not to have severed international relations. Marge and I commiserated, searched the most unlikely places for hidden bottles and preached temperance daily, with no effect.

Life was filled with one huge domestic crisis after another. Finally our battles reached such splendid emotional heights that I had to have Jack placed under a peace bond for my own protection and the preservation of my sanity. He was not at all sporting about it. He came to the apartment in a white-hot rage, charged around like a wounded buffalo and in a rousing finish, pulled the telephone out of the wall. I knew it was time for a strategic withdrawal and ran out of the apartment to the nearest phone and called the police. Since he'd violated the peace bond, he was carted off to jail where he spent a thoroughly uncomfortable ten days. Then, because he was threatened with an indefinite stay, I went down and bailed him out. At that point I could have had him committed to a state institution for a drying-out period but I refused and instead he was remanded to my custody. That idea wasn't particularly appealing. I had no wish to play custodian to anyone except my baby, and after that final blowup, I refused to take him back.

Humor, at the moment, seemed exceedingly well disguised. I was eighteen years old with a two-month-old baby, the father of whom was a hopeless alcoholic when he wasn't in jail, and lack of money was an everpresent fear. My overblown pride was at stake, too, and although my family had sent us money from time to time and may have had some vague idea of my troubles, I was too proud to share the whole story or admit my sizable error. All in all, the prospects were bleak. My marriage was a graveyard, and I felt a little like Eliza crossing the ice, jumping from one icy dilemma to another to escape the bloodhounds of despair.

Nevertheless, the realities were clear: minus one husband, plus one daughter. I had to get on with the business of making a living, and after my final separation from Jack, I limped along and on a couple of occasions found extra work in the movies to keep going. One job was a film with Corinne Griffith and the other, *Power,* starred Bill Boyd. During work on the latter film, I met another extra named Jane Peters, later known as Carole Lombard.

While all that was going on, after a lengthy tour through the South in *The Barker,* Father and Aimee returned to San

Francisco to continue the run there. One night he called me in Los Angeles but I missed the call and instead he talked to the nurse. After a few leading questions, she broke down and spilled the whole dreary tale of my marital disaster. Predictably, Father went into a blind rage and came flying down from San Francisco, waving a gun and threatening to shoot the father of my child unless I got a divorce. It was already chillingly clear that my marriage to John Marion Fox would never succeed, and amid Father's threats of homicide I instituted divorce proceedings.

By early summer, *The Barker* had closed in San Francisco, and Father was beginning to prepare for a new production in New York called *Jarnegan,* a play about Hollywood based on Tim Tully's novel. He told me he'd give me the ingenue role of Daisy Carol but, he said, I'd have to get myself East on my own. He wouldn't help beyond that, except to suggest I sell the furniture to pay for the trip.

With all my inflexible ideas about avoiding the theater, there I was, about to be the next one of the fifth generation to walk out on a stage. Just because I was born of a theatrical family didn't mean I'd automatically turn into an actress. On the other hand, it was the only thing I knew even a little about, by osmosis if nothing else. But more important to me at the time, it was a job. I decided to give it a try until I could figure out something else. The furniture went on the block, and I made preparations for the trip to New York.

My greatest quandary was five-month-old Adrienne. It seemed perilous to drag her cross-country in the summer heat; in those days before air-conditioned trains, I thought of it as an impossible task. Also, facing a debut in the theater, I knew I'd have about all I could handle alone in New York. After much hesitation, I decided to leave her in the nurse's care, and I felt more secure about it when Marge Kelley promised to pay them a daily visit. After writing out two or three acres of memos for Adrienne's care, I headed for New York in late July.

I was in for a shock when I arrived at the theater for the first day of rehearsal. Another actress Frances Fuller, was onstage rehearsing the role of Daisy Carol. Immediately, I went to Father for an explanation. "For God's sake," he said, "keep quiet and leave everything to me!" In those days, supporting actors were put on a kind of probationary period. If their work proved unsatisfactory within five days, managers had the right to dismiss them. Father invoked the ruling and I started rehearsals the next day. Miss Fuller later became the president of The American Academy of Dramatic Arts, and to this day I wonder if Father is remembered for his blatant nepotism. I knew he'd given me the opportunity to help myself, but I also knew he wouldn't have given me the chance if he hadn't thought I could deliver. Later on I learned that being a Bennett might have opened the door more easily, but it was more difficult once I'd walked through it.

So I started to work. And I mean work! During the rehearsal period, I stayed with Father and Aimee, and every night he drilled me in the part at home. A photographic memory helped me to learn lines easily and quickly, but I had then what might be described accurately as a tiny voice that drove Father to distraction. We rehearsed the scenes from a distance with two rooms between us. "My God," he told his leading lady, Margaret Mower, "I must do something about that voice. She was born a racehorse and I have to teach her to run!" It was a frustrating time for both of us. I worked all day at rehearsals and went home at night to Rasputin.

Every spare moment that was left to me, I spent telephoning Los Angeles to get detailed reports on the baby. Each time either Marge Kelley or the nurse would assure me she was flourishing and that would pacify me for a few hours. Then I'd think of something else and given the slightest breather in rehearsals, I'd run to the telephone again.

Father gave me no quarter. At the theater it was all business and serious work, and the fact that I was his daughter was of no importance. I've always been grateful for that and probably learned more in that one production than if I'd spent a year in a school of drama.

I learned early that I was only part of his preoccupation. Possessed of a magnificent voice himself, he made the entire company rehearse with more voice than would ever be used in performance. No aspect of the production escaped his notice and no detail was missed. He intruded himself into every corner and generated excitement throughout the entire company. His intrusions may have been a reason for the sudden departure of our director. After the preopening try-out in Brooklyn, George Abbott took over the direction, and I remember he wrote in an extra scene for me.

Opening night arrived on September 24, 1928, at the Longacre Theater, with all the customary flurry and excitement. There were wires from Mother, Constance and Barbara, all too far away to attend. It seems incredible now, but I was hopelessly blasé about the whole thing. Not a qualm in a carload, I was completely nerveless, and just too inexperienced to know any better. I didn't give a thought to what was expected of me, what to expect of myself, or even what the notices would be like. Father, on the other hand, was stiff with stage fright, and no doubt his fear was as great for me as it was for himself. His eyes bulged with terror, his hands shook, and my calm, stupid detachment made him furious. I remember I sat on a staircase in the wings just before my first entrance in the second act, calmly lapping up an ice cream sundae. "For God's sake," he hissed, "what do you think you're doing?" I didn't know what I was doing. I was just hungry.

His greatest pleasure of the evening was the father-daughter curtain call we took together. Then came his curtain speech, a ban which had been lifted for opening night only. He hoped the audience liked the play, his performance and his daughter. "But it doesn't matter whether you like me or not," he added. "I'm a habit!"

A searing indictment of Hollywood, *Jarnegan* was generally

well received by the press and though most critics noted the shortcomings of the play, they were unrestrained in their praise of Father's performance as the swearing, drinking, lecherous movie director. Again he was labeled "brilliant," "overpowering," "electric." He was no less pleased to find that I'd been generously acknowledged by the critics and marked the suitable passages, which he pressed on anyone unable to flee in time.

Once the good reviews were in, I was given a raise and a run-of-the-play contract, and when the possibility of a decent run seemed assured, the first thing I did was to send for the baby and the nurse. For a brief time they stayed with friends in Pelham, New York, until I could get settled. Meanwhile, Mother had returned to New York after another trip to England. She wanted me near her, and the nurse, baby and I moved to an apartment in the same building on East Forty-eighth Street where she lived with Eric.

Working with Father was rather like working with Niagara Falls. He was terribly demanding with every member of the company. I remember once I went blank for a moment and didn't answer a cue, and instead of sliding over it and covering for me, he just stood there waiting. He gave the cue twice and looked me right in the eye as if to say, "I want that line, young lady, and I'm going to wait right here until I get it no matter how long it takes." If he was a perfectionist with the rest of us, he sometimes took outrageous liberties himself, and would ad-lib or paraphrase lines, tricks at which he was a total master. When director George Abbott cautioned him about it on occasion, he played the wide-eyed innocent and said, "Good heavens, George, did I say that? Really?" But before long, a sly ad-lib would slip through again.

Even at his most outrageous he could be fun and amusing, and loved teasing people if he thought he could get away with it. If they rose to the bait, so much the better. Once, in a scene with his leading lady, he sat with his fly unbuttoned, the nightmare of every actor, but Margaret Mower found out later it was not accidental, and Father roared with laughter at her discomfort.

I think Father got more pleasure out of *Jarnegan* than anything he'd played in a long time. There was not a little of Richard himself in the title role, and he loved scourging Hollywood eight times a week in profane language. In the final scene of the play, he leaped to a platform and addressed the guests gathered at a wild Hollywood party. "If I were the Electrician of the Universe I'd pull the main switch and close down this city of painted shadows! I'm living in a dunghill, in search of a lily!" And the curtain descended amid thunderous applause from the gallery gods.

Offstage, he still played the heavy-handed father and often took me to task for my behavior or choice of companions, but it wasn't long before I adopted my sisters' tricks of defying him. One thing that was sure to loose havoc was George Jean Nathan. I dated George quite often and because he was one of Father's favorite enemies, his very presence was enough to invite apoplexy and a stream of abuse. "I don't want that snake slithering around backstage and, furthermore, I am withdrawing from him the privilege of calling me 'Dick.' He must learn how to address his betters!"

It was George Jean Nathan who told me he thought I should rename the baby. For some reason he didn't think Adrienne suited her and suggested she was more of a Renee. She, however, took matters into her own hands, and when she later began to talk, "Ditty" somehow came out of the baby gibberish and we called her that from then on.

The five-month run of *Jarnegan* was a memorable time for me. I had a steady job and a growing, healthy baby to look after and from time to time fortified my income with occasional jobs as a photographic model. Then I was asked to make a screen test, filmed in Manhattan, for Fox Studios. I don't remember much about it, but it must have been forgettable because the studio was mercifully silent. Shortly after, I met Walter Wanger for the first time. I was escorted to a party of Conde Nast's by George Jean Nathan that was also attended by Walter. My hair was long then and worn down around my shoulders, and when we were introduced, he said, "Well, Ophelia, where's your garland of flowers? Who do you think you are, Lillian Gish?" I thought he was somewhat more attractive than his smart greeting and then forgot it, until he sent me a message asking if I'd make a screen test for Famous-Players-Lasky at the Astoria Studios in Long Island. At the time Walter was general manager of all film production for Jesse Lasky and his chief aide. I did make the test but it didn't make any more of an impression than the one for Fox Studios, and Walter confided to Mother, "Your daughter is very sweet, Mrs. Pinker, but she'll never photograph!"

With the end of the New York run of *Jarnegan* in sight, Father made plans for the road tour, and I went into rehearsals of another play called *Hot Bed,* a property that had been negotiated by Mother and produced by Brock Pemberton. For awhile I was kept busy, dividing my time between daytime rehearsals of the new play and evening performances with Father. One night I was told that Joe Schenck of Feature Films and his assistant, John Considine, Jr., would be out front and wanted to talk to me after the play. Sam Goldwyn, then a copartner of the newly formed United Artists with Charlie Chaplin, Mary Pickford and Douglas Fairbanks, Sr., had asked Joe Schenck to look for an ingenue from the New York stage to play opposite Ronald Colman. The proposed film was *Bulldog Drummond,* scheduled to be Colman's first sound movie. Father was present and took over his parental duties at once. "If there's any talking to be done, they'll have to talk to me!" But I decided the time had come for me to speak for myself.

During the meeting with Mr. Schenck and John Considine, Jr., John asked me if I'd be interested in testing for Ronald Colman's leading lady in his first talkie. Without a second thought, I gave him a flat "no." My first two tests had been unsuccessful and I figured that if a studio wanted an actress badly enough, they'd sign her first and then do everything possible to make her look good. Besides, I thought, a screen test wasn't always a fair barometer. My refusal produced two pairs of arched eyebrows, but I was adamant. No, I wouldn't test, and that was final.

Apparently, they didn't find anyone they liked better and eventually I negotiated a five-year contract with United Artists Studios, making the decisions and the deal on my own, much to Father's annoyance. On the other hand, Mother, who'd always preferred that I concentrate on a stage career, was all for my going and realized it was a simple matter of finances. I had a child to support. I was getting a hundred and fifty dollars weekly in the theater and had been offered five hundred dollars a week for the film contract. Since Mother was still my legal guardian she arranged my release from the Brock Pemberton play and the run of the play contract with *Jarnegan,* so I was free to leave, despite strong warning against going to Hollywood from George Abbott and theater critic, Richard Watts.

Though Father detested Hollywood, the fact that I would make my film debut with an actor as distinguished as Ronald Colman seemed to pacify him somewhat. He gave me his grudging approval and promptly took the credit himself. "She is the hit of my show, but I don't want to stand in the way of my child's future. However, I'm willing to forfeit any claim on her services, and will cheerfully do so."

Nevertheless, he kept my name on the program as Daisy Carol when he later took *Jarnegan* on tour, even though the role was played by Elaine Temple. He like the public-relations ideas of a father-daughter team and didn't go out of his way to announce my replacement on the road. Many times in the future, people would insist they'd seen me in Chicago, Milwaukee, Omaha or San Francisco, though in truth I never played the role outside of New York.

Privately, however, Father was quite proud of the way I'd handled things, and as I made preparations for the trip to the West Coast early in 1929, he confided to a friend, "You never can tell about Joan. She has all kinds of possibilities!"

# 7

I suppose being one of the fifth generation in my family to enter the profession should have filled me with an awesome sense of responsibility, but frankly, at the time, I didn't give it much thought. I'd appeared in one Broadway play and was on my way to Hollywood as a means of making a living. I'd always taken my theatrical background for granted and didn't really know enough to be awed or frightened by my first experience. The family tradition meant very little to me then, although even in childhood I think I always felt there was something "different" about theatrical people.

I really don't know what sets them apart from others as a distinct tribe, for it seems to me most everyone dramatizes himself in some way and at one time or another. Children begin to "play-act" at an early age, and the urge for self-dramatization seldom dies completely. We often exist in realms of make-believe and fantasy where, governed by imagination, we mold life nearer to the heart's desire. Too, I think most people will admit to harboring a secret ambition to act, however fleeting. No matter what a man's chosen profession, the smell of greasepaint is a powerful lure.

Since the human impulse is to leave something of oneself in the way of an imprint, it seems a regret that the actor's art is such a transient one, for of all the arts acting is perhaps the most personal.

In the theater, the spectator is aroused or stirred or bored, as the case may be, but an hour or a day after the final curtain the performer's impact fades and only a general impression remains. Of the past, the best one can do is regard the theater as a series of experiences to be relived in the form of reminiscences, old playbills, programs and an occasional glimpse from a contemporary of a given time. I can only rely on these things to revive the spirit of my ancestors.

For an artist to ask for a direct invitation to impermanence seems a strange perversity. Furthermore, the theater is a chronically overcrowded business, and I've often wondered why people go about deliberately choosing it as a lifelong profession. What private reasons are there to give oneself to other men's dreams? I suppose there are as many answers to that as there are numbers of players in the twenty-five-hundred-year history of the theater. In my case, of course, the profession had been passed from parents to children, and when it got down to me, though I'd hoped for another career, I first walked through a stage door to perform because it was expedient.

Certainly, by its very nature, the theater is a precarious business, but I'll place odds it was just as shaky in ancient Greece. It's small wonder that George S. Kaufman dubbed the theater "The Fabulous Invalid," though the fabulous invalid is also a raving hypochondriac. Talk to any actor nowadays and you'll find that things are much worse this season than they were last year, a generation or a hundred years ago. No matter what the period, there are always "the good old days" to fall back on for rich comparison.

But in fact, when the first member of my family entered the profession in England almost two hundred years ago, the theater and its players were really having a rough time of it. My great-great-grandfather, William Wodin, was born in Wales about 1770. I have no idea what first prompted him to leap into the hazardous life of a performer, but he must have had what an English drama critic once called "a studied madness." Undoubtedly he fell under its spell at a country fair or saw his first performance from a barn hayloft, but whatever his introduction, he never found a cure for the virulence of stage fever. In any case, he left Wales for London around 1789 to join a band of strolling players. Since the theater wasn't at all a respectable profession, but a "tool of Satan," he changed his name to Wood to protect the innocent and conceal his identity.

No wonder great-great-grandfather Wodin changed his name. Actors were branded as "rogues, vagabonds and sturdy beggars," though suffering under so many deprivations and indignities, it's not likely they were sturdy for very long. In certain sections of rural England, my long-ago grandfather risked a brush with the law. If an actor was caught playing his hateful trade without a royal patent or license from the Lord Chamberlain there were stocks and pillories waiting, and in more extreme cases of church and civic reprisals the penalty of flogging wasn't unknown. In our time, it's a privilege reserved generally for the critics.

On arriving in London, Will Wood went first to one of several inns in the neighborhood of Covent Garden, which were used as central meeting places for managers to hire actors. In those days before agents it was an effective system, for the inns were frequented by all ranks of actors from the beginners, like nineteen-year-old Master Wood, to a well-dressed gentleman of the Theater Royal, to a "country player without a shirt." There, Will talked himself into his first job.

My great-great-grandfather Wood, however, wasn't entrusted immediately with the responsibility of carrying any sizable role. As an apprentice, he ran errands and was assigned to the first business of a company on arrival in a new town, that of beating a drum or blowing a trumpet to attract crowds, and distributing posters and handbills. When a tragedy was to be performed, the notice was printed in red; when a comedy, it was printed in black.

The stroller's life to which Master Wood pledged himself

involved setting up a playing area at an inn or town hall, a platform in an open field, or a booth at a fair, playing a night or a week, sometimes even a month, and then packing up and moving on again. All summer he was on the move, and when the summer was over, if lucky, he went with the strollers to winter quarters in some country town.

Permission from the authorities, plus hiring a suitable playing area, was known as "taking the town," and on the success of those first advance men depended the success and comfort of the actors. They lodged in inns when they could afford it, or in rooms with local tradesmen. Sometimes, even a barn hayloft served as a resting place.

Almost any enclosure was used as a theater. Audiences were extremely vocal in their praise or contempt, and often they were eager for a brawl. Will Wood learned early that if one of his colleagues whispered, "The goose is in the house," it meant the audience was hissing, and he'd better gear himself accordingly. The cry of, "Ladies out! Ladies out!" was the ominous warning that trouble was about to start out front.

Many smaller companies were short on actors, and it was no novelty for an actor to perform two or even three characters in the same play. The shortage meant backbreaking work and demanded a quick brain for rapid study of roles. One great advantage for the young strolling player of the eighteenth century was the versatility he acquired in playing a wide variety of parts. The provincial strolling companies were the training ground for many famous English players, among them George Frederick Cooke, Edmund Kean and Roger Kemble.

Life for my great-great-grandfather was one of strict discipline and never-ending hardship, to say nothing of the Puritan opposition which the strollers often encountered. Poverty and hardship developed a shield of bravado and self-esteem in some actors, which was reflected in their public behavior. "No people show themselves off so much," wrote a social critic. "They talk loud in the streets, are overbearing in public company and at the theater break out into all the insolence of self-importance." But "going a-strolling," as it was called, presented actors with so many indignities, it's not surprising if they sometimes indulged in fits of self-advertisement to compensate for their miseries.

That maternal great-great-grandfather of mine certainly had a durable, intrepid character with great physical endurance and old-fashioned grit to persist in a wandering life so demanding and fraught with peril.

Of necessity, strolling players were an insular lot. They married within the boundaries of the theater and, as gypsies in an unsettled life, had little opportunity to develop personal relationships beyond their own circle. Following the pattern of the time, Will Wood married an actress and had three children: William F. Wood, born in London in 1799, and later two daughters, Mary and Sarah Wood. The children were indoctrinated in the ways of the theater from early childhood, for there was little chance for formal education or training in other more stable trades. But the theater itself was a strict teacher for the Wood children. For them, education meant the collection of all kinds of fascinating information: training in the powers to observe, and a more worldly enlightenment than the deadly dull textbooks which only informed them that kings were born, ascended the throne and died on certain dates.

When their father played *Richard III*, they would not forget that Edward V was born in 1470, a tragic little boy of thirteen when he and his smaller brother were murdered by the humpbacked Duke of Gloucester. And when *Henry VIII* was performed, they knew the history of England was changed because the king illegally divorced Katherine of Aragon to marry Ann Boleyn, and that she in turn became the mother of England's greatest queen, Elizabeth I. Education and history were in the plays and in the world around them.

To do intelligent work in the theater, the three strolling

Wood children learned that they must thoroughly understand a play and its period in history, for the active mainspring of many of the plays of the time was political. The customs, manners, costumes and even the furniture styles of various periods and countries were important sources of information. Mary and Sarah were taught to sew and make wardrobes and William F. learned lettering so that he could print out the playbills. To study parts, of course, they had to read and they were taught early and well, along with the actor's tricks of pantomime and memorization. Writing was also essential. Manuscripts of plays were either printed or written out by hand, and they were passed among the actors, who copied their own parts in longhand. Singing, dancing and learning to play musical instruments were part of the curriculum, too, for music was an integral part of the theater.

Raising and educating children in an atmosphere of want and hardship must have been extremely difficult, but in defense of a life in the theater in the eighteenth century, a young actor wrote, "We see the world, and by study and observation, acquire a greater knowledge of men and manners than twice the number of years would give to a person tied to one situation."

I like to think that Will Wood was just such a man with a similar view of life on the stage. Above all, he must have had a sizable supply of hope, the constant fellow traveler of the actor, though undoubtedly there were times when hope seemed a frail ally.

Literally, the word "pantomime" means "the imitator of all," and not necessarily speechlessness or dumb show. To most of us nowadays, pantomime means telling a story without words, with gestures or expressions alone. But to the English it has another connotation: a theatrical production that includes songs, dances, music, dialog and mime, all incorporated within a loose story framework.

English Pantomime was born at Drury Lane Theater in the early seventeen-hundreds and had derived its form from an Italian company of "Commedia dell'arte," brought to England in the same decade. A Venetian clown in the company named Arlecchino gave his name to the central character, which in the Anglicized version became known as Harlequin. The other Italian characters were gradually altered to English equivalents and became the classic characters of Clown, Columbine and Pantaloon.

Pantomime in England became the mirror of society and reflected the changes in behavior and social custom. Above all, it was topical and made irreverent jokes about the events of the time and local celebrities. There was plenty of "inside" gossip, slapstick comedy, songs, dances and snappy chatter. From the beginning, "Pantos" were an extremely popular form of entertainment and went through several transitions in the following generations. A higher tone gradually took over when morals were stressed, patriotism incited, virtue lauded and useful information distributed. Originally, Pantos were not intended for children, but eventually they turned to fairy tales for their plots and many of them are still played in England today.

With all of its burlesque and vaudeville atmosphere, it was no disgrace to play in Pantomimes, and some of the greatest actors of the day appeared in them in the early stages of their careers. A "pantomimist" was not only a silent mime, but an actor who could sing, dance, show his comedic talents and acrobatics, all of which demanded huge energy and a special performing technique.

My great-grandfather, William F. Wood, son of the family's first strolling player, became a specialist in the Pantomime form of entertainment. Like his father, he gained his early experience in the tough school of the provinces and in London's smaller theaters. His sisters, Mary and Sarah, gradually performed less and less and eventually married outside the acting profession; Mary to a London tradesman named Fields and Sarah to Frederick Vokes, a theatrical costumer. The

Vokes's children would one day eclipse their theatrical predecessors and become the pillars of Pantomime at Drury Lane for an entire decade.

But it was William F. Wood who carried forward the family tradition in his own generation. He married a young Scottish dancer named Sarah Campbell, a descendant of the Duke of Argyll, head of the Campbell clan, and he made of her a strolling player like himself. Sarah and William F. spent the next several years trouping the hinterlands.

Gradually, great-grandfather Wood's career spiraled upward, and by 1830 he was a featured player at some of the more prestigious London theaters, such as The Haymarket, Drury Lane and Covent Garden, specializing as an "actor-pantomimist." He became successful not only in Pantomimes, but as a dramatic actor in short dramas played as after-pieces, many of which were written for or adapted by him. On those nights, to signal the performance of a tragedy, a large green baize cloth called a "tragic carpet," was spread on the stage to prevent the falling corpses from soiling their costumes.

Somewhere along the line, William F. acquired a remarkable dog named Bruin, a large black-and-white hound of indeterminate heritage. Bruin was stagestruck from the very beginning, and great-grandfather found him a willing partner in such mainstays of pantomimic drama as *The Cherokee Chief and His Poor Dog Tray, The Deserter and His Dog, The Foulah Slave* and *The Disowned and His Wonderful Dog*. Bruin always got second billing and became a kind of nineteenth-century "Lassie."

One of the most delightful theatrical traditions of the period was the "Penny Plain or Twopence Colored," a miniature edition of the contemporary theater. It consisted of printed sheets of theatrical characters, copies from the latest productions at Covent Garden, Drury Lane and the minor theaters of London. The term "Plain Penny or Twopence Colored" was derived from their cost; a penny for plain black-and-white reproductions, and twopence for color. At first they were probably intended as a kind of theatrical souvenir, but the idea proved immensely popular with children and was eventually adopted as a toy.

There's a Penny Plain of my great-grandfather Wood in a heroic pose from *Conrade, the Marquis of Montserrat,* dressed in the chain mail and plumed helmet of a crusading knight, one arm outflung and the other carrying a fluttering banner. Bruin, caught in midair, is leaping at his throat, whether in savage fury or overwrought devotion I've never been able to determine. The background of palm trees and tents seems overly tropical for chain mail and fur coat, but I guess those crusaders got around a lot.

The Woods's first son, William A., was born January 23, 1833. The family was living in London, since great-grandfather's career was flourishing in the larger theaters by then, and the necessity for playing the provinces was confined to the summer. They lost no time in introducing the little boy to the theatrical trade, and in June of 1836, at the age of three and a half, he made his debut with a few comic steps in a London Pantomime. Later that year another son was born, and they named him Albert.

I'm not sure of the circumstances that prompted my maternal great-grandparents to move to the United States, but a new and expanding country undoubtedly presented them with fresh challenges and opportunities. In the eighteen-thirties and -forties, the American theater wasn't American at all; its actors and plays were English. With the exception of Edwin Forrest, the first great native tragedian, the big box-office names were British: Edmund Kean, Charles and Fanny Kemble, William Macready, James K. Wallack and Junius Brutus Booth. American audiences and critics were anglophiles and felt that if a performer was "imported," it was an automatic sign of excellence.

Among actors, there was a fever of migration to America in spite of the rumors of discomfort brought back by their colleagues: filthy inns, vast distances between towns that could only be reached by stage coach or river boat, rude manners, an irritating condescension to foreigners, and a terrible climate. English actors could expect poorly equipped theaters, inferior supporting companies and ignorant audiences. However, the theater's general popularity and the guarantee of sizable earnings made up for the rough, often dangerous Atlantic crossing and the reported discomforts of an American tour. Above all, it presented new artistic worlds to conquer in an ever-restless profession.

Queen Victoria had been on the English throne only slightly more than a year when William F. Wood, Sarah and their two sons, William A. and Albert, arrived in New York in the fall of 1838, and accompanied, of course, by Bruin.

Almost immediately, great-grandfather found a willing public. He was billed as a "pantomimic melodramatic actor," which left nothing to doubt, and made his American debut at the Franklin Theater in New York, November 1, 1838, in a piece called *The Dumb Man of Manchester*. Success came quickly and one theatrical historian wrote, "Wood was quite the featured person of the establishment. The public admired him prodigiously."

An evening in the theater during that period was likely to go on hour after hour and included a great variety of entertainment. Several interludes were played between at least three major pieces: the curtain raiser, the principal three- or four-act drama, and the after-piece, which was a short but complete play. It was the last offering of the evening in which William F. made his starring mark, and some of the titles give an idea of their general style: *The Yellow Kid, Nabob for an Hour, The Smuggler, The First Fratricide* and *The Murdered Boatman and His Dog*. Bruin was in there pitching, too. Most of great-grandfather's roles were in comic farces, but not all, for he played a heavy dramatic part in *The First Transgressor,* and to close one season, he played the tragedy of *Gaulantus* for his own benefit performance.

Sometimes a play was given in a series of tableaux which told the story in poses and mime, like the harrowing temperance drama, *The Bottle*. William played the leading role of the doomed alcoholic and also staged the production. It all may have been too harrowing. Repeat performances were few. However, it was one of the first temperance dramas in America, and came long before its more famous counterparts, *The Drunkard* and *Ten Nights in a Barroom*.

Within two months of his New York debut, great-grandfather went to Philadelphia, a city that only recently had been equaled by New York in theatrical activity. He made his first appearance there at the Walnut Street Theater* in January of 1839, then played the Arch Street Theater where a particular favorite with the public was *The Spectre Pilot*. The playbill, headlining William F. Wood, assured the public that it would be "produced with every essential aid necessary to its perfect representation."

The Woods's sons, William A. and Albert, were also introduced to American audiences. In the 1839 season at the Chatham Theater in New York, "young Master Will Wood enchanted for some nights in the Highland Fling and other dances." Though he was all of six years old, Master Will was already a veteran of the theater, and both he and his younger brother were featured performers before they could read their press notices.

In November of 1841, three years after his arrival in the United States, great-grandfather, bound for New Orleans, left Sarah and his smaller son in New York. He'd accepted a three-week engagement to play the St. Charles Theater, an offer that included young Master Will and the irrepressible Bruin. By then, New Orleans had been part of the theatrical "circuit" for more than twenty years and was visited by most of the important stars of the day. Either by sea or the inland water route, the trip was long and arduous, and the fact that so many actors undertook its hardships indicates that engagements in New Orleans were as profitable as those in New York or Philadelphia.

At the time great-grandfather played the six-year-old St.

* The oldest existing theater in the United States.

Charles Theater, it was the largest and most beautiful structure of its kind in the country, with a seating capacity of 4,100. Also, it was the first theater in America to be lit entirely by gaslight. Audiences gossiped and strolled in spacious foyers and splendid arcades and refreshed themselves during intermissions with gulf oysters, fruit or strong liquor. In the sultry New Orleans weather they fanned themselves with programs which, in addition to the cast list and other useful information, contained the notice: "Slaves Will Not Be Admitted Without Exhibiting Passes from Their Masters."

Due to pressing competition from other local theaters, Caldwell, the manager of the St. Charles Theater, dwelt more on equestrian, musical and pantomimic features to begin his season of 1841, and for three weeks William F. Wood was starred in his most celebrated roles. He opened in his perennial favorite, *The Dumb Man of Manchester,* and two nights later introduced to Louisiana audiences a nautical drama, *The Murdered Boatman and His Dog,* assisted by "the wonderful dog, Bruin." Eight-year-old Master Will Wood did his Coconut Dance, "in character," according to an eyewitness. Master Will also appeared in *Timour, the Tartar* with T. S. Cline, a famous "equilibrist" (tightrope walker) of the period. Father and son then performed together in *Philip Quarl and His Monkey* and *Jack the Giant Killer.*

As in England, benefit nights were a regular part of the schedule in the American theater. When an actor "took his benefit," he received all box-office receipts over actual expenses. On his benefit night and farewell to New Orleans, great-grandfather played Androcles in *The Grateful Lion,* which was described as "a grand Oriental spectacle," with Bruin frolicking in the Roman bacchanalia. Then with his son and Bruin, and the usual paraphernalia of the traveling actor, great-grandfather made the long trek back to the East Coast and continued to ply his trade between New York and Philadelphia.

In 1844, another son was born to the performing Woods

in New York City. William F. and Sarah's roots in the theater's traditions were reflected in the fact that they named their third son Frank Motley, "motley" being the term for clothing of mixed colors and patterns worn by a clown or harlequin.

Master Frank made his debut a few years later when he appeared with his brothers in an evening of "Living Statues." Directed by their father, who was billed as "the sole living illustrator of the great Greek and Italian sculptors," the piece was composed of a series of tableaux that depicted famous statuary groupings. Performed at the Bowery Theater, it was called *The Twelve Classic Groups of Adam and Eve, or The First Murder.* It was an evening of considerable variety. The Woods appeared on the same bill with a glass blower, an Irish giant, a lady magician, The Lilliputians and O'Connell, the Tattooed Man. Bruin had the night off.

My great-grandmother, Sarah Campbell Wood, had discontinued her career when the family came to the United States and contented herself with the career of homemaker for her growing brood. Four actors in the family were quite enough, and she coped with the problems of an often absent husband and the education of her three talented sons. Certainly she was outnumbered by the males in her immediate family and, since it's only fitting that a theatrical troupe have at least one feminine member, on June 21, 1845, in New York City, she presented William with his only daughter, and named her Rosabel.

William saw to it that his daughter also had an early introduction to the theater. In 1848 he took her to Philadelphia's famous Chestnut Street Theater where, like her older brother, she made her debut at the age of three and a half in *The Dumb Man of Manchester.* She was billed as "La Petite Rosabel," which up until the turn of the century was a designation given to any child actress who could meet the diminutive description, and to some who could not. Some years later, as a young and independent performer, she changed her name to Rose, and Rose Wood eventually became my maternal grandmother.

For four years, La Petite Rosabel appeared at the various theaters in New York and Philadelphia as a "danseuse," and her father and brothers also divided their time between the two cities. By 1850, however, the family had established a more permanent home in Philadelphia, since the National, the Chestnut, the Walnut and the great Arch Street Theaters were demanding more and more of William F.'s talents. After that, he made only occasional trips to New York, and no Philadelphia season was complete without "the best-liked of pantomimists, the celebrated William Wood."

Then, suddenly, William F. Wood died in Philadelphia in January of 1855. By then La Petite Rosabel was nearly ten years old. William A. was a young man of twenty-two and had taken an engagement at a Baltimore theater, where he was billed as "the young and daring pantomimist," and appeared in many of the old Wood standbys. At once Rosabel joined her brother in Baltimore and played a year with that company. But by 1856, she was back in Philadelphia dancing again at the Walnut Street Theater, and the following season at the Arch Street, where she was hired as a twelve-year-old "premiere danseuse" by John Sleeper Clarke, Edwin Booth's brother-in-law. It was there that Grandmother began to use Rose Wood as her professional name. She remained with Clarke's company for three years, while her brothers, Albert and Frank Motley, struck off on their own and appeared singly in New York and Boston. Only their mother would live permanently in Philadelphia, close to the dim shadow of William F. Wood, the "melodramatic actor-pantomimist" and son of a strolling player who had brought his performing bag of tricks from the old world to help build the traditions of the new.

Nothing is known of the fate of the astonishing dog, Bruin, but whatever it was, he left some first-rate press clippings behind him.

# 8

In the same year that La Petite Rosabel was born in New York, her future husband was born in the British West Indies. He, too, would figure prominently in the family's theatrical history. His father, an English tradesman named Morris, had bought a sugar plantation in Jamaica. Next to the Morris plantation was a family with thirteen children named de Cordoba, of Spanish heritage and with deep roots in the islands. Pedro, a grandson of the de Cordobas, also became a famous actor in America and was closely linked with my family personally and professionally in the years to come. Through his neighbors, the English Mr. Morris met and married the dark-eyed daughter of the Carvalhos, also a Spanish family with a long history of sugar commerce in the Caribbean. My maternal grandfather, their son and only child, was born in Kingston, Jamaica, on September 4, 1845, and was named Moritz W. Morris. Soon after, and for unknown reasons, the family name was changed to Morrison. Grandfather would use Lewis Morrison as a professional name in the theater.

The Morrisons flourished for the first few years after Lewis was born, and certainly it was a pleasant outdoor life for a young boy, with acres of sugar cane to chew on and the Caribbean Ocean for a swimming hole, plus a neighboring houseful of de Cordobas for playmates. But Lewis's father was a stern, unrelenting character, and in violent fits of temper, his discipline was swift and severe. The plantation horses were exercised and bathed in the ocean, and Lewis and his friends thought it was great sport to hang on to the horses' tails and be dragged through the surf. As an absolutely forbidden sport, it was doubly attractive, and Morrison, Sr., caught his son in the lie more than once by merely tasting the back of his hand. If his skin tasted salty from evaporated sea water, he was whipped unmercifully, and Grandfather remembered more than one brutal beating.

As time went by, his mother's fiery temperament collided with the ill temper of his father more and more frequently. By the time Grandfather was eight or nine, the conflicts of his parents finally resulted in their separation. His mother's solution to a hostile domestic life was to put as much distance as possible between herself and her husband and she took Lewis to the protective Brooklyn, New York, home of her older brother, David Carvalho. With no hope of reconciliation, Morrison, Sr., sold his business interests and returned to England where he vanished from the family history.

The Morrisons, minus one, took up a new life of freedom from domestic tyranny in Brooklyn. Lewis was sent to a private boys' school where he showed a talent for mimicry and in his early teens became a leading young actor in amateur theatricals. He chose photography, then a newly expanding field, as a profession, and his Uncle David promised to set him up in a photographic business after his graduation. First, however, Grandfather planned a return trip to the West Indies to photograph the islands and their inhabitants, as a kind of pleasant vocational prelude to his career. After graduation, and accompanied by a friend, Lewis packed his equipment and returned to his birthplace in Jamaica, while his mother and uncle moved south and took up residence in New Orleans just before the outbreak of the Civil War.

Lewis returned from his tour of the islands late in 1861

with the intention of joining the Confederate Army. Though he deplored secession, like many English colonials, his sympathies lay with the South. He rejoined his family in New Orleans for the Christmas holidays, then set out one day early in 1862 to join the army. On his way to the recruiting center, he was distracted by a crowd that stood around a group of hoodlums, and watched them deface and burn the American flag. Feelings were running high and the crowd applauded the incident, but Lewis was so outraged, he turned around and went home. Within a few days, he was on his way North to join the Union Army, in which he was given a lieutenant's commission.

In six months he'd become a brevet captain and was leading a colored regiment of freed slaves. At one point, he headed a "forlorn hope" mission, charged a Southern command post, and was wounded in the process. Then, during the blockade of Port Hudson, he was cited for bravery when he swam the river to deliver messages to the Northern lines. After two years of fighting, Lewis returned to his mother and uncle in New Orleans, a hardened veteran of nineteen.

By then he'd given up all thoughts of a photographic career and was entertaining the more provocative idea of becoming an actor. The Varieties Theater in New Orleans was then under the management of Lawrence Barrett, who later became one of America's greatest stars, and John Lewis Baker, himself an excellent actor. Baker had known the Carvalhos in Brooklyn and had seen Grandfather perform there in nonprofessional productions. One night Lewis went to the Varieties to see a performance of *London Assurance,* a popular melodrama of the time, and then went backstage to see his friend, actor-manager Baker. By sheer chance, one of the actors was about to leave the company, and Baker asked Lewis to join as a replacement.

Certainly Grandfather had all the attributes to make a successful actor. He was a tall, imposing figure with strong heavy features that would carry across the footlights, the dark, expressive eyes of his Spanish mother, and a naturally resonant voice. He wasted no time in accepting Baker's offer, and on an evening in August of 1864, he made his professional debut as a "walking gentleman" in *Loan of a Lover.* "At least," he recalled later, "I didn't fall over the furniture."

It was a time, in the stylized plays of the period, when ladies suffered a good deal in libraries, generally from melancholia, and gentlemen invariably were shot in smoking jackets. For an actor, there were principal "lines of business," and in an artistic sense those lines bound the players in an inflexible system. A company generally was composed of a leading man, juvenile, heavy, first and second old man, first and second comedian, walking gentleman and utility man.

"Walking gentlemen" weren't necessarily ambulatory. They just sat around and expressed a solemn interest in everything and were often called upon to announce a sudden inheritance or identify a baby locket.

Of the feminine lines of business, first came the leading lady, then the ingenue, the character woman who sometimes played heavies, the soubrette who doubled in boys' parts, the utility woman, and finally "the ladies of the ballet." The last were young girls who danced specialty numbers between acts or in ballroom scenes, and occasionally had a few lines to announce the arrival of very important persons.

It was in this atmosphere that my grandfather learned the terrain of the actor, the stagecraft and mechanics of the theater. He learned the technical terms of the profession and the backstage lingo that is peculiar to the theater alone, and the odd abbreviations. OP was opposite the prompt side, where the stage manager prompted the actor whose memory failed and rang two bells for the close of each act: the first a warning to the curtain man up aloft in the flies, and the second a signal to lower the curtain. RUE and LUE were right or left upper entrance; RC, right of center stage; and CD, center door. DS or US meant that he'd do well to go down or upstage, while X to C directed him to cross to center stage.


At the time when Lewis had started for the West Indies on his photographic trip early in 1861, my grandmother, Rose Wood, had already been active in the theater for well over a dozen years. In 1860, after her three-year engagement at the Arch Street Theater in Philadelphia, she made her first New York appearance since childhood, dancing in John Sleeper Clarke's production of *The Naiad Queen* at the Winter Garden Theater. *The Naiad Queen* was America's first "leg" show. A rousing success in its many revivals, it had been an early vehicle for Charlotte Cushman before she made her brilliant mark as America's first great native tragedienne. An eyewitness to the Winter Garden production declared, "Such a display of ladies' legs no mortal could resist the opportunity of seeing!"

After that seductive display, Grandmother went to engagements at Boston's Museum, then home to her mother in Philadelphia and the Arch Street Theater, then to New York again to appear with her brother, Frank Motley, under P. T. Barnum's management. In March of 1864, she worked again with the distinguished comedian, John Sleeper Clarke, in *Dr. Pangloss* at Ford's Theater in Washington, D.C., the theater that would soon witness the assassination of Abraham Lincoln. There, the actress was born, for Clarke gave Rose several important ingenue roles during that period which netted her first glowing press notices as a dramatic actress.

In the second year of the war, her brother, William A. Wood, joined a Three Month Volunteer unit under the Union flag. While in the army he contracted flu during a severe epidemic and died in Philadelphia at the age of twenty-eight. Meanwhile Rose's other brothers, after serving briefly with volunteer units, were kept busy in the theater:

Frank Motley as an actor-pantomimist, who married an actress named Kate James, and Alfred, who lived in New York and worked as a musician.

August of 1864 found Rose at the Varieties Theater in the same company with Lewis Morrison, who was making his debut as a "walking gentleman." By then a young lady of nineteen, Grandmother first performed at the Varieties as one of the "ladies of the ballet," and danced specialty numbers with her sister-in-law, Kate James Wood. Then she made her first important dramatic appearance of the season in the role of Madelain in *Satan of Paris*.

Within a few months, the company was sharing the news of the impending marriage of the new actress, Miss Wood, and the promising young actor, Mr. Morrison. The future looked particularly bright. Both had blossoming careers and were employed in one of the most distinguished theaters in the South, but best of all, the tragic war was drawing to a close. On that night of April 9, 1865, they watched the fireworks that burst over Lake Ponchatrain, and joined in the celebrations that signaled the war's end.

Then, five days later, came the staggering news of Lincoln's death at the hands of the actor, John Wilkes Booth. Actors were horrified and fearful of how the mindless act would affect an already damned profession. Suddenly, the world of the theater was not so bright a place. Their fears were not unfounded.

The assassination at Ford's Theater in Washington brought forth many ugly demonstrations against actors throughout the country, not only in the North. The most offensive thought of all was that Abraham Lincoln had met his death in a theater, "the playground of folly, lewdness and infamy." For weeks after the tragedy it was the subject of many a Sunday sermon filled with the fervent wish that "Mr. Lincoln had fallen elsewhere than at the very gates of Hell." Actors were the subject of violent attacks in the newspapers and were openly derided in the streets. Sullen crowds milled around stage doors. For a time, business in the theater was affected seriously and some companies were forced to close.

Grandmother mourned for the Booth family whom she'd known since childhood. Before joining the Varieties company, she'd played a number of engagements with John Sleeper Clarke and his wife, Asia, John Wilkes Booth's sister. William F. Wood had worked with Junius Brutus Booth in the late eighteen-thirties, and the Arch Street Theater in Philadelphia, where all the Woods had been headliners, was managed by Edwin Booth and Clarke.

But as the months passed, the theater gradually began to recover from the terrible effects of Lincoln's murder. Rose and Lewis dismissed the dark predictions of the theater's future and were married in New Orleans on August 28, 1865.

Among other advantages, it meant that Lewis could enter his wife's dressing room at the theater and speak to her from inside the door. In spite of public opinion, the theater of the nineteenth century had many puritanical customs, and some of them still prevail. If an actor found it necessary to speak to an actress in her dressing room, he knocked politely and asked, "Are you decent?" If she was presentable, she then opened her door and spoke to her visitor from the doorway. Under no circumstances would an actress permit a man to enter her dressing room, unless he was her husband. A "greenroom" was the only proper place for social encounter and conversation.

The greenroom of the theater was the clubhouse and parlor of my grandparents' day. There, Rose and Lewis read through the play on the first day of rehearsals, studied their parts, waited for entrance cues until they were called into place by a "call boy," received visitors after a performance, and put up their Christmas trees.

Conditions for the Morrisons weren't really much improved over what they'd been in the days of my great-great-grandfather, the family's first strolling player. Actors had no clubs or trade unions, they were required to pay their own transportation fares to a new engagement, they were not paid for rehearsal periods, and for three weeks out of the season, Holy Week, Election Week and Christmas, received only half their salaries. Being stranded on the road was so common that a trade paper, *The New York Clipper*, printed a weekly column of stranded actors, listing their whereabouts, as a service to families and friends.

Immediately after their wedding, Rose and Lewis began a month-long tour of Texas and the South before opening the fall season of 1865 in New Orleans. Touring the hinterlands was a dismal life. Travel was difficult and uncomfortable, and there was seldom decent food or inside plumbing. Dressing rooms were invariably dirty and had no running water; a row of hooks, a chair, a shelf and a mirror were all they expected. Most theaters were overrun with rats and mice, and the modern superstition of good luck which surrounds the theater cat started out as a practical means of eliminating the rodent population. Since rats have a peculiar affection for greasepaint, an actor's tin makeup box was a necessity.

After the tour, New Orleans was a welcome haven. In all, my grandparents spent five years as resident members of the Varieties company, often playing in support of visiting stars. Starring actors brought no company or scenery to an engagement, but were supported by resident "stock" members· of a theater who were required to learn the repertory of the visitor. Usually, the leading player devoted little time to rehearsals. He merely indicated where he would play his most effective scenes, and the other actors were expected to tag along somehow. The stage manager made note of the star's favored positions onstage and maneuvered the rest of the company around him.

In New Orleans, my grandparents appeared in the popular dramas of the period, such as *East Lynne, Oliver Twist, Under the Gaslight, The Ticket-of-Leave Man* and *Camille,* as well as in Shakespeare and Restoration Comedy.

Frequently, plays were revived from year to year, but new plays were added to the repertory constantly. The system had no particular rule governing the length of a run; sometimes the company would perform a play for a few nights, sometimes a few weeks. Long runs were uncommon, study and rehearsals never-ending, but the system was a great proving ground for young actors learning their trade.

New Orleans had been kind to the Morrisons, and they would always regard that city with affection. They'd married there, their careers had developed satisfactorily, and they'd established a more or less permanent home for nearly five years that centered around Lewis's mother. Then in 1869, Rose took time out from their final season at the Varieties to give birth to their first daughter, my aunt, Rosabel Morrison. But there was really no "home base" for the Morrisons, and they left New Orleans to join a touring company in the Midwest until the fall of 1870, when they returned to the Walnut Street Theater in Philadelphia, under the management of Edwin Booth and John Sleeper Clarke. Their first test of the season was the starring engagement of Edwin Forrest.

In many ways, Forrest was unique in American theatrical history, for he was the first native-born tragedian whose talents could claim equal rank with his English contemporaries, Edmund Kean, William Macready and Charles Kemble. He'd made his debut at the age of fourteen at the Walnut Street Theater, fifty years before my grandparents worked with him. But Forrest refused to concede to the defeat of age and illness, even after he'd suffered a stroke in 1865 that partially paralyzed him, and he hugged close to the myth that between himself and his public there was an undying bond of appreciation. When the Morrisons supported him in Philadelphia in 1870, he was still playing the heroic roles of his prime. But despite his uneven performances and diminished powers, Grandfather recalled that Forrest, at times, yet summoned moments of great beauty and passion.

One of Forrest's first appearances in the Walnut's fall season came in September when he played *Richelieu*. Grandfather had been cast in a minor role, but during the rehearsal before the evening's performance, the actor playing the villain, Baradas, was taken ill and Lewis was handed the part. He not only succeeded in learning the lines by curtain time, but acquitted himself with honor and won Forrest's admiration. He'd gone from "walking gentleman" to principal "heavy" in one evening. "From then on," he said, "I was associated with many villains of high and low degree."

After that, when the Walnut's resident leading man, Charles Walcott, took occasional leaves of absence, Lewis was assigned to his roles, and on one of those occasions he played his first Romeo to the Juliet of Adelaide Neilsen, a capricious English star. Also, he made a personal hit as Bill Sykes in *Oliver Twist*, opposite Lucille Western. Both grandparents then supported her in the tear-provoking tale of woe, *East Lynne*. The adaptation from the popular novel had been originally commissioned by Miss Western, and for the dramatization that had made her famous and wealthy, she'd paid the embarrassingly modest sum of one hundred dollars.

But the highlight of the Morrisons's first season at the Walnut Theater was the engagement of Edwin Booth. It began on December 5 with *Othello*, in which Booth alternated in the title role and Iago. *The Merchant of Venice* followed; then *Richelieu*, with Lewis again as Baradas; and *Macbeth* and *Hamlet*, with Grandfather as Laertes. To Grandfather, Edwin Booth was a god, "a somber genius who had an extraordinary capacity for melancholy." Later, he would pattern his own Iago after Booth's portrayal. Both Lewis and Rose were struck by Edwin's kindness and courtesy to the company, and they recalled that he even suggested to one actor that he keep his hat on during rehearsals, "lest you catch cold."

My grandparents were kept busy in the early months of 1871 playing in *The Rivals, Our American Cousin* and *She*

*Stoops to Conquer,* and on February 15, Lewis took his benefit in *Cricket on the Hearth. East Lynne* was revived in May, this time with Rose as the tearful Lady Isabel. The following month, Philadelphia audiences welcomed back one of the most beloved actors on the American stage, Joseph Jefferson, in *Rip Van Winkle.* By then Jefferson's Rip, like Booth's Hamlet, had become a national institution. In his lifetime, he played the role thousands of times over a span of thirty-nine years, and from his opening performance to his last he wore the same wardrobe, merely adding patches from time to time. Jefferson's engagement at the Walnut in June of 1871 was the beginning of a long and cherished friendship with Rose and Lewis, and later, with their daughter, Rosabel.

During my grandparents' second season at the Walnut in 1872, Edwin Booth returned to Philadelphia and paid Lewis the compliment of an invitation to play his own celebrated theater in New York City, the Booth. However, the Morrisons had already accepted an offer to play the California Theater in San Francisco in support of the handsome Irish actor-manager, John McCullough. Reluctantly, Lewis had to forego the distinction of playing the Booth for the lengthier and better paid engagement on the West Coast.

Altogether, the two years at the Walnut Street Theater under the Booth-Clarke management had been extremely rewarding for my grandparents. Each had graduated to more important roles in support of some of the most distinguished figures in the American Theater, and the prospects that lay ahead in California seemed equally inviting. One event, however, marred the time—when Rose's mother, Sarah Campbell Wood, died in the early spring of 1871.

Philadelphia held many memories for Rose Wood. She'd made her debut in that city at the age of three and a half, and she, her father and brothers had returned many times to perform in its half a dozen thriving theaters. Also, since 1850, the Wood family had established a somewhat permanent residence there, and Philadelphia had become the nearest thing to home base for the family's vagabonds. Now Rose left those memories and three graves behind: mother, father and brother. In May of 1872, the Morrisons and their three-year-old daughter, Rosabel, began preparations for the long trip to California's El Dorado.

While the fortunes and careers of the Wood family were developing in America, the members who'd stayed in England had not been idle in the theater. Another troupe was materializing in London that would become a pillar of Drury Lane for an entire decade, and at its end, would rock those hallowed halls in a sweeping controversy.

My great-grandfather, William F. Wood, had left two sisters, Mary and Sarah, in London when he came to the United States in 1838. Sarah had married Frederick Vokes, a theatrical costumer and wigmaker who owned a shop at 19 Henrietta Street in Covent Garden and advertised as "Makers of Grand Fancy Costume Ball, Theatrical and Historical Dresses."

Three years after my grandmother, Rose Wood, was born in New York, the first of her Vokes cousins was born in London in 1848. All four, Fred, Jessie, Victoria and Rosina, were born within a year or two of each other. True Cockneys, they were all born within the sound of the bells of Old Bow Street Church.

Many theatrical people frequented the shop on Henrietta Street, and the first language the children heard was that of the theater and actor's "shop talk." Creswick, the Drury Lane star, was particularly fascinated by the Vokes's precocious brood, and spent time between costume fittings teaching them bits of Shakespearean verse.

They were further encouraged in their childish theatrics by their mother's sister, Mary, now a music teacher. Her tradesman husband had died shortly after their marriage and she'd gone to live with the Vokeses, from then on devoting herself to the children's training with the quiet approval of their mother.

Father Vokes didn't think much of the stage as a profession and looked on his sister-in-law's coaching as just plain meddling. But Creswick prodded him into allowing two of the little girls, Jessie and Victoria, to appear with him at the Surrey Theater in London in 1855. Rosina, six months old, was carried on wearing her long white christening dress. The girls succeeded each other in a series of child parts which included Prince Arthur in *King John,* the little Princes of Wales and York in *Richard III,* and Mamillius in *The Winter's Tale.*

Soon it became apparent that the young Vokeses were developing into something more than talented amateurs. Mary began forming them into a unified act and wrote short Pantomime farces, tailored especially to their youthful abilities. The strong point of the family was its acrobatic dancing. Fred was known as "The Boy with the Elastic Legs," and developed such an amazingly agile style that a critic later coined the term "legomania" to describe the phenomenon.

Fred, Jessie, Victoria and Rosina, aged thirteen, ten, eight and seven, made their first professional appearance as a family troupe at the Opera House in Edinburgh, Scotland, on Christmas night of 1861, billed as "The Vokes Children." They were an instant hit and a short year later made their London debut at the Lyceum Theater in the Pantomime, *Humpty-Dumpty.* For the next six years they plied between the provinces and London until September 4, 1869, when they found a permanent home at Drury Lane, Theater Royal. They created a furore there and, billed as "The Vokes Family," soon became the darlings of the British public.

The year of the children's debut at Drury Lane, their father became "the sole Producer of all the grand dresses at the Theater Royal, Drury Lane." The advancement was due to the phenomenal success of his children and no doubt was the inducement that softened his harsh view of the theater.

Their number rose to five when a young actor named Frederick Fawdon was given a part in *Belles of the Kitchen* and proved himself such a valuable addition to the act that he was adopted unofficially by the family. Thereafter he was known as the second brother, Fawdon Vokes.

From the time of their debut at Drury Lane in September of 1869, the Pantomime season was under the singular domination of the Vokes family. Their popularity with audiences was enormous and made them the most idolized group of performers in the mid-Victorian era.

News of the miraculous family soon reached the United States, and offers began to appear from American managers. Anticipating an American tour and responding to the news of the death of her aunt, Sarah Campbell Wood, Jessie was prompted to write to her cousin, Rose Wood, in Philadelphia. My grandparents were just ending their first season at the Walnut Street Theater, and Jessie's letter arrived at a time when they were appearing jointly in *East Lynne*.

Liverpool
May 26, 1871

My Dear Cousin:

Permit me at once to introduce myself. I am the eldest daughter of your late father's sister, Sarah Vokes. Therefore, I trust our relationship will be sufficient introduction for my thus addressing you.

My mother has forwarded me your letter and wished me to write to you, which I do with great pleasure, and express how delighted she was to hear from you.

She was deeply grieved to hear your dear mother is no longer upon this earth and regrets much that Fate has kept her in ignorance for so many years of the welfare of her brother's family. Furthermore, I have often heard her speak of him in terms of the deepest affection.

Believe me, your family has often been the subject of

conversation. Ever since we were children we considered ourselves much more fortunate than our companions, for we had some wonderful cousins in America, and as we grew up, the desire to hear more of you grew with us.

And now I trust a little account of ourselves will not prove uninteresting to you. In the first place, my parents are both alive and I am thankful to add enjoying the best of health. My brothers and sisters and myself, like you, are in the theatrical profession and at present enjoying a very prosperous career, and we all perform in our own pieces. I have two dear sisters, Victoria 18 years, and Rosina 17 years of age. Then, there is my elder brother, Frederick, 23 years.

We have an adopted brother, who has performed and traveled with us since we were children, so you see I have as good as two brothers.

My Aunt Mary (your Aunt also) has lived with us all our lives and has educated us. When we leave home she travels with us which is no light responsibility I assure you, to look after five such troublesome boys and girls.

We were thinking of paying a visit to the United States of America, but we are afraid we should not be able to remain more than two or three months on account of returning in time for our London Drury Lane season and it seeems so long a journey for so short a time.

There is a manager in New York who is trying to map an engagement, a Mr. Colville, if you know him. But I'm afraid we shall have to let it rest until after we have concluded our Drury Lane engagements. He seems very much interested and promises to do it.

How anxious we are to meet you, after missing you all our lives. . . .

Believe me my dear cousin
Yours very sincerely,
Jessie Vokes

PS A letter to my home
19 Henrietta Street
Covent Garden
London W
will always find me. You see, I am urging you to write me.

Eventually, it was A. M. Palmer, an astute New York impresario, who succeeded in bringing the Vokes family to the United States, and they made their American debut on April 15, 1872, at the Union Square Theater, three years after their first Drury Lane appearance. Their success in New York was no less a sensation.

Jessie's wish for a meeting with the cousin she'd never met was realized when the family played Philadelphia soon after their first New York engagement. Rose and Lewis were finishing their second season at the Walnut Theater and playing with Edwin Booth when the Vokeses arrived to play the neighboring Arch Street Theater. From then on, they corresponded frequently and often played the same cities, though they never performed together.

The success of the Vokes family in the United States more than fulfilled their most hopeful expectations. Americans idolized them as much as the English audiences. Their financial rewards were enormous, but on their fourth tour of the country in 1876, Fred's reckless speculations on the New York Stock Exchange nearly cost them their entire earnings in America. Barely averting disaster, they returned to London and the Pantomime season at Drury Lane.

There the family continued its extraordinary success until 1877, when an event occurred which began its decline. It was Rosina's marriage to Cecil Clay, a London barrister and composer of the popular "Songs of Araby." Clay was a man of means and social position and persuaded Rosina to retire and devote herself to the social life of London. At her retirement, Fred, Jessie, Victoria and Fawdon regrouped, and the next Pantomime season found them once again at Drury Lane. In the season of 1878–79, their mother, Sarah, joined the troupe and appeared with them in the Pantomime of *Cinderella.*

By then they had monopolized all the principal parts in the Christmas Annuals for a decade, and Drury Lane gradually began to suffer from "too much Vokeses." The public began to balk and the critics grumbled. There's no doubt that the absence of the plump and vivacious Rosina from the group had made a difference to the public, for she was its most popular member.

Fred's autocratic business methods added to their troubles. Their celebrity and popularity had convinced him that the Vokeses were eminently indispensable to the amusement world and he saw no reason to change their style or update their material to satisfy a few dyspeptic critics.

F. B. Chatterton, the genial manager of Drury Lane, was a popular figure in the theater, but a man occasionally misled by his judgments. His tenancy had shown shaky financial signs earlier in the 1878 season, and by the time *Cinderella* opened he was in serious trouble. To pull himself out, he staked all on the Christmas Pantomime, but the public had grown tired of undiluted Vokeses and showed it in a sharp drop at the box office. To avoid closing, Chatterton asked his company to take a voluntary 50 percent cut in salary. As business spokesman for the family, Fred Vokes refused to appear until full salaries were paid. Without its principal players, Drury Lane suddenly closed its doors at midseason in early February of 1879, "in consequence of unforeseen circumstances," leaving the field clear for the rival Pantomime at Covent Garden.

Ordinarily, internal theater conflicts weren't shared with the general public, but news of the Drury Lane closing erupted into full-blown outrage. Newspapers and public took up the cudgels and the Vokeses went from the pampered darlings of the English stage to the assassins of Drury Lane. The scandal raged on for weeks. Newspapers carried headlines on "The Drury Lane Catastrophe!" and magazines printed sternly accusing articles headed, "Disaster at Drury Lane" and "Theatrical Tyranny!" Managers and performers in other theaters throughout England took sides.

Fred, in the unaccustomed role of public apologist, wrote a lengthy letter to major newspapers to exonerate himself of the accusation that his selfishness had been the immediate cause of closing, and he lamely replied to the charge that he was "responsible for the cruelty of allowing hundreds of employees to be thrown out of work and the ruin of Chatterton." Then he offered the services of the family for one week without pay, but by that time it was too late.

Deprived of performing at Drury Lane for the first time in ten years was like being homeless, though Fred, Jessie, Victoria and Fawdon continued to perform in other theaters, both in London and the provinces, and made several "farewell" tours of the United States. Their final tour of America as "The Vokes Family" was in June of 1883. The previous year had brought the sudden death of their Aunt Mary, and when the family returned to England, Jessie was already suffering from malaria, which she'd contracted in the South. August 7, 1884, Jessie Vokes died at the age of thirty-three.

Meanwhile, things had gone badly for Rosina and her husband. For seven years after her marriage and retirement from the theater, she'd shone in London's social circles, but financial ruin overtook Clay in 1884, and the pressures forced Rosina to return to the stage. There's a hint that snobbery was responsible for bringing Rosina once again to the United States. As an "ex" actress she flourished in society as a popular hostess, but as a working performer London's bluebloods found her less acceptable. To avoid the humiliations she felt might confront her, Rosina formed a troupe of her own and brought them to America. She never again performed in England.

Most of her repertory was composed of the old-favorite comedies and burlesques that had made the Vokes family famous. For the next several years, she spent most of each season doggedly touring America, and although her own popularity was revived, the overall success of the company was only moderate.

In New York in 1888, four years after her return to America, Rosina received news of the death of her brother in London. Fred, the agile young "legomaniac," died at the age of forty. By then only Fawdon and Victoria were still appearing in England, making the beaten rounds of provincial theaters and performing singly.

On September 16, 1893, Rosina began what proved to be her final tour at the Arch Street Theater in Philadelphia. By the time the company reached the Western states, audiences began to comment on her changed and shocking appearance. "I am not dancing so much this season," she told a San Francisco reporter, "but of late my ankles have taken to swelling, and so I have been compelled to conduct myself very sedately." Rosina was dying of tuberculosis, but she insisted on continuing the tour until the company came East again and arrived in Washington, D.C.

On December 9, they presented a triple bill, though Rosina appeared in only one of the farces, *A Pantomime Rehearsal,* her most popular vehicle and one written by her husband. The next morning, Cecil Clay quietly confided to the Washington theater manager that it was unlikely she would ever appear on a stage again. But Rosina cheerfully announced that she would die in England or not at all and Clay, convinced she would never survive the trip, booked passage from New York on December 13.

After their departure, it was suddenly made clear that Rosina had more than extended herself to her friends during her final years in the United States. Known as one of the most charitable women in the profession, she'd given away a fortune to her fellow actors and departed for England with little to show for a long career but her wardrobe trunk and her memories. She left behind, however, a theatrical maxim that has always appealed to me. "I believe most earnestly in the old plan of good stock companies in the theater, and no bonnets in the audience!"

A. M. Palmer, who had first engaged the Vokes family in the United States, began to organize a gigantic benefit for Rosina in New York, but his good intentions came too late. She died at her home at Babbicombe in Devonshire, England, on January 27, 1894, aged forty.

Three months later, Victoria died in London at the age of forty-one, the last of my grandmother's Vokes cousins. Only Fawdon, the foster brother, was left, and he continued to perform in the smaller variety theaters until his death in London in 1904.

For an entire decade the incomparable Vokes family had been the most celebrated and adored variety performers on the English-speaking stage of two continents. The very pillars of Pantomime in one of the world's greatest theaters, they had contributed to shuttering the doors of Drury Lane one of the few times in its long and colorful history. It seems curious that an entire family should streak across the theatrical scene like a flashing comet, then suddenly pass from view in a fading shower of sparks. Ours is a strange profession.

# 9

As far as the theater was concerned, San Francisco in the eighteen-fifties took second place to no city in the country. With the explosive rise in population after the first gold strike, theatrical opportunists had built several new theaters which rivaled in splendor any of those in the East. Barbary Coast audiences took to the theater wholeheartedly, and a tide of actors began to flow westward. To tempt actors into undergoing the hazards of travel across the country, managers charged higher admissions and paid higher salaries. In 1869, when the first transcontinental railroad linked California with the East, the flow of players became an avalanche. By the time my Morrison grandparents decided to improve their fortunes in 1872, California exercised a powerful attraction in its prospect of greater salaries and the challenge of conquering tough, exacting audiences.

The trip from Philadelphia took ten days. There they joined a company under the management of John McCullough who had taken over the California Theater and established in it a highly popular stock company. A handsome Irishman and fine actor, McCullough led off each season with a dazzling procession of visiting stars, supported by the resident company of stock actors. My grandparents played with both McCullough and his partner, Lawrence Barrett, and again with Edwin Forrest and Edwin Booth. Grandfather repeated his Romeo to the Juliet of Adelaide Neilsen, and in that production, there was an eager young man in the crowd of extras who carried a spear on the side of the Capulets—David Belasco.

The Morrisons played a full season at the California Theater, then returned to Philadelphia's Walnut Street Theater in March of 1873, to perform with the most admired actress of the time, Charlotte Cushman. The first production was *Henry VIII*, in which the star appeared as Queen Katherine, Lewis played Buckingham, and Rose the role of Anne Boleyn. *Macbeth* followed with Grandfather "laying on" as Macduff, and Miss Cushman's overpowering portrayal of Lady Macbeth.

The first American actress to achieve fame in England, Miss Cushman's supreme reputation, both as an actress and a woman, reflected the rise of the theatrical art in the United States in the mid-nineteenth century. England had acclaimed her genius, intellectual distinctions, and immaculate personal life; but her entire dramatic training and development had been acquired in America, and as a native product, she became a symbol of immense national pride. Many of the parts in which she excelled were male roles; Romeo, Hamlet and Cardinal Wolsey, but the peak of her genius was reached as Lady Macbeth. When my grandparents worked with her in Philadelphia, she was already stricken with cancer, which took her life three years later, and though some of her brilliant power had diminished, Grandfather recalled her performances as "terrifying and wonderful."

Then it was back to the West Coast for another season at the California, though by December of 1874, Rose and Lewis had returned to engagements in New York and Grandfather's dream of playing the prestigious Booth Theater came true. To play the Booth had been the summit of his ambition, although the play, *Red Tape*, with John Sleeper Clarke, was a failure. Until late in 1875, the Morrisons plied between San Francisco and the East, when Lewis found a more permanent home at the Union Square Theater in New York, where the leading star was the dashing and handsome James O'Neill, Eugene's father, and their association was the beginning of an enduring friendship.

While Grandfather was appearing at the Union Square, a particularly auspicious time was approaching for my grandmother as she began rehearsals at the Park Theater in George Fawcett Rowe's comedy, *Brass*. The opening night on February 16, 1876, was a milestone in her career, and *Brass* was to be one of her greatest successes. It was something of a record breaker for the time, and the annals of the New York theater state, "*Brass* opened with the handsome and talented Rose Wood, and ran for an unprecedented one hundred performances."

By the mid-eighteen-seventies, a new era had begun for the American stage. In all parts of the country tremendous expansion was taking place. New theaters were being built in rapidly growing cities, and among the vast network of railroads there were few towns of even moderate size that didn't have their own "Opera House" or "Museum," polite terms that cloaked the "tool of Satan" in the more acceptable auras of music or antiquity. Audiences in the smaller towns throughout the country began to look to New York for entertainment, to the greatest stars, native and foreign, as well as to the most successful plays. The Golden Age of the Road had begun.

In the season of 1876, while Grandmother was enjoying her new stardom in *Brass*, A. M. Palmer induced Grandfather to leave the Union Square Theater for a national tour, starring jointly with James O'Neill. They played the leading roles in *The Danicheffs, A Celebrated Case, French Flats*, and other plays that had been successful in New York. That period cemented Grandfather's friendship with James O'Neill, an irresistibly romantic figure in the theater.

While Palmer's Union Square company was touring the country, Grandmother stayed in New York with her five-year-old daughter, my aunt Rosabel, and continued the run in her current hit. Her performance attracted the attention of the great Lester Wallack, and until the winter of 1877, she played leads opposite him in a series of comedies for which he was famous: *The Shaughran, All for Her* and *Wild Oats*. She was now one of the most sought-after leading women in the business, and although still a young woman of thirty-two, she'd been in the theater close to three decades. It was a far cry from the moppet who danced in her father's production of *The Dumb Man of Manchester,* to the leading actress in one of the country's finest theaters opposite its distinguished actor-manager.

In November of 1877 my grandparents joined forces again to form their own dramatic company for a three-month tour of the Midwestern states. Billed as "The Miss Rose Wood and Lewis Morrison. Company," it was their first attempt at actor-management, and a successful one, for the press and public greeted them with enthusiasm in Nebraska, Kansas, and Missouri. One of the dramatic highlights of the tour was their production of *Camille,* with Grandfather as Armand and Grandmother as the pulmonary heroine. They returned to New York for a brief rest before rejoining the Union Square Stock Company. Then in March of 1878, accompanied by James O'Neill, they began the long train trip to the Pacific Coast for an extended engagement at the Baldwin Theater in San Francisco.

In the center of the Western theatrical scene at the time was a wild Irishman named Tom Maguire, one of the miracle men who sprang from the variegated theatrical history of San Francisco. Sailing into the city at the height of the gold rush, he emerged as an impresario and soon began building pretentious playhouses, engaging the most noted actors and actresses to play in them. He called his theaters "Temples of Thespis." An inveterate gambler, he made and lost fortunes with equal aplomb, and the 1877–78 season found him reinstated as manager of the Baldwin Theater, after having lost fifty thousand dollars the previous year.

By then, David Belasco, the young spear carrier from

Adelaide Neilsen's *Romeo and Juliet,* was working at the Baldwin as stage manager, sometime actor, hack playwright and secretary to Tom Maguire. At twenty-five, Belasco had already shown signs of the qualities that would make him the high priest of show business in the eighteen-nineties and early twentieth century. He was a curious combination of charlatan and genius, a wizard with other people's ideas, and one of the most astute plagiarists in the business. The copyright laws were much less stringent than they are today, and the future "Bishop of Broadway" could practice theatrical thievery at the Baldwin without much fear of the consequences.

The company, headed by James O'Neill and the Morrisons, led off on March 5, 1878, in the popular drama *A Celebrated Case,* produced with "new and beautiful scenery." Playing a supporting role in the production was a young actress from Salt Lake City named Annie Adams. The play also required a child actress in one scene, and Maguire hired Annie's six-year-old daughter, Maude Adams, for the role.

Three resounding flops followed. Then came Belasco's retouched and rearranged adaptation of Boucicault's *The Octoroon,* a controversial drama about slavery. The production provoked a letter to one of San Francisco's newspapers from a playgoer who declared he had never before seen such really bad acting with so much good scenery. Even an obvious admiration for Grandmother in the role of Zoe failed to move the writer, and O'Neill's and Grandfather's contributions were greeted with scorn. The public responded at the box office, however, and that season a more partisan critic reflected that "O'Neill, Morrison and Rose Wood can do no wrong."

By the late summer, David Belasco had finished laboring over a script of *The Vicar of Wakefield,* a dramatization of Oliver Goldsmith's novel. He called his version *Olivia,* and Grandmother was cast in the title role, with Grandfather as

Squire Thornhill and O'Neill as Mr. Burchell. Adhering closely to the original tale, the play won favor as the first big hit of the season. *Olivia* opened September 2, 1878, and during its run, James O'Neill's first son, James Jr., was born.

Christmas of 1878 for Rose and Lewis was something of a contrast to the previous year's holiday, which had found them on their successful Midwestern tour. The floundering Maguire was sometimes in the habit of settling a claim for their salary with "six-bits for breakfast." The 1879 season, however, held a brighter promise, for Belasco's dramatization of *Within an Inch of His Life* opened February 17 of the new year and was an instant success.

For my grandparents, O'Neill and the entire Baldwin Theater company, a time was approaching that would arouse one of the fiercest controversies in San Francisco's theatrical history—the opening of Salmi Morse's *The Passion Play* in March of 1879. A religious zealot, Morse was a man with a passionate mission. His greatest preoccupation was the dramatization of the life of Christ, which he claimed was the result of twenty years of research in the Holy Land. Hoping to enlist the powerful support of the Catholic Church, Morse read the play to the Jesuit fathers of St. Ignatius College, who received it kindly but gave him little encouragement for an actual production. Tom Maguire, who entertained a wondrous view toward all things foreign or properly antiquarian, heard the reading with tears in his eyes. As an intrepid theater man and gambler, he wasn't at all intimidated by the novelty of the idea, and promptly took an option on the play. James O'Neill, himself a devout Catholic, agreed to play the role of The Christus, and Grandfather was cast as Pontius Pilate. Since there was no appropriate role for Grandmother, she stayed home to spend rare and precious time with ten-year-old Rosabel, while the company plunged into rehearsals.

But long before the play was unveiled, criticism and angry protest exploded in the newspapers, encouraged by a small group of Protestant ministers. *The Passion Play* provided them with the right excuse for an outcry in the name of civic virtue and religious scruple. Although in an atmosphere of reverence and faith a similar play had been performed every decade for nearly two and a half centuries in the small Bavarian town of Oberammergau, the presentation of such a spectacle in a theater before a paying public was too radical a notion in San Francisco. Early in the rehearsal period at the Baldwin, it was clear that the undertaking was going to be a perilous one.

A hurricane broke from the pulpits, and ministers all over the city denounced the production and the theater in general, raising their voices against the immorality and sacrilege that had descended on the fair city of San Francisco. At the Tabernacle, Reverend Dr. Smith fervently called upon the thunders of Sinai to destroy the Grand Opera House. The call went unheeded.

O'Neill, convinced that *The Passion Play* was inspiring and beautiful, was bewildered by the criticism that was hurled against him and his fellow actors. Grandfather maintained a discreet, if apprehensive silence and considered the not unremote possibility of a jail sentence.

Amid the gathering storm, the company rehearsed in a biblical atmosphere. At the center of the feverish preparations, Grandfather recalled, was young David Belasco. With a prompt book under one arm and a conspicuous Bible under the other, he scoured San Francisco's museums to gaze at religious paintings, rounded up one hundred nursing mothers and an equal number of babies for the tableau, *The Massacre of the Innocents,* and took on the riotous job of tending a flock of real sheep that were to follow Joseph and Mary down the hillsides of Jerusalem.

The boards of the stage became the Holy Land. To do justice to the most notable impersonation of his career, O'Neill scorned worldly habits and the sins of the flesh, and became a dedicated ascetic. He gave up smoking and liquor, guarded his language, denied himself all physical pleasures and demanded solemn rehearsals, after which he retreated to his dressing room for solitary vigil and contemplation.

Despite ominous threats of legal action and the opposition of an irate religious community, *The Passion Play* opened on schedule. The results were breathtaking. When O'Neill appeared on the stage with a halo around his head, a number of women in the audience wept and fell to their knees in prayer. In the scene in which he was stripped, dragged before Pontius Pilate and crowned with thorns, several of the more vulnerable patrons fainted. A group of Irish Catholic members of the audience were so moved by the realistic portrayal of Christ's martyrdom that they stormed from the theater after the final curtain looking for San Francisco's Jewish population. The outraged Irishmen managed the wholesale destruction of several Jewish pawnshops, wreaked havoc in other Jewish-owned businesses, and assaulted a number of individual Jews.

The critics did not share the high emotionalism of *The Passion Play*'s viewers, however. Reviews were frigid. One critic suggested that "after last night, San Francisco should wash its hands of Lewis Morrison."

In the days that followed, lines lengthened at the box office, while editorial pages continued to ring with protest and the clergy called for an "end to this impious presentation that has made the Passion of Christ the subject of flippant criticism in the newspapers and in the idle conversation of the ungodly."

Threatening and anonymous letters began to pour into the Grand Opera House, and several of them contained threats on the life of manager Tom Maguire. Knowingly or not, the prospective assassins had struck an exposed nerve. Maguire's morbid fear of death was so pronounced that a casual remark dropped about his appearance or health could plunge him first into despair and then into bed. Feverish with fear, he closed *The Passion Play* eight days after its opening, despite the standing-room-only attendance.

My grandparents and the rest of the company returned to

the Baldwin Theater in a hastily substituted production of *The Miner's Daughter,* supporting the illustrious star, Rose Eytinge. However, it was rather lukewarm fare after the excitement and controversies of Salmi Morse's *The Passion Play.*

Reeling under the clamorous demands of the opposition, San Francisco's Board of Supervisors passed a prohibitive city ordinance within a week of *The Passion Play's* closing. The terms of Order Number 1493 were not uncertain:

> It shall be unlawful for any person to exhibit, or take part in exhibiting, in any theater, or other place where money is charged for admission, any play or performance or representation displaying or intended to display the life or death of Jesus Christ, or any play, performance or representation, calculated or tending to debase or degrade religion.

Created in 1879, the ordinance remained on the statute books until October of 1938.

Passage of the new law was a mortal blow delivered right to Maguire's box office. After the heady entertainment at the Grand Opera House, offerings at the Baldwin seemed pale to the public by comparison. Determined to test the legality of the city ordinance and shaking off the pall of death, Maguire announced the reopening of *The Passion Play* for Holy Week, beginning April 15. There was an immediate clamor for tickets.

The cast for the revival again was headed by James O'-Neill as Jesus of Nazareth and Grandfather in the role of Pontius Pilate. Though most of the cast was unwavering, a couple of actors resigned rather than risk arrest.

Long before the curtain time on the evening of April 15, a huge crowd—a milling mob of the outraged, the curious, and determined—poured through the doors of the Grand Opera House and spilled over into the streets. Belligerent supporters of *The Passion Play,* and its equally hostile enemies, waited for a sign to do battle. Backstage, the reverent silence imposed by James O'Neill remained unbroken, while out front Tom Maguire was torn between joy and despair by the musical sound of hard cash and the presence of two San Francisco police officers who waited in the background with arrest warrants.

The moment of truth arrived. David Belasco called the actors into place, the musical director played the overture, and the curtain rose slowly on the first scene, *The Presentation in the Temple*. There followed *The Massacre of the Innocents, The Death of John the Baptist, The Last Supper, The Agony in the Garden* and *The Crowning with Thorns*. As each scene unfolded, the atmosphere grew heavier with expectation, both in front and in back of the footlights. Just before the final tableau depicting the removal of the Savior's body from the cross, the policemen went backstage and removed O'Neill, Grandfather and six of their colleagues from the Holy Land of the Grand Opera House. Belasco escaped arrest by hiding in a cellar. Still clad in the robes of the Christus and Pilate, James and Grandfather went along without protest, as befitted their station, but several of the rabble put up some resistance at being carted off in costume.

The police led their prisoners through a shouting, angry mob and took them to jail to await the pronouncement of justice the following morning. Fortunately the management furnished bail and saved the actors the indignity of spending a night in jail clothed in biblical robes. A further hearing was set for April 22, at which time the judge sustained the Board of Directors and upheld the actors' convictions. The actors pleaded guilty on advice of counsel, and as the figure of the most celestial importance, O'Neill was fined fifty dollars, while Pontius Pilate and the supporting cast were fined only five dollars. O'Neill gallantly paid the court for the entire troupe.

A brief notice appeared in *The Alta California*.

GRAND OPERA HOUSE—The management has the honor to announce that in deference to public opinion *The Passion* will no longer be presented.

Grandfather was somewhat cautious in his opinion of the experience, and asked for his impressions of *The Passion Play,* he replied with customary reserve, "It was a most enlightening experience." O'Neill's wife, Ella Quinlan, was mortified and humiliated by the whole affair, while James believed it was the end of his career as an actor. There was no nonsense in Grandmother's view. She called it "The Holy Circus."

With profound relief, the Morrisons, O'Neill and company returned to the Baldwin Theater to play routine melodrama.

Lester Wallack arrived in San Francisco for a starring engagement at the competing California Theater. The Morrisons renewed their acquaintance with Wallack, and he recalled his joint appearances with Grandmother at his own theater in New York three years before and her personal triumph in *Brass.* Looking ahead to his approaching season as an actor-manager in New York, he offered Grandmother a contract to appear at Wallack's Theater beginning in September of 1879. It posed something of a problem for Lewis and Rose, since it meant another long separation and another adjustment for their daughter, Rosabel. But an offer to play one of the most distinguished theaters in the country again was not to be refused. Grandmother accepted the New York offer and began to make plans for the trip East, accompanied by Rosabel.

Meanwhile, Lester Wallack was totally unprepared for his reception at the California Theater. Audiences greeted him with towering indifference, and he chafed with impatience to leave San Francisco for the unqualified success he knew awaited him in New York. As one of America's foremost actors and the son of an illustrious one, there was nothing in his successful past to shake his confidence or self-esteem. After a few weeks of suffering audience apathy, at the point of his departure an ill-chosen question from a reporter brought a sharp retort from the princely Wallack. "Sir, you can judge what I think of the average San Franciscans when I state my opinion that if Jesus Christ himself came down from Heaven, they would give James O'Neill preference in the character!"

In the rapidly changing kaleidoscope of the theater, Wallack's Theater seemed the one fixed point. It was New York's premiere theater, the home of high comedy, a social institution. One of the largest in the city, the theater was built at Broadway and Thirteenth in the early eighteen-sixties, and its architecture and furnishings reflected the last word in opulence. Orchestra seats sold for a dollar; the parquet and pit for fifty cents. Gallery gods paid a quarter for seats in the "family circle," so called because of some odd reluctance to call a balcony a balcony. Opening nights drew the most distinguished audiences, who attended the theater more to be seen than to see.

For actors, to play Wallack's was the best of all passports to fame. Salaries weren't very impressive, but the prestige of acting in the country's leading playhouse more than made up for the financial deficiencies.

My grandmother had played Wallack's as early as the 1876 season and became one of its favorite performers when she rejoined the company in 1879. Often she played in support of Lester Wallack himself and there, too, first performed with the extraordinarily handsome Maurice Barrymore, father of Ethel, John and Lionel, as well as with the prolific playwright and sometime actor, Dion Boucicault. Until the mid-eighteen-eighties, Grandmother was one of Wallack's leading actresses, though she also performed in other New York theaters during that period. For her and for Wallack's, however, the high point of the decade was a celebrated revival of Sheridan's *The Rivals*, with Joseph Jefferson as Bob Acres, Mrs. John Drew, grandmother of the Barrymores, as Mrs. Malaprop, and "the pleasing and handsome Rose Wood" in the role of Lydia Languish.

.   .   .

On the West Coast, shortly after Grandmother's departure, Grandfather and James O'Neill made a month-long tour of the Pacific Slope towns and then returned to the Baldwin, still under the management of the unpredictable Tom Maguire, for the fall season of 1879–80. After the tempestuous engagement of a leading female star, Clara Morris, followed by a number of undistinguished dramas, James and Lewis became increasingly dissatisfied with their lot, and Maguire searched desperately for some suitable material to gratify them.

Grandfather wrote a complaining letter to Rose in New York, for by then his only wish was to rejoin her and his small daughter since the family had been separated for nearly a year. Oddly enough, it was *The Passion Play* that made their reunion possible.

In the spring of 1880, a year after the riotous production at the Grand Opera House, *The Passion Play*'s author, Salmi Morse, persuaded Tom Maguire to seek a New York production. In New York, *The Passion Play* was accepted by producer Henry E. Abbey, who promptly engaged the Booth Theater, altered the name to Booth's Tabernacle, and sent a hurried wire to James O'Neill and Grandfather in San Francisco. The experience of the past had no effect on either actor, for both agreed to re-create their portrayals of Jesus Christ and Pontius Pilate. Abbey and Morse quietly began elaborate preparations for the new production, scheduled to open at Booth's Tabernacle the second week in December. Lewis and James began to wind up their final season at the Baldwin.

September of 1880 brought a new celebrity to San Francisco's Palace Hotel in the person of Ulysses S. Grant. The city rolled out the welcome mat and Tom Maguire, with creditable grace, arranged a testimonial performance for the general and expresident, combining it with a benefit for the Baldwin's charming actress, Miss Nina Varian. The theater program for September 24, 1880, declared: "Grand Gala Night—Occasion Extraordinary!" First on the bill was a scene from *Romeo and Juliet*, played by Grandfather and Miss Varian. Then came The Double Male Quartette, followed by Victorien Sardou's drama of intrigue, *Diplomacy*, with a cast led by James O'Neill.

As soon as the notes of The Double Male Quartette died on the air, Grandfather boarded a train for New York. After the long-awaited reunion with his family, he went to the Park Theater to appear with Agnes Booth in *Legion of Honor*. By then, Grandmother was reigning at Wallack's and for a few months at least, all was serene.

But a new storm was gathering over the approaching production of *The Passion Play*. When the opening of December 6 was announced, once again protest erupted in the press and from the pulpits. New York was no less outraged than San Francisco had been, and the ministers predicted the rebirth of Sodom and Gomorrah. Despite the ominous rumblings, Henry E. Abbey and Salmi Morse continued their feverish preparations at the Booth, while James and Lewis reviewed their roles. In the scene shops, a huge drop curtain was painted depicting snowy-winged angels in upward flight on Easter morning, and a statue of William Shakespeare was removed from the top of the proscenium arch and replaced by a large cross.

But the mounting objection and harassment directed at *The Passion Play* was too much to bear. Amid the deafening protest, Abbey withdrew his support, the preparations came to a halt and Salmi Morse had to be content with a public reading of his play at the Cooper Institute. William Shakespeare was hoisted back up on his pedestal over the proscenium and Booth's Tabernacle was restored to Booth's Theater. Henry Abbey redeemed himself the following year by introducing Sarah Bernhardt to American audiences.

The week of December 6, 1880, found both my grandparents and James O'Neill performing together in *A Celebrated Case*, instead of *The Passion Play*. A New York amusement column printed the following perfunctory note: "There had been promised this week a much-advertised *The Passion Play* arranged by Salmi Morse. Public clamor prevented its production."

December 27, Grandfather made a smashing personal hit at Booth's Theater as Simon Legree in *Uncle Tom's Cabin*. The twenty-seven-year-old *Uncle Tom* was already an American classic, and again it played to solid houses clear through the first two months of the new year, a long run for the time.

For Rose and Lewis, 1881 was a year filled with activity when both were in constant demand. Often, the Morrisons were on the road either together or separately, while Rosabel was relegated to the attentions of the Convent of the Sacred Heart. My twelve-year-old aunt planned on becoming a nun, but after years of soaking up the theater's atmosphere, she, too, would eventually make her debut in the profession.

After appearing in a few more conventional dramas, a period that included a revival of *A Celebrated Case* with James O'Neill, Grandfather began to prepare for his biggest challenge to date, his first Iago in *Othello*. It was a production scheduled for mid-April of 1882 and marked one of the most curiously variegated plays in America's professional theater.

The previous year, an American representative of foreign stars went to Italy to engage the great Italian tragedian, Tommaso Salvini. He presented Salvini with the idea of playing his celebrated *Othello* in Italian, with an English-speaking cast for a tour of the United States. The famed Milanese actor had already achieved phenomenal success in America seven years before with an all-Italian company, a success that had been crowned by his portrayal of Shakespeare's tortured Moor. Despite the language barrier, Americans had wildly acclaimed his inexhaustable passion and dramatic power. But Salvini posed what to him was the insurmountable problem of understanding his cues, and he wondered how American actors would know when to speak if they didn't understand Italian. The American agent overcame his objections, convincing him that American actors could work like mathematicians, memorizing the cues from phonetic spellings. Salvini signed the contract with great misgivings, and when the first announcement was made of the bilingual *Othello,* he received many protesting letters from his American fans.

His fears proved to be unfounded. The company had made a meticulous study of the cues in Italian. Grandfather recalled that the American actors were letter-perfect when, at the first rehearsal, a nervous Salvini floundered through the opening scenes until finally he recovered his composure.

In April of 1882, with Grandfather as Iago and Clara Morris as Desdemona, the bilingual *Othello* opened in New York. Once again, Salvini's performance made New Yorkers gasp with its brutality and excitement, and he swept his audience before him in a storm of raw emotion. He refused to perform more than five times a week and declared that an actor's life in America could be summed up in three words: "theater, railroad, hotel." But in spite of the discomforts of touring, the financial rewards of the dual-language experiment were so great, he repeated it on his two subsequent tours of the United States.

Late in 1882 an item in a theatrical trade paper noted, "Rose Wood was to have appeared in *False Shame,* but Alice Wyndham took her place." Grandmother's withdrawal from the play was for a good reason; it began her confinement before the birth of her second child, my mother, Mabel Adrienne Morrison. Fourteen years after her sister Rosabel was born, Mother was born March 1, 1883, at the Morrison home on Eighty-sixth Street in Manhattan. The previous month had found Lewis on tour not only playing Iago to Salvini's Othello, but also supporting him in two other bilingual productions, *The Outlaw* and *The Gladiator,* both long-time starring vehicles for the great Italian actor. On the night Mother was born, however, he was playing Armand to Marie Prescott's Camille in New York and so was home for the arrival of his new daughter.

Within a few weeks Grandmother was back in theatrical

harness and in October of that same year was playing *Cricket on the Hearth* at the Union Square Theater with Joseph Jefferson. In one scene, she carried the seven-month-old Mabel Adrienne on in her arms, and although there's no record of the effect of Mother's debut, the early influences must have been considerable. She, too, would become a highly successful leading woman on the New York stage.

The following year of 1884, on May 12, the Morrisons's third child, a son, was born, the only member of the family who would have no interest in the theater. He was named Victor Jago as a namesake of Grandfather's favorite Shakespearean role, though it was given the Spanish spelling instead of the Anglicized Iago, perhaps out of deference to Lewis's Spanish mother. Eventually, Uncle Victor was sent to a military school and Mother, like Aunt Rosabel, attended St. Gabriel's Convent and the Convent of the Sacred Heart.

Meanwhile, Rose and Lewis continued their busy lives in the theater, appearing singly or together, and at the same time tending a growing family. By then Rosabel was nearly sixteen years old, and Lewis persuaded her to try her wings as an actress.

Early in 1885, he began to prepare her for her debut in the approaching summer and planned for another fling as an actor-manager himself. Grandmother went contentedly from home and family to Wallack's Theater, little realizing that her husband's next most important production would lead to theatrical tyranny for him and disaster for their marriage.

# 10

If Wallack's Theater seemed a permanent fixture in the theatrical scene of the eighteen-eighties, other traditions were being abandoned or fostered. In the larger cities, people began to dine later and, as a result, performances started at eight o'clock, or even later. The old system of providing a farce as an after-piece, which had been great-grandfather Wood's specialty, was discarded, and actors began to complain that they were working too hard when Saturday matinees were added to the weekly schedule of performances.

Also, it was a period when actresses surrounded themselves in an atmosphere of mystery. Glamor was a star's most valuable asset, and some of them went to great lengths to protect and encourage their legends. But with the increasing use of colored lithograph posters in advertising, images of performers were exposed everywhere to the public gaze. One highly celebrated beauty of the period was incensed at finding her portrait displayed in the window of a saloon, and that evening she stormed into her dressing room in a welter of indignation. Mrs. John Drew, who headed the company, tried to calm the enraged lady and made a statement that was more prophetic than she knew. "My dear, don't be a fool. We will all be obliged to come to it, and God knows where we will next see ourselves pictured. But wherever it may be, we actresses will have to submit!" Eventually, the new means of publicizing plays and players would have a telling effect on the profession. Grandfather Morrison began to use it widely in the most successful theatrical venture of his career.

Sometime early in 1885, he began work on a production that v.ould make his name a household word as the devil incarnate in cities throughout the country for more than two decades, actually until his death in 1906. It was an elaborate production of *Faust,* in which he starred as Mephistopheles. Written in five acts by Grandfather and George Lipsher, it was adapted from Goethe's work, with a nod here and there to Gounod, and in the profession it became known as "the Morrison version."

In January of 1885, Grandfather performed the famous "screen" scene from *School for Scandal* opposite Rose Coghlan and gave a fencing exhibition for an Actors' Benefit in New York, but most of the months that followed he concentrated on his massive production of *Faust,* writing furiously and working toward a tryout in Chicago planned for later in the year.

Between performances at Wallack's and the Union Square Theater, Grandmother directed a busy household that included my mother, Mabel Adrienne, who was then two years old, and the year-old Victor Jago. Between them, Rose and Lewis coached their older daughter for her theatrical debut in *A Celebrated Case.* Grandfather took her to Chicago, where she appeared opposite him for the first time on June 15, 1885, in the role of Adrienne, a role her mother had played before her. The newspapers predicted a bright future for the sixteen-year-old Rosabel Morrison. Then, Grandfather began to groom her for the role of Marguerite in *Faust.*

In November, the first performance of the Morrison *Faust* was seen at the Columbia Theater in Chicago, then under the management of J. M. Hill. Mr. Hill paid for the scenery and Grandfather furnished everything else: the company, the play, his own performance as Mephisto, the direction and costumes. "My finest contribution, however," he said later, "was my daughter, Rosabel!"

Great-grandfather, William F. Wood, and Bruin
in *Conrade, Marquis of Montserrat,* London, 1835

The Vokes Family

My maternal grand-
mother, Rose Wood

Grandfather Lewis Morrison as
Mephistopheles in *Faust*

Aunt Rosabel in *The Squaw Man,* 1906

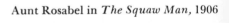

Mother as Juliet, age 14

Mother as Marguerite in *Faust*

My mother, Mabel
Adrienne Morrison

Father, the juvenile leading man

Richard Bennett, the matinee idol

Father during *Winterset* period

Family portrait, Constance, Barbara and me with mother and father

Early frolics on the lawn at Palisades, New Jersey.
Barbara, Joan and Constance.

Me, at 14, ready for a costume party

With Constance, our cloche period

The gentle Bennett, Barbara

My stage debut in *Jarnegan* with Margaret Mower and father

Jack Fox

Gene Markey

Introducing Shelley Wanger, surrounded by Walter, Stephanie, Mims and Ditty

Mr. and Mrs. Walter Wanger, a night out

The Rolands, Lorinda, Constance, Gyl and Gilbert

With Donald Cook in *Janus*

Cary Grant and Constance contemplate the hula in *Topper*

Constance, before she broke the habit

With Bing Crosby in *Mississippi*

With Fredric March in *Trade Winds*

I face scandal and the press
with my lawyer, Grant Cooper

With George Arliss in *Disraeli*

Constance, a studio portrait

The brunette look in *Secret Behind the Door*

*Pursuit of Happiness*

Smoldering in *Scarlett Street*

*Man in the Iron Mask* with Louis Hayward

Ditty, Mrs. Diana Anderson

Mims, Mrs. Joseph Bena

Shelley Wanger

Stephanie, Mrs. Frederick Guest

The first reviews were a comforting sign that *Faust* was headed for success, and Grandfather's portrayal of Mephisto was greeted with particular acclaim. He was delighted with the critical reception, and especially pleased with his daughter's success in the leading feminine role. It was an auspicious time for my Aunt Rosabel, and a clear indication to Grandmother that she would ably lead the family theatrical tradition into the fourth generation.

The first performances in Chicago, however, generated more interest among the critics than with the general public. *Faust* was anything but a blockbuster at the box office. But Grandfather had faith in the production and, at the end of the Chicago run, bought the scenery from Hill for thirty-seven hundred dollars. By then his total financial outlay was something over ten thousand dollars, which represented every cent he had in the world. The only way to recoup his investment was to play hell on the road, though he knew it was a long chance and would be immensely costly to tour. However, he stinted on nothing and lavishly mounted the road production with splendid costumes, a large cast and extravagant scenic effects. He carried his own electrical plant and a playbill of the time proudly informed the public, "Electric effects are by the Edison Incandescent System."

The first few months were disastrous. He lost money with distressing regularity and, to make matters worse, all the expensive scenery was burned during the run in Worcester, Massachusetts. Still, he clung doggedly to the road, confident that his production would make money eventually.

In Cincinnati, Lewis met an eager young man named Edward J. Abrams who persuaded him to "paper the town" with posters, particularly the colored lithographs of Mephisto, and further ingratiated himself by writing a love song to Rosabel, which he sang to her at every opportunity. When the company left Cincinnati, it had a new general manager in Mr. Abrams, and within a few weeks, Grandfather had a son-in-law.

When the season closed, Grandfather spent the summer at

a house in Asbury Park, which he'd bought two years before as a summer residence, and helped Grandmother to organize her own touring repertory company, booking her first performances in the West for the fall of 1886. After *Faust's* financial disaster of the previous season, she tried to dissuade him from a repetition of failure and urged him to join her, but Lewis gritted his teeth, rehired Aunt Rosabel as Marguerite and her new husband as general manager, and once more pulled on the red tights of Mephisto. He borrowed money to replace the scenery that had burned in Massachusetts, and opened the second season fully sixteen thousand dollars in debt, while Grandmother left in a huff for her own tour of the Western states. The first three months the road company *Faust* repeated its previous financial calamity, and to keep afloat, Grandfather sold the summer house in Asbury Park, an occurrence that Rose found less than endearing. Occasionally, in the larger cities, the play was received with some enthusiasm, but the deeper it went into the hinterlands, the deeper it went into box-office poverty.

After several weeks of one-nighters and a few split weeks, Lewis looked forward to New Orleans, a large city in which he felt he could play a longer engagement and, hopefully, make up some of his recent losses. Also, for him, New Orleans was a place of fond memories. His mother was buried there, he and Grandmother had been married there twenty-two years before, he'd made his professional debut at the Varieties Theater in that city, and it was Rosabel's birthplace.

*Faust* was booked into the Grand Opera House, and the spirits of the company rose with each mile that drew them closer to New Orleans. It had always been a great theater town, Grandfather assured his actors, and already he was banking the profits, at least on paper. But the rosy prospects vanished when the company arrived to find the advance sale was virtually nonexistent, due in part to faulty advance publicity, but mainly because P. T. Barnum's circus had arrived to play simultaneously and had swept the town clean of ticket-buyers. As the world's greatest drumbeater, Barnum and his three-ring circus had blinded amusement seekers to any other theatrical presentation, and the competition meant catastrophe for Grandfather. It was too late and too costly to publicize *Faust* against such odds.

Desolated, Lewis, Rosabel and Edward Abrams huddled together in the lobby of their hotel, trying to think of a way out of the predicament and wondering where in hell their next meal was coming from. At that moment Phineas T. Barnum himself walked into the hotel lobby. He and Grandfather had met on a few occasions in New York; Barnum recognized him, gave him a hearty greeting, and asked what he was doing in New Orleans. When Lewis spilled out his woes, Barnum laughed and accepted it as just another challenge to his formidable talents as a showman. He laid out a plan for the evening's performance, and with a "nothing to lose" attitude, Grandfather put it into effect.

An hour before curtain time, he took several cannisters of red fire, used to produce the effect of flames in the Brocken scene, to the roof of the Grand Opera House and, along with some other fireworks, set them all off at once. The explosion unleashed instant pandemonium. A cry of "Fire!" went up from all directions and people came flocking to watch the pyrotechnics, drawn by the thrilling prospect of watching the Grand Opera House burn to the ground. Fire wagons thundered onto the scene, harassed police jockeyed the milling crowd into line, and there above them all was the frightening figure of Mephistopheles silhouetted in flames. Three-sheet lithograph posters out front advertised the presentation of *Faust*. and, shortly, the spectators realized they'd been taken in true Barnum style. It produced a reprimand from the authorities, and an immediate run on the box office. With Barnum's help, Grandfather talked himself out of a charge of attempted arson, and salved the city's police and fire departments with free tickets. The opening night curtain was held for twenty minutes to accommodate seating of the audience. The next day, all of New Orleans knew *Faust* was in town, and Barnum had further proof of his genius for bally-hoo. By popular demand, the New Orleans run was extended twice, and the company never played to an empty seat.

It proved to be the turning point in the ebbing tides of *Faust,* and the fortunes of Lewis Morrison. Although he played it on tour in a repertory with other popular dramas of the period, it was *Faust* that the public wanted to see. After the initial success, Grandfather felt he could tour the country with it for several more seasons, but soon he realized it could play an unlimited number of return engagements, particularly in split-weeks or one-night stands in the smaller towns. Eventually its popularity was enormous, his personal success as Mephisto, no less so. Occasionally, he played with other companies for brief engagements as a guest artist, but mainly, for the next twenty-one years he toured at the head of his own company, chained to the theatrical tyranny of repeating a single role thousands of times.

Years later, in a one-night stand in the South where he'd already played Mephistopheles for fifteen consecutive engagements, he asked the theater manager to let him appear in *Richelieu* instead. Over strong objections, the manager finally consented and the result of that single performance of *Richelieu* was box-office lethargy, where before he'd played to standing room. The public simply resented seeing him in anything but *Faust.*

Everywhere he played the pattern was repeated as he crossed and recrossed the web of cities throughout the country. Rochester . . . El Paso . . . Seattle . . . Ashtabula . . . Omaha . . . Denver . . . Butte . . . Fort Worth . . . Tampa. The list was endless and the same territory was retraced each year.

Though it meant critical recognition and affluence, Grandfather was patently aware of the artistic pitfalls of being so completely identified with one part and, inevitably, he felt moments of regret. "There is a great drawback," he wrote, "in becoming identified with one role. No actor with creative instincts cares to limit his work to the impersonation of a single character, even if he is sure of making money."

There were other actors of the period who were also forced into artistic slavery. Among them were his friend, James O'Neill, who began his perennial triumph in *The Count of Monte Cristo* about the same time Grandfather introduced *Faust*, and played the Count in over six thousand performances. Joseph Jefferson, despite many other brilliant portrayals, is known to this day as Rip Van Winkle, and William Gillette was bound hand and bank account to *Sherlock Holmes*.

By the time Grandfather first produced *Faust* in 1885, when he was forty, he'd become a wonderfully versatile actor who had played literally hundreds of roles and shared honors with some of the theater's most illustrious figures. He'd received particular personal acclaim for his Romeo, Shylock, Iago and Richard III, and had played most of the standard comedies and melodramas in the successful repertory of the time. Like most actors, he felt that versatility was a prime requisite, although for some reason, the display of variety didn't meet with great success with theatergoers. For its stars, the American public demanded specialists, one actor to play tragedy only, one to devote himself to romantic drama and duels, another to dress-suit satire. Others were relegated to the drawing room and smooth "cigarette" parts. Actresses were no less fettered by the system of specialization. If an actress could cry easily, then she wept relentlessly throughout her career, and if she was a comedienne, she was terribly jolly until she died of hysterics. No matter what his contrasting skills, it was box-office woe to the star who stepped out of those boundaries.

There's no doubt that Grandfather's acting techniques would be considered "hammy" by today's bottom-scratching methods. But it was a time for excesses, though even then, critics occasionally were moved to denounce them. The exaggerated style of the period was called acting in the "grand manner," vigorous, colorful, expansive and filled with infinite detail, and Grandfather could chew scenery, and "split the ears of the groundlings" with the best of them. It may have been "ham" served up with all the trimmings, but audiences loved it and felt cheated unless they were blasted in their seats by the trumpet tones of a powerful voice. Ineffectual lighting systems also demanded exaggerated gestures and posturing to carry tragic messages across the footlights, and Lewis was in his element when he could clutch, gasp, stagger, reel or, in the stage directions of the time, "exit left, wiping tear from eye." In any case, his Mephisto could not be faulted in the eyes of his public.

I never saw either of my grandparents on a stage, for Lewis died and Rose retired before I was born, but from what I've heard and read, Grandmother was the finer, subtler artist. Despite the supremacy of her acting, it was Grandfather who left the deeper mark on the American theater of the nineteenth century. Fortunately there was no competitive feeling between them. She idolized him and thought him the world's greatest actor.

Above all, he was known among his colleagues for his genial disposition and the liberal treatment of his actors. One of his contemporaries wrote, "Thorough in his methods, patient and encouraging as a director, he is to members of his company, both instructor and example. To be acquainted with Mr. Morrison is to know a scholar, to be the friend of hospitality and a gentleman—always a gentleman."

After Barnum's riotous rescue of *Faust* in New Orleans in 1886, Grandfather happily paid his creditors and reveled in his new success, while his son-in-law, Edward Abrams, continued his duties as company manager, and Rosabel made her nightly ascensions to Heaven on piano wires to the celestial music of Gounod.

Meanwhile, Grandmother's own ventures in the theater kept her busy on annual tours of the Western states and the

Pacific Coast. Advertised as "Miss Rose Wood's Company," the troupe toured for three years, beginning the first season simultaneously with Lewis's *Faust* in 1885. Although at that point Grandfather's production was still limping, Grandmother's tours spared no expense on the acting company, the scenery or the advertising, and they turned out to be financial successes.

Separated all season, Rose, Lewis and Rosabel were reunited each summer in New York with Mother and Victor Jago, and in 1887, the family reunions included Rosabel's son, Lewis Abrams. During the summer vacation of 1888, both Grandfather and Rosabel were disquieted by disturbing signs of instability in Rose's behavior. She was given to fits of depression, long sullen silences and sudden unexplainable rages. Occasionally she suffered from "the vapors," a vague Victorian term for most any mysterious disorder which ladies of the period relieved with smelling salts and a good deal of vigorous fanning. Doctors diagnosed her condition as "melancholia," but rest and a vacation from work improved her spirits, and by the time her next road tour was ready to open, she seemed her normal self again.

That fall, Rose and Lewis went their separate ways, Grandmother to the Western states and Grandfather to Cincinnati to open his season with *Faust,* accompanied by Rosabel and her husband, Edward Abrams. Lewis had added a larger repertory of plays to his season that included *Victor Durand, Richelieu, A Celebrated Case, London Assurance* and *Romance of a Poor Young Man.* The ingenue roles were played by Rosabel and all of them, with the exception of Marguerite, had been played by her mother before her. In the larger cities, Grandfather alternated in his own repertory and as a visiting star with resident stock companies. By early spring of 1889, Grandfather's company had swung into the Western leg of the tour and settled in at the Baldwin Theater in San Francisco for an engagement of several weeks.

In the resident company at the Baldwin, there was an

eighteen-year-old novice named Florence Roberts, whose first stage appearance had been made the previous year as a super in the crowd scenes of Boucicault's Irish drama, *Arrah-no-Pogue*. Her cousin, the prominent actor Theodore Roberts, was also in the company, and it was he who'd introduced her to the Baldwin's management. Florence, who was young, beautiful and impetuous, fell in love with Grandfather at once, not overlooking the fact that he was one of the country's most prominent actors. For her, there seemed no obstacles in the facts that she was only two years younger than her idol's daughter, that Lewis was twenty-six years older than she, or that his wife was still very much in evidence, if removed by distance and the circumstance of separate tours. In the past, it wasn't unknown for him to respond to other impressionable ladies smitten by his charms, but those had been passing encounters. At first, he played the benign role of benefactor, but the harmless game became less of a game as time went by and when the company left San Francisco, there was a new ingenue in the small role of Martha in *Faust*. Eventually, she assumed the role of Marguerite and later costarred with Lewis in the rest of his repertory.

It's an obvious comment that theatrical families, of necessity, are often separated for long periods of time. Ideally, of course, husband and wife work together, and many of them do with great success and harmony. But there are also times when separation breeds discontent. For most of the five years that followed 1885 and the introduction of *Faust*, Lewis had been roaming the country, while Rose had been involved in an independent career. It's probable, too, that her increasing emotional problems and peculiar behavior had alienated him further, and Florence's provocative attentions no doubt offered him a refuge of greater stability. The break was inevitable. Late in 1890, my grandparents were divorced after a marriage of twenty-five years, and Lewis married Florence the following year. The Morrison children, Rosabel, Mother and Uncle Victor Jago, were then aged twenty-one, seven and six. To his credit, Lewis provided for Rose and the children until his death. The adjustment was difficult for everyone concerned, but particularly for my Aunt Rosabel, since the swift decline of her mother forced her to assume full responsibility for raising a brother and sister, as well as her son, Lewis. In 1894, another son, Harry, added to her responsibilities.

In despair over the divorce, Grandmother retreated into a secluded twilight world, and after a career that had spanned forty-two years, she never worked in the theater again. As time went by, she became fey and "irresponsible," or quite simply, unhinged. For years she lived with my aunt and later, Mother and various other members of the family looked after her. In 1932, at the age of eighty-seven, she died of "melancholia" at her home in Tenafly, New Jersey. She'd outlived Grandfather by twenty-six years, which seems a rather long time to be melancholy.

Family legend says that Grandmother's decline was due to a broken heart, which may have a ring of truth, for her great love for Grandfather was well known, and it's possible that the loss of that love contributed to her derangements. On the other hand, she may have been the victim of a view expressed by Schopenhauer.

> My own experience of many years has led me to the opinion that madness occurs proportionally most frequently among actors. But what a misuse they make of their memory! Daily, they have to learn a new part or refresh an old one; but these parts are entirely without connection—nay, are in contradiction with each other, and every evening the actor strives to forget himself entirely and be some quite different person. This kind of thing paves the way for madness!

I prefer the more romantic legend of a broken heart.

# 11

From the beginning, it was patently clear that Florence Roberts would not win any popularity contests with the rest of the Morrison clan. Green-eyed, sharp-tongued and imperious, she led Lewis around on a tightened leash and bullied him into reviving plays that would show her to best advantage as a leading actress in his company. She reveled in her position as the wife of a celebrated actor, a circumstance which brought her into many charmed theatrical circles. Lewis, Florence and Rosabel managed to work together, at least with some harmony, for three seasons, from 1889 to 1892, and performed together at the Star Theater in New York for Florence's Broadway debut in *The Schatchen*.

As time went on, however, Rosabel and her husband decided to branch out on their own and with Lewis's help, formed their own traveling company. Edward Abrams was also known for his forceful personality, and undoubtedly there was friction between him and Florence, who inherited the role of Marguerite. Having played the part herself for six years, it was no loss to Rosabel, though she would return to it from time to time and later estimated that she'd been launched toward Heaven in *Faust* over twenty-five hundred times.

While Abrams continued to book and manage Grandfather's company, in 1892 he and Rosabel prepared for the opening of their own road tour. As the main feature of their first season, Rosabel chose *The Danger Signal,* a four-act melodrama depicting the perils of railroad life which had been rewritten expressly for my aunt by Henry de Mille, the father of William and Cecil B. The main attraction of the play was its extraordinary scenic effects: a snow avalanche, an express train that simulated a speed of fifty miles an hour, flashing railroad signals, and a real engine that rang bells, blew whistles and belched smoke. The climax was a spectacular wreck between a passenger-freight and a mail train, followed by a thrilling rescue of the hero's mother.

*The Danger Signal* proved to be a great success for the newly formed company, and for over two years Rosabel played Rose Martin, a female track-switch attendant and telegraph operator, known as "the wild flower of Laramie Bend." The newspapers called her "charming and sprightly, a real soubrette" . . . "remarkably talented and handsome" . . . "a consummate actress." She contributed further to the realism of the drama by learning the Morse code and sending a fateful, frantic message in the telegraph scene with authentic dots and dashes on a genuine key. In Ohio, a telegraph operator in the audience read aloud every word of Rosabel's message for the enlightenment of his fellow townsmen in neighboring seats. There was some suspicion that Miss Morrison's husband had staged the incident, since it was immediately related in *The Daily Irontonian,* and widely repeated with elaborations.

Abrams wasn't at all averse to staging things for the benefit of publicity, and proudly maintained, with some reason, that some of "Barnum's bunk" had rubbed off. Another of his contrivances also received attention in the press. "Rosabel Morrison, daughter of Lewis Morrison, who is starring in *The Danger Signal,* showed what she knew about running a locomotive last week by getting into the cab of a New York and New England Railroad locomotive, pulling the throttle and sending the train flying on its way between Fishkill, New York, and Danbury, Connecticut." There may be no connection, but Rosabel's understudy played the balance of that week.

Eventually weary of portraying "the wild flower of Laramie Bend," she returned to New York late in 1893 to spend some time with her young son, Mother and Uncle Victor. Her second son, Harry, was born in January of the following year. By then, Rosabel had taken on the full guardianship of her brother and sister, and in her absence Mother was placed in the Convent of the Sacred Heart, Victor in military school and, on occasion, they were placed in the care of servants and friends. But each time she returned to New York, Rosabel brought a trunkful of presents for the children and tried to make up for her all too infrequent visits home. Grandfather by no means neglected his children and made visits to them whenever he was in the New York area.

Shortly after he and Florence Roberts were married, Grandfather began to build a country home in Peekskill, New York. Built in 1892 as a summer haven from his seasonal tours, he named it "Morrison Manor." From then on, his children and Rosabel's spent their summer vacations there. A big, rambling house with wide verandas and spacious lawns, it still stands in the rolling countryside of New York state. Uncle Victor's initials are still distinguishable in a windowsill, where he carved them when he was nine.

When the Morrison family congregated at Peekskill in the summer of 1896, my mother, Mabel Adrienne, was thirteen years old and had begun to show signs of theatrical ambition. She was dark-eyed and beautiful with a sweet and trusting nature, a small replica of her sister, and like Rosabel, lured by the smell of greasepaint. Too young for *Faust's* Marguerite, Grandfather agreed to let her try her wings in the small role of Anita in a forthcoming production of *Carmen*, starring Rosabel in the title role. Rosabel had found a suitable adaptation of Merimee's novel and was planning a new production for the fall of 1896. It meant Mother would have to leave school, but that was a minor consideration to a budding actress and a doting father, proud of her ambitions.

In November, the *Carmen* tour opened in the South with a first-rate company headed by the "clever and vivacious Rosabel Morrison," handsome Edward Ellsner as Don Jose, and a vigorous Escamillo played by Harold Hartsell. Advertisements were careful to inform playgoers that they were being offered a dramatic version of *Carmen,* not the musical one, for Bizet's opera had become a popular standard in the operatic repertory since its American premiere in 1878.

No mention was made of nepotism, or the similarity of names in the cast list, but of Mother's debut, the New Orleans review declared, "Miss Mabel Morrison appeared as Anita and demonstrated that she has ability and knows how to display it."

*Carmen* played successfully until the late spring of 1897 when the Morrison sisters returned to New York and broke up the act. Lewis, highly pleased with Mother's initial efforts, decided to launch her in his own company beginning with the fall season, and that summer in Peekskill, he began to coach her in Juliet. She was delighted with his view that Shakespeare would do her more good than school, and he hired a tutor for the tour to make up the deficit.

During that same summer, Rosabel prepared another production of *Carmen* and headed for a New York opening. Critics predicted she was on the high road to fame and, in glowing terms, described her graceful figure and perfect brunette beauty, also noting that she spoke fluent French and was an excellent musician. As the Spanish gypsy, she attracted the attention of the great Joseph Jefferson who, in 1898, offered her an engagement in *Cricket on the Hearth*. It seemed an odd coincidence that my grandmother, Rose Wood, was playing that same role with Jefferson when she carried my seven-month-old mother onstage for her first taste of the theater.

Mother was fourteen when Grandfather introduced her as Juliet, the age Shakespeare intended for his tragic heroine, although Juliet was a part she always said she disliked. She also appeared with her father in *The Master of Ceremonies,* and inevitably graduated to Marguerite in *Faust* when the role was temporarily vacated by Florence Roberts.

For the next several years, Mother toured with the Morrison company, playing a variety of parts, as well as the airborne Marguerite, and developing her skill on tour. As it has always been, the road was a tough and demanding school in which discipline was the first requisite and, like most young actors, she learned the hard way.

By then, audiences usually overflowed the theaters for a performance of "Morrison's meal-ticket," as *Faust* was called in the family, and a night in 1899 at the Opera House in Peekskill, New York, was no exception. A packed house watched the play unfold with my beautiful mother holding forth as the doomed Marguerite, downstage center. Without warning, the curtain suddenly descended in the middle of her scene. Grandfather, in the scarlet costume of Mephistopheles, stepped in front of the curtain and addressed the audience with splendid gravity. "Ladies and gentlemen, I beg you to pardon the unseemly conduct you have just witnessed on this stage. With your very kind indulgence, my daughter will now proceed to play this scene over again!" He bowed and disappeared, the curtain went up again and the entire scene was replayed. The "unseemly conduct" for which he'd punished Mother was a fit of uncontrolled giggling induced by a wisecrack from a local wit in the audience. In the months that followed, she played that scene some three hundred times, but never again with a single giggle. It was a lesson in professional behavior she never forgot.

In spite of Grandfather's stern measures, at times it was difficult to keep from breaking up onstage. During a performance in Cairo, Illinois, the trap door through which Mephisto made a spectacular descent to the infernal regions wasn't in good working order, and halfway to Hell the machinery jammed while the head, hat and feathers of the devil remained in full view of the audience. Grandfather spent several agonized moments urging the frantic stagehands to greater effort. Every straining attempt failed and after a long interval, a voice from the top of the gallery, shouted, "Hell's full, there's no more room for us!" There was nothing left to do but ring down the curtain.

The early years of the twentieth century moved in the usual circles for the Morrison side of my family. Aunt Rosabel and Edward Abrams roamed the country in their own touring company and spent their summers in a home in Yonkers, New York, not far from Grandfather's Morrison Manor in Peekskill. Their home base in Manhattan was a house on Ninety-third Street, and the household included my grandmother, Rose Wood, who lived with the Abrams's in a private, disordered twilight. Mother and Uncle Victor also lived with them when both were still under Rosabel's guardianship.

In those years of the century's first decade, Grandfather was still including *Faust* in his touring repertory and spending a long season of stock each year at the Alcazar Theater in San Francisco, starring jointly with his second wife. Then, David Belasco signed Florence for a tour of the Pacific Coast in roles which had been made famous by one of his leading stars, Minnie Maddern Fiske. Florence played *La Tosca, Tess of the d'Urbervilles, Zaza, A Doll's House* and *Martha of the Lowlands*. That left Lewis without a leading lady, and although he found several temporary replacements, both Rosabel and Mother rejoined his company as often as their own work permitted. Once again, one or the other of the Morrison sisters was seen in the role of Marguerite.

In the beginning, Grandfather never stopped making alterations in his version of *Faust* and constantly studied Goethe's text to find new dimensions for himself and the other characters. Often, he made innovations in the scenic features of the play and in a span of eight years introduced three entirely new productions. As the years passed, however, his interest began to wane, and he paid less attention to the luster of the production and the actors. It seemed to make no difference to his audiences, and still they came as he trudged wearily from town to town, caught in the artistic despotism of one part. His greatest wish was to regain his reputation as an all-around actor in the profession, and he began a partnership with an unknown "capitalist" in New York to organize a massive repertory of plays made famous by Henry Irving and Edwin Booth. As early as 1896, he began to announce his retirement from Mephisto, but his mysterious partner withdrew and Grandfather returned to the old standby. Once, he was asked what new plays he'd presented in the recent past, and he answered sadly, "None."

In the twenty-one-year reign of *Faust,* he played Mephistopheles more than five thousand times. His familiarity with the role was so great that he could go to sleep in his dressing room, rise on cue, walk onstage and play the scene, and return to his dressing room and doze until his next entrance.

In 1902, he was still announcing his retirement from the play, and cheerfully admitted that his farewell appearances exceeded those of Adelina Patti, the great Italian diva who retired industriously every year. His playbills announced "Positively Closing Performances" and "Goodbye Engagements," but by then *Faust* was a national institution in the smaller cities and the faithful refused to allow his retirement. It was much adieu about nothing.

A reporter of the time estimated that Mr. Morrison made his final appearance ten times, his positively last engagement seven times, and permanently retired from *Faust* five times. "I am now getting ready to retire again," Grandfather declared, and distributed the following handbill to prove it.

TO MY FRIENDS—THE PUBLIC

While I do so with great regret, it is my duty to inform you that this will *positively* be my *last appearance* as Mephisto in *FAUST* before you. In connection with this announcement, I also beg to advise you that in order to appropriately close my long career in this part, I have secured one of the best companies I have ever had and the best production this famous play has had in the many years I have presented it.

Thanking you for the many times repeated proofs of your good will toward me and my company, and assuring you that this has always been highly appreciated, and as nearly as possible reciprocated by me, and hoping that this, my final appearance before you will meet with your approval, I am

Yours very truly,

Lewis Morrison

But, indeed, he never did retire from *Faust* until his death closed one of the longest runs in theatrical history. No matter how hard he tried or how many times he announced a farewell, it remained his most popular vehicle. He made one last valiant effort to remove it from his repertory in 1906 and firmly announced that the following season he would shelve the play once and for all. This time it seemed to have a ring of authority. After the long domination of one role, he was infinitely weary of it all, and he was no longer a young man. Also, he knew that both he and the play had lost individuality and spontaneity long before, and he made public his plans to abandon Mephisto forever and produce a series of lighter plays the following season.

The pace of the tour that season of 1905–06 slowed somewhat, and he took fewer bookings, preferring to spend more time supervising the building of a new house. Morrison Manor in Peekskill had been used by the family as a summer residence only, and Grandfather chose Nepperhan Heights in Yonkers for the site of a more permanent home. Although spurred on by the repeated demands of his wife, it was a project he undertook only gradually and with waning energy.

Early in April of 1906, at a matinee in the Colonial Theater in Akron, Ohio, he was suddenly stricken with illness during the famous Brocken scene, and collapsed onstage. Doctors revived him, and he finished the performance and appeared again that night, but it was with no little effort that he finished out the season and then went immediately to Rosabel's home in Yonkers. Florence Roberts had returned earlier that year after a long starring tour of the Northwest, then made her New York bid for stardom in a play from her repertory, *The Strength of the Weak*. At the time Grandfather closed his tour with *Faust*, Florence's production was running on Broadway at the Liberty Theater with golden results.

Lewis spent the first few weeks of the summer packing away the production paraphernalia of "the Morrison version," and began to lay plans for the fall season. He was arranging a trip to San Francisco to adjust some affairs at the Alcazar Theater when symptoms of his illness flared again and mid-August found him undergoing surgery for gallstones at St. John's Hospital in Yonkers. But the surgical measures came too late. He died in the hospital, August 18, 1906, five days after my sister, Barbara, was born. Aunt Rosabel, her son, Lewis, and Florence Roberts were at his bedside. Uncle Victor, who had begun his military career the year before, was serving in the Philippines with the Marine Corps. They kept the news from Mother, for fear of the emotional shock so soon after her recent childbirth.

After private services in Yonkers, Grandfather was buried at Woodlawn Cemetery in Mt. Hope, New York. Tributes were paid by the profession throughout the country. A memorial plaque was placed beneath his portrait in the lobby of the Alcazar Theater in San Francisco where years before he'd been a guest of honor at the laying of its cornerstone. In New York, actors accorded him a final salute in services that took place at The Little Church Around the Corner. It seemed a fitting setting for a man who had served the profession for over forty years. That particular church, properly known as The Church of the Transfiguration, has occupied a special place in the affections of actors for a hundred years. The traditions began with an incident in 1870 when Joseph Jefferson approached the pastor of a fashionable Fifth Avenue church to make arrangements for the funeral of a friend, George Holland. The pastor refused on the basis that Holland was an actor, but he recommended "a little church around the corner where it might be done."

In spite of its demise after a long, eventful career, *Faust* wasn't through by any means. Aunt Rosabel, goaded by a failing marriage, financial pressures and the responsibility of her young sons, unpacked her father's scenery and once more began her celestial flights as Marguerite. Edward N. Hoyt portrayed Mephistopheles, and many other actors who'd played *Faust* with Grandfather in the past joined Rosabel's revival. In 1908, two years after Grandfather's death, "the Morrison version" hit the road again. Incredibly, people flocked to see it. My aunt maintained the high caliber of the production and acting company that had been associated with it in the first decade of the original, refurbishing the scenery and costumes and improving some of the scenic effects. Highly successful at the box office, receipts for a week in Denver in 1909 totaled eleven thousand dollars, which was extraordinary for a time when tickets were twenty-five cents, fifty cents and a dollar. As a businesswoman, the new producer of *Faust* was her father's peer. Avoiding the tank towns that Lewis had played the last few years of his life, she booked the larger cities and found that her improved production standards had paid off. Furthermore, her unique advertising methods would have pleased Barnum. In Minneapolis, with the cooperation of a local newspaper, she offered a hundred tickets to those people who would call the paper and admit they'd sinned, "just the little white sins, whispered in your ear." And she added the restriction, "Only those sinners over eighteen years of age will be given tickets." Minneapolis showed its eagerness for salvation by mobbing the newspaper. There was plenty of activity in Hell yet, and Aunt Rosabel played *Faust* on tour for the next three years.

The circumstances which had forced her to revive the play were personal. Four years before, she'd separated from her husband, Edward Abrams, after a marriage of eighteen years, much of which was spent unhappily, due to his outbursts in public and his tyranny in private. He was given to mysterious absences which were explained when, on more than one occasion, he was seen in the company of brightly rouged ladies in dimly lit saloons and my long-suffering aunt was finally moved to seek the nearest lawyer. Armed with a brace of detectives, she paid a visit to a certain hotel on Fifty-ninth Street in New York, and what she saw there furnished grounds for divorce. During the years of their separation, he refused to contribute to the support of their two sons and Rosabel was forced to struggle alone, often hard-pressed. But it wasn't until 1907 that she finally divorced Abrams and when she went to court, she was given custody of the two boys and legally changed their name to Morrison.

At the same time, Rosabel, as the elder spokesman for Mother and Uncle Victor, was further burdened with the complications of her father's estate. Grandfather had left a sizable sum of money and a good deal of property, due mainly to the fortunes of *Faust,* and it was understood that his wife and three children would share in them equally. His will, someone remembered vaguely, was probably in San Francisco where he'd conducted many of his business affairs. Immediately after Grandfather's death, Florence Roberts made a hurried trip to San Francisco and returned to Yonkers to begin the project of redesigning the house that he was building when he died. By the time it was finished, it had been enlarged to the size of Versailles Palace and appointed like The Louvre. There, for several years, she lived in ostentatious splendor. The suspicion lurks in the family to this day that there was skulduggery in Yonkers.

Several years later, Florence became the object of additional news interest when she was named corespondent in a divorce case between a former leading man and his wife. Details of the case are lacking, but she indignantly demanded a retraction and promptly married Frederick Vogeding, an actor from the Royal Dutch Theater who later went into films. After a decade of touring in stock and vaudeville, Florence died in Los Angeles in July of 1927, aged fifty-six.

Though 1911 was a productive and happy year for the Bennetts, it was marred for Mother by a staggering loss, the death of her sister. Early the year before, Rosabel married Mitchell Lewis, an actor whom she'd met in *The Squaw Man* when she succeeded Mother in the leading feminine role. It was a happy marriage, and they toured together successfully in her production of *Faust,* in which Mitchell played the role of Valentine. Returning to New York in 1911 from her annual rounds, Rosabel then went into Paul Armstrong's courtroom drama, *Romance of the Underworld.* On the evening of December 18 at Hammerstein's Victoria Theater, she performed as usual until the scene when she appeared on the witness stand to give testimony. Near the close of the act, she suddenly toppled forward and fell into the arms of an actor who was standing close by. As he carried her offstage, unconscious in his arms, the audience, thinking it was part of the play's action, applauded the exit. But unknown to anyone, at that moment she was dying. Her husband and her older son, Lewis, were watching from the front of the house and rushed backstage to her dressing room to find her still unconscious. The family physician was able to revive her somewhat, and by midnight she was resting more comfortably at home. By morning, her condition had deteriorated so alarmingly that Mitchell frantically summoned the doctor again. Rosabel died before his arrival. The cause of her death was given as "overexhaustion due to working in a rundown, nervous condition." Whatever the medical reasons, it seemed a dramatic if untimely death for someone who had so loved the theater and served it for twenty-eight years.

Mother was heartbroken. She and her brother, Victor Jago, had looked on Rosabel as a second mother, which indeed she was. She'd played the role gallantly and with love; now she was dead at the age of forty-two.

# 12

In the first half-dozen years of the twentieth century, legitimate actors seldom would admit to working occasionally in the movies that were being made in Ft. Lee, New Jersey, across the Hudson River from Manhattan. The standard pay scale was a straight five dollars a day, whether an actor played a large role or a small one, and frequently, he doubled in more than one part. If he was absent from his regular haunts along Broadway, often it was because he'd sneaked across the river for a few days' work in the "illegitimate" medium, and invariably, he was evasive about his absence. His colleagues looked upon him as a traitor. Movies were "The Enemy." In 1912, however, films were legitimized when Sarah Bernhardt made a four-reel version of her celebrated stage success, *Queen Elizabeth.* "This is my one chance for immortality," she said. Almost immediately, the Divine Sarah was followed by other great actors of the time when Adolph Zukor produced a series called *Famous Players in Famous Plays,* beginning with James O'Neill's *The Count of Monte Cristo.*

By the time Father made *Damaged Goods* in 1915, the movies were here to stay. As he said, "The enemy is encamped, we are surrounded!" Despite his own forays into the motion picture industry in the years that followed, he continued to resist on the premise that "If you can't fight 'em, insult 'em!"

By the early nineteen-twenties, New York's brief glory as the nation's film center was doomed, and the sleepy suburb of Los Angeles, called Hollywood, had already made its name synonymous with the movie industry. By 1924, when Constance first went to Hollywood, New York, at least for the business of movie-making, was a ghost town.

The damaging effect of the movies on the legitimate theater was undeniable, but there were other influences at work in the nineteen-twenties that were equally to blame, and even Father admitted that films alone didn't kill the theater; it committed suicide. "The theater today," he said, "is an art conducted like a business by bad businessmen. It has become a speculating playground for rich, untalented amateurs. Tickets are astronomical, a condition for which the unions are partially responsible, but the stagehands cannot be blamed for the nefarious practice of swindling the public, by sending out without scruple, third- and fourth-rate companies and thereby alienating large numbers of theatergoers."

The swift technological growth in movie-making continued to enchant the public with new devices and improvements to catch its fancy. The development of powerful mercury-vapor lamps allowed filmmakers to move indoors, and by the early nineteen-twenties a number of studios were erected in Hollywood, expressly designed for the purpose of making films. The transition from New York was nearly complete.

Even then, moviemakers were dabbling in primitive sound experiments, and in 1921, D. W. Griffith's *Dream Street* used a phonograph behind the screen, synchronized to the lip movements of the hero and heroine in a love duet, though the era of the "talkies" on any significant scale was still in the future. At the same time, color experiments were developing. As early as 1908, experimental films in Kinemacolor were shown in London, though it wasn't until 1920 that movies captured living color for the first time when Dr. Herbert Kalmus introduced the first Technicolor camera. One of the earliest uses of color in commercial filmmaking was in Constance's first Hollywood film, *Cytherea,* when two dream sequences in color contributed greatly to its box-office success. The only thing I can remember about the film was that her hair had been bleached a lighter blonde, and I thought she looked ravishing.

When I entered films in 1929, Hollywood was in the middle of the talkie revolution, a period fraught with change for the entire industry. Most producing companies rushed frantically to convert to the sound system, but others ridiculed the idea and put up a stubborn resistance, much as television was resisted two decades later. Walter Wanger at Famous-Players-Lasky haunted the sound stages of Warner Brothers, the studio which had introduced the first all-talking film in July of 1928. He returned to a meeting with his studio bosses to sell them on the inevitable. In the middle of the conference, a telegram arrived from one of Jesse Lasky's colleagues.

ALL BEST MINDS IN INDUSTRY AGREE SOUND WON'T LAST DON'T LISTEN TO WANGER.

Walter kept that wire as a memento for years. Famous-Players-Lasky had no equipment and no great amount of faith in the new idea of sound, but Walter took a baseball picture that Richard Dix had completed, inserted crowd cheers, the crack of baseball bats, some badly dubbed dialogue and a musical score and went forth joyfully to compete with Warner's Vitaphone. It made him a boy-wonder in the industry.

After selling Lasky on the idea, Walter had to help convert the exhibitors, and one of the arguments that cropped up among the theater owners was memorable. "People come to our theaters to rest, often to take a nap, and they won't like this sound business one bit!" The movie that helped sway the exhibitors was Walter's production of *Animal Crackers,* starring his four fiendish finds, the Marx Brothers.

The public went wild over sound, box offices were stampeded and by the spring of 1928, the worst sound movie was outdrawing any of the silents. With the sound barriers broken, chaos and panic reigned for a time, and the period brought with it some casualties. Most of the already established silent stars looked on talkies with great uneasiness, and many of them went in for intensive voice training. But to the stage actor, the new system presented no obstacles; it was merely the same old business of speaking lines aloud. The exodus from Broadway began.

By the time I went to Hollywood under the United Artists contract, the conversion to sound was nearly complete, and by the middle of that year of 1929, the era of the silents was over for all time.

With only one stage play under my belt, what I knew about acting makes me blanch today. Even then I knew that one play did not an actress make, but working with Ronald Colman in *Bulldog Drummond* was certainly a wonderful send-off for any neophyte. I felt insecure and intimidated at the very thought of working with him. Not too long before, he'd been one of my cherished idols, and I'd gone reverently to see his movies with Vilma Banky. But he couldn't have been sweeter or more helpful, and I'll always remember his encouragement at a time when it really mattered.

Everyone knew, of course, that I was a rank beginner, and most people were kind. In particular, Lilyan Tashman and two other cast members of *Bulldog Drummond*, Claude Allister and Montague Love, gave me helpful advice. Lilyan called me "Snoopy" because I was so nearsighted I couldn't see a thing until my nose hit it. Through Ronald Colman I met one of his good friends, William Powell, and Bill took me to lunch and explained camera angles and other techniques that proved valuable aids in the future. Also, I met Mary Pickford, one of the stockholders of United Artists, and she gave me the nickname of "Pollyanna Borgia" because she said I looked so quiet and sweet. "But underneath that demure exterior," she said, "watch out!" To Mary at least, I had a hidden wellspring of strength and confidence, although I could find no evidences in myself.

I'd gone through the makeup and wardrobe tests, then we rehearsed for a week, and after the first two or three days of shooting, I was quaking with fear. When Sam Goldwyn saw the first results on film, he came to me and said, "Where's the Bennett fire? Why don't you come across like your sister?" That did nothing to inspire my confidence and I could only answer, "I'm sorry, Mr. Goldwyn, but I'm not my sister." Then he commented on my father's spark, and I had no defense for that except to say that my father had had a great deal more experience than I, almost forty years more. It was a hesitant and difficult time for me.

In those days before the union controls of The Screen Actors' Guild, directors could work their companies around the clock if they chose, and the filming of *Bulldog Drummond* brought me the first brush with Hollywood temperament—not mine, but the director's, Richard Jones. At one point, the company worked until three in the morning, with a seven-o'clock makeup call the next day, ready to shoot on the set at nine. Ronald Colman put up with the schedule for a few days, then announced that he would not appear the following day until noon, no matter what the call might be, and if we had scenes with him we could take our choice of arriving before then or not. At that point I was so tired I jumped at the chance for a few extra hours of rest and the next day reported to the makeup department in plenty of time to be on the set when Colman arrived. The director greeted me with a blast. "What do you mean by not reporting at nine o'clock?" I explained that since all of my scenes were with Mr. Colman, I saw no reason to appear earlier just to watch the crew set up the scenes. "You do as you're told, young lady," he answered. "You're new at this business." Certainly he was right about that, but I felt his demands were unfair and unreasonable.

Between Sam Goldwyn's futile search for the Bennett fire

and Richard Jones's lectures on my inadequacies, it wasn't a particularly ego-building time, but I stuck with it because it was a matter of survival. I had a child to support; it was that simple. It wasn't until later when I was offered better parts and the challenges grew that I began to pursue a career with more desire and energy.

In that same year I did one more film for United Artists, *Three Live Ghosts,* which didn't win me any acting awards either, and the studio released me from my contract. I began to free-lance after that, and the first film I made on that basis was *Disraeli,* directed by Al Green and starring George Arliss, for Warner Brothers.

Robert Benchley once complained that a whole generation grew up thinking that every great man of history had looked like George Arliss, for in the late twenties and thirties he was cast as Disraeli, Voltaire, Alexander Hamilton, Cardinal Richelieu and other historical figures. When I worked with him, he was almost a legend and I was hopelessly in awe of him. He had a professional reputation for perfection and it was well deserved. Extraordinarily meticulous in his work, we rehearsed two weeks before the shooting began, a rarity in those days, and he demanded everything planned out ahead of time. Although he was a sweet and gentle man, he was absolutely inflexible about his working schedule. On the very stroke of five o'clock, he doffed his toupee, handed it to his valet, Jenner, and walked out. It was the signal that Mr. Arliss was through, and no amount of cajoling or pleas for "just one more take," had any effect whatever.

While I was taking my first tentative steps in motion pictures, the rest of the family was involved in various projects, both personal and professional. Father on tour with *Jarnegan* was still confounding the critics, fighting the censors, lecturing his audiences and generally having a grand time. Since the road tour was under his management, he reinstated his privilege of addressing audiences. In Boston, he became annoyed one night because his viewers weren't laughing in the right places. "This is a comedy," he told them sharply. "When the lines are funny I'll clap my hands together, like this—so you'll know." Also in Boston, "that sumphole of iniquity," the Board of Censors had cut the most objectionable lines in the play. At the final performance at the Wilbur Theater, he told his audience that Boston censorship was stupid, put back all the lines that had been deleted, and left town for good.

In the three years since Barbara's association with the international dancing star, Maurice Mouvet, she'd danced in Broadway musicals and taken infrequent jobs in movies, merely because they were offered to her, not because she was overly ambitious. In 1929, she appeared in a movie called *Syncopation*, filmed at the old Cosmopolitan Studios in New York's Harlem, and one of the first full-length sound musicals. Included in the cast were Fred Waring and a young Irish singer named Morton Downey. Shortly after, Barbara called me in California to say she was going to marry Morton.

"Morton who?" I asked, since his career was still in its early stages, and the name meant nothing to me. Billed as a singer from Ireland, although born in Wallingford, Connecticut, he'd been a nightclub and band singer with a ship's orchestra and, after some twenty Atlantic crossings, returned to the United States to make three films, one of which was *Syncopation*. From the first, his relationship with Barbara seemed perfect, and all things conspired to make theirs an ideal marriage. Morton was personable, his singing career was promising, and his religious background satisfied Barbara's own leanings toward Catholicism. A career had never meant much to her, and at last she could fulfill her great love of family and domesticity. Above all things, having children was her greatest desire.

They were married three weeks after they met, on January 28, 1929, in New York City. For a time, Barbara's life was productive and happy and, as a family, we were delighted that her emotional security and happiness seemed assured.

Since her marriage to Philip Plant in 1925, Constance had divided her time between the resorts of Europe and Florida. It was a glittering way of life that seemed to suit her perfectly, and she'd given little thought to her erstwhile movie career. But eventually, the pleasures of that life faded. Although Philip was an extremely attractive and likable companion, his weaknesses ran to alcohol and, occasionally, to other delights. By the middle of 1928, their public tiffs were well known and provided plenty of material for society gossips and the press. Near the end of that year she separated from him and went to London.

March found her back in Paris undergoing an emergency appendectomy, with Phil at her bedside, though within two weeks a divorce was pending in the French courts. But there was another visitor at the hospital, Gloria Swanson's husband, Henri Falaise, the Marquis de la Coudraye. As the European representative of Pathe Films, Falaise was one of the first to reach Constance with a movie offer when news of her separation from Philip Plant became common knowledge. Until then, she'd kept her promise not to do any more films, but once back in circulation, studios began cabling bids for her services. Through Henri Falaise, Pathe beat the field and Constance signed for her first film in nearly four years, conveniently forgetting the obligation she'd left behind at MGM.

Always looking for a chance to confuse the press, on her return to the United States she told reporters who met the ship in New York that her five-month-old son, Peter Bennett Plant, was really her niece, Ditty Fox. Ditty was then about eighteen months old and Peter was still a babe in arms, so it must have raised a question or two in the minds of reporters. But she'd been irritated by all the recent gossip surrounding her divorce and the attentions of Henri Falaise, and vowed on more than one occasion that she'd get even with the press some day. From then on she did everything possible to confound the newspaper people, particularly when it came to her personal life, which earned her a lifelong reputation for being "difficult and uncooperative." Often an avalanche of newspaper criticism was launched at her blonde head, but she had no awe for the sacred cows of the press and like Father, took great delight in reducing their absurdities to the proper levels.

All of the Bennetts, for that matter, had little but contempt for sham or favor-carrying. In Constance, the running battles with news reporters and columnists satisfied a natural tendency for high tension, and when she rankled, she never kept it a secret. People seem to resent independence, and my older sister had it in abundance. From the moment she returned from Europe it was clear she'd brook no nonsense on the publicity surrounding her return to films.

She found great changes in the motion picture industry when she arrived in Hollywood, for in the nearly four years of her absence, movies had converted to sound and all of her films before her marriage to Philip had been silents. But she made the transition easily and in mid-1929 filmed her first sound movie, *This Thing Called Love,* a fast-moving comedy with Edmund Lowe. Few remember the fact, but Jean Harlow made a brief appearance as an extra.

Three talkies later, Constance did *Common Clay* for Fox Studios, costarring with Lew Ayres under the direction of Victor Fleming. Based on Cleves Kinkead's play and originally a vehicle for Jane Cowl, *Common Clay* turned into one of the box-office hits of the year 1930 and thrust Constance once more into the front ranks of Hollywood leading women.

Soon, she became known for her demands at the bargaining tables. Two years and seven films after *Common Clay,* she negotiated her way into making two films for Warner Brothers for an unprecedented sum, adding to it the provision that Warner's not only pay the income tax on her salary, but her agent Myron Selznick's fee as well. "I'm a businesswoman," she said, "not a philanthropist." The arrangement made her the highest salaried film player in the history of the industry up to that time and gave her a lasting reputation for being the shrewdest businesswoman in Hollywood.

But shrewdness wasn't always the factor that drove her. A little known fact at the time was that Constance didn't really care if she worked or not, and often made the most outrageous demands with the certainty that they'd never be accepted. Frequently she was as surprised as anyone to find that, indeed, they were acceptable, and her indifference only seemed to place her in greater demand. Her reputation for business acumen prompted a friend to remark to Father, "I don't know why Constance works so hard. After all, she can't take it with her"; to which Father replied, "If she can't take it with her, she won't go!"

For some reason I've never been able to understand, Hollywood gossips tried to spread the rumor that Constance and I were involved in some sort of sisterly rivalry, but there was never a shred of truth in that. We always had an affectionate relationship, and although normal differences of opinion cropped up on occasion, they never interfered with our strong attachment for each other. The most opinionated of women, she sometimes played the older sister and volunteered lectures and orders with a generous hand, but I never minded that. It was merely the chemistry of being Constance Bennett. Furthermore, we were never competitive in the business. For years I was the sweet blonde ingenue and Constance the brittle blonde sophisticate, so we were never placed in a position of professional rivalry. Whenever our schedules permitted, we saw a great deal of each other and shared many of the same friends.

Constance and I had a lot of fun in the Hollywood of the nineteen-thirties. The industry was at a peak of excitement with the advent of sound, and almost daily there was a new technical development or an exciting personality to keep things interesting.

It didn't matter that some of the early moviemakers seemed ill-equipped for the business of mass entertainment. They'd come West to the movie gold rush from such professions as glove salesmen, junk dealers and penny arcade operators. When I first knew it, the film industry held a combination of nuts, genuine talents, charlatans and authentic geniuses, all of whom were still in the process of learning, bumbling and creating with a fury and innocence that outstripped any other period in its history. The colorful types like Sid Grauman, Goldwyn, Schenck, Mayer and Zukor had a passionate love for the business, not just for the money to be made, and many of them I remember as people of taste and sensitivity.

Today, it seems to me, it's strictly a big business, based on dollars and cents. I suppose the monumental, always rising costs of producing have made that a necessity, but the industry has lost some of its swagger, glamor and excitement. Then, everyone seemed to have growing pains. It was an industry of youth, and the expansion brought with it a unique kind of freedom and unrestricted creativity, combined with a good deal of preposterous ballyhoo and wonderful nonsense. It also brought forth a great deal of editorial sniping and criticism from many quarters, and not the least vocal among its detractors was my articulate father. "Hollywood is an intellectual sewer, a cesspool of folly!"

I can only say that when I first entered the business in 1929, I thought that Hollywood was an extraordinary community, filled with wonder and excitement, and as Samuel Behrman wrote of that enthralling time, "It was a Golden Era. It had never happened before. It will never happen again."

Admittedly, the philosophy of Hollywood publicity was built on the idea that almost any news was good news, and the result was an incredible accent on trivia. Over two dozen fan* magazines and countless syndicated columns, aided by platoons of press agents, magnified the smallest details of movie-making and movie folk. If nothing of particular interest unfolded to feed the insatiable publicity machine, then it was invented. Glamor was made remote and unapproachable. There was no such thing as the girl or boy next door, and the nightlife of the gods was reported from Olympus,

* A term derived from the word "fanatic."

sheathed in a mysterious, rosy glow. Quite unlike today, when interviewers lead the reader to the bathroom and lock him in, the industry protected its stars. Publicity was carefully channeled through a studio's own department, and there was always a studio representative present for interviews with the outside press. The industry policed itself and its actors and, frankly, I don't think there's much romance or glamor in the present system where bad taste and bad manners are often rewarded and applauded.

And while I'm dealing indirectly with romance, I didn't exactly retreat from it myself after my divorce from Jack Fox in August of 1928. During the run of *Jarnegan* in New York, I'd met John Considine, Jr., the Feature Films executive who'd asked me to test for *Bulldog Drummond*. My refusal to make the test had apparently attracted his interest, both professionally and personally, and I was not only signed for my first movie, but I won him as a constant companion as well. John was a wild, attractive Irishman whose father had been a copartner in one of America's largest vaudeville circuits.

For years, Considine, Sr., and another theater magnate operated competing circuits on the West Coast, and their bitter rivalry continued until John Jr. began a romance with the Considine competitor's attractive daughter. It was a tempestuous relationship, given to frequent skirmishes and retreats, followed by reconciliations. John had broken off the romance "once and for all" by the time I met him in New York, and several months after I arrived in Hollywood we became what was then called "an item."

What I didn't know until later was that he played the cavalier in both camps. He'd fight with one of us, go rushing back to the other until the next battle, and then return to outpost number one, breathing charm and contrition. When I finally discovered the double deal, it brought on a fine burst of fury, and an even finer one when I learned he'd arranged a rendezvous with the opposition in Palm Springs. I chartered a plane, not a little private one, but what passed for an airliner in the nineteen-thirties, and was flown to Palm Springs, rattling around inside as the only passenger. Planes rarely flew at night in those days, but the pilot reached the desert town after sundown and the ground crew had to light flares on the runways so we could land. Once I'd found the offending parties, I presented them with a large piece of my mind, laid on a Bennett curse, and flew right back to Los Angeles. A slight case of melodrama, perhaps, but at the time I thought it was a splendid gesture.

By early 1930 I'd made half a dozen films, and my career had risen enough for me to think maybe I'd found my niche after all. With each movie I was gaining experience and learning the craft, and the parts were also improving. I even did a musical during that period, *Mississippi*, with Bing Crosby and W. C. Fields, in which I sang a duet with Bing. I can't think of any other performer who was as easygoing as he. Even in those days when his movie career was beginning to flower, he was as relaxed as Jello and much more fun. I sang in several movies after that and, for the record, my singing wasn't dubbed, it was my own voice. At this point, I may as well confess to a secret desire to do another musical some day.

Another memorable experience of those early days in Hollywood was working with John Barrymore in *Moby Dick*, although at first I was terrified at the thought of working with one of the great actors of the time. I'd known him since childhood, but that didn't lessen my feelings of intimidation. His eccentric behavior and his drinking habits were well known, and I approached the first few days of filming with a fine case of nerves. I could have saved myself the trouble. He couldn't have been sweeter or more considerate. Barrymore was then married to Dolores Costello and expecting their first baby, and he was on his best behavior, at his most charming and cooperative.

During that period at least, the Bennett sisters were thriving in both the professional and romantic departments. Constance had made her smash hit, *Common Clay*, and was deep in a developing romance with Henri Falaise.

I was about ready to give up free-lancing after half a dozen films with various studios to sign a contract with Fox Studios, a development that had been paved by John Considine, Jr. My relationship with John was just as tempestuous as ever, and things were lively and interesting for awhile until the emotional demands became too heavy a load to carry and it became clear that eventually I'd have to close the door permanently.

Barbara and Morton Downey, by then living in Connecticut, had adopted a little boy, whom they named Michael Joseph. As it often happens, they were afraid at first they couldn't have children, but after they adopted Michael, they proceeded to have four of their own in the following years. It was about that time, too, that Morton's career began to spiral upward, and in that year of 1930, he made his successful radio debut. All was well with Barbara, deeply happy at the prospect of a family of her own.

Meanwhile, Mother busied herself with the Pinker-Morrison Agency in New York and in October, 1930, added a new project to her involvements by launching a six-month season of plays for children. She organized a company of adult actors, called it The Children's Players, and began a series of matinees in one of the midtown Manhattan theaters. It was a labor that was very close to her heart, and she looked after every detail of the productions. Her ultimate goal was to help build audiences for the future.

The first season was composed of six plays with one given each month in Friday matinees, and the series proved to be equally successful with children and parents. The Children's Players became Mother's pet project and continued for several years, until tragic developments in her personal life put an end to it.

Mother was always on the lookout for a suitable play for

either Constance or me, and occasionally Father would come forth with an offer to appear in one of his productions. Throughout the years, Constance and I talked about doing either a play or a movie together, but unfortunately we never found the right script. Not long after I made the first couple of movies under the United Artists contract, I took another flyer into the theater and did a costume play with Doris Keene. We opened in Santa Barbara and played two weeks at the Biltmore Theater in Los Angeles, but the play was so undistinguished I've even forgotten its title.

In the fall of 1930, Father was preparing a Broadway production of Lawton Campbell's story of a decaying South, called *Solid South,* and offered me the ingenue role of Geneva. But my film career was progressing and the financial security for Ditty and me seemed assured, so I refused the offer and the part went to a young actress named Bette Davis. "Ah, yes," Father recalled later, "she turned out to be quite a nice little motion picture actress." I didn't know it then, but my refusal of the part saved me from disaster.

Goaded by an unhappy marriage, Father's hostilities toward the world in general had produced in him an even more outrageous behavior pattern, if possible. His battles with Aimee and personal discontent made him more irascible and intractable, more impossible to control. The result was that he paid less attention to his acting skills and more attention to drowning his personal sorrows in alcohol, and his performances were often inconsistent. He was fifty-eight years old, and he was tired and ill. Tirade against the critics was expanded to king-sized proportions, and he addressed his audiences with more magnificent insults than ever.

Managers regarded him now as a calculated risk. Offers were not quite so plentiful as they once had been, and instead of creating original portrayals, on several occasions he was forced to play roles originated by other actors. Also, his treatment of his fellow actors was sometimes inconsiderate and overbearing. They were traits he'd never shown before, for he loved actors and had the utmost respect for them. "There are no bad actors in the theater," he was fond of saying. "They're all in Washington!"

The company of *Solid South*, which included Jessie Royce Landis, Bette Davis, Elizabeth Patterson, Owen Davis, Jr., and director Rouben Mamoulian, suffered through his tantrums at rehearsals. The play left something to be desired, but the role of Major Follonsby offered Father the opportunity to bluster and boom to his heart's content. He had a lovely time, but when the play opened at the Lyceum Theater on October 14, 1930, for the first time in his career the critics were divided in their opinions of his performance. Their criticism was harsh and to the point. Father blasted them as "mental degenerates," suggested they should be taken out beyond the twelve-mile limit, and attacked their taste and intelligence until there was nothing left of them but a graveyard of their inadequacies. In the middle of one performance, he lambasted the audience for not laughing in the proper place, then walked off the stage, leaving Miss Davis and Elizabeth Patterson aghast and stranded.

*Solid South* played only three weeks at the Lyceum, then closed quietly, "due to Richard Bennett's illness," according to the management, but "due to Bacchus" according to Bette Davis.

Unperturbed, Father took the play to Chicago the following May and opened at the Harris Theater with a different cast. On matinee days, he was driven up to the stage door in a chauffered car, and surrounded by the usual crowd of fans and well-wishers, he alighted and stalked grandly to his dressing room clad only in pajamas, robe and slippers. Since matinees were played so early in the day, it seemed only natural to him to leave his bed and go right to the theater just in time for a two-thirty curtain.

The play fared somewhat better in Chicago than it had in New York and ran all through the summer season, but his speeches became more inflammatory, his temper more volatile, and at last *Solid South* was closed for good. With one brief exception, five years would pass before Father acted again in a stage production. Suddenly, he was adrift in the theater with nothing in view that attracted his enthusiasm in the least. Also, the word had been passed in the business. There were dark rumors of his drinking habits, temperamental scenes, his untrustworthy and erratic performances. Slowly but inevitably, he'd worked himself into a one-man wrecking crew.

Then Hollywood beckoned again, just in time to rescue him from himself, and he accepted an offer to do a series of films in the fall of 1931. That year found three Bennetts entrenched in Hollywood: Richard, Constance and Joan. When Father arrived to fulfill his movie contract, he was asked by a reporter what it felt like to be the father of two celebrated daughters. "How the hell do you think it feels," he growled. "It feels just fine!"

# 13

For the American theater, the decade beginning with 1920 was a time to remember, a tumultuous period filled with experimentation, a new wave of realism, and an outburst of native playwrights overflowing with talent. But two events in the late nineteen-twenties contributed to the destruction of that cherished time. The Wall Street crash of 1929 struck a damaging blow and brought an immediate decline in production and attendance. The stock companies throughout the country floundered and disappeared almost overnight, and theaters that formerly had housed the legitimate were turned into motion picture pleasure domes. With the coming of talkies particularly, many theater producers saw a serious threat to the theater's existence.

When Father went to Hollywood after the debacle of *Solid South,* his attitudes did a complete about-face. Until then, he'd labeled motion pictures as "a vortex of corruption and ture, a temple of intellect and truth. Now, however, the theater became the villain of the current scene and when at last folly." His beloved theater represented the epitome of culture the movies talked and sang, he saw them as a new art form of enlightened entertainment and communication. Once films were articulate, his enthusiasm was unbounded. In rapid succession he made three films in 1931, *The Five and Ten, Arrowsmith* and *Bought!* The third, in which he played Constance's father, was made for Warner Brothers, and it was the first and only time they worked together. "It seemed funny," he wrote, "to be playing second fiddle to one of my own kids, but I didn't resent the idea. It was rather stimulating."

Ignoring his own violent criticism of Hollywood over the years, he hotly defended the movie business. "Anybody calling the movies by degrading names is a damned jackass! I wouldn't budge a foot toward Broadway until they can do better than Hollywood for real stories. I wouldn't give up my part in this movie [*Bought!*] for anything on Broadway. Besides, I'm working with my daughter and that's a pleasure not to be missed. For both of us. As for actors, there are only three great actors still alive in America today, Maude Adams, Feodor Chaliapin, and Lionel Barrymore. Four, if you count me."

Until then, Father and Aimee had made their permanent home in Palo Alto, California, but the house burned in July of 1931, a total loss, and they moved to a home in Santa Monica where they stayed for the next five years. His marital difficulties had not improved with time. The walls of the Santa Monica house bulged with melodrama, and his battles with Aimee reached grand proportions.

With my thirteenth movie in Hollywood, though it may have no connection with ill luck, I was the victim of a disastrous accident. Despite an indifferent script, *She Wanted a Millionaire* seemed to start out very well. I was still under the Fox Studios contract, I liked the director John Blystone, and working with Spencer Tracy was a huge treat. I remember him as a rather private person, taciturn, though he had a delicious sense of humor. He teased me unmercifully, and it always pleased him when I rose to the bait, which was most of the time. There was one thing that seemed contradictory to his rugged screen image: he dressed impeccably, sartorially splendid at all times.

Spencer was known in Hollywood as "an actor's actor," and his intense powers of concentration were legendary. I never had the feeling that he was acting, but that the truth of the scene occurred at the very moment he spoke, and no matter how many times we repeated a scene, that spontaneity was always there. Like George Arliss, he was extremely meticulous in his work and methodical in his schedule. He took two hours for lunch and quit every day at five o'clock, and that was that. I worked with Spencer several times after that, and it was always stimulating and rewarding for me.

Late in July, 1931, about halfway through the filming of *She Wanted a Millionaire*, we were shooting on location in Stone Canyon. That section of Bel Air was threaded with bridle paths then, with a big stable at the bottom of the canyon. I was riding a horse up a hill, headed for the filming area, accompanied by a stable groom and one of the actors from the company. He was a skillful actor but an unskilled rider and began to have trouble with his mount, a huge animal called "Gilda Grey." She got more and more skittish as we rode along, and since my horse was friendly and mild, I finally suggested we exchange mounts. I'd been riding since early childhood and saw no reason for alarm just because Gilda was in a temperamental mood. I climbed into the saddle, and the groom told me to give her her head, which I did. Already unnerved by her previous rider, she headed right back to the Bel Air stables, and I pulled her around to go back up the hill toward the filming site. By then some of the crew had seen the struggle, and someone jumped into a camera car and started down the hill to the rescue. In all fairness, I don't think Gilda meant to be so ill-mannered; she was just overwrought, but after one look at the approaching camera car, she shied and I went off into space. A tree stopped my flight and I ended up in a heap like a discarded rag doll with a hip and three vertebrae broken, and a beautiful black eye. I was most relieved to find I hadn't broken a single fingernail.

Our director, Jack Blystone, had the good sense to give orders I wasn't to be moved. Someone phoned for an emergency police ambulance, but I refused to be taken to the receiving hospital and two hours elapsed before an ambulance arrived from The Cedars of Lebanon Hospital. It must have been providence, but a week or two before the accident, I'd been talking with a friend who extolled the virtues of her orthopedic surgeon. For some reason, through the haze I remembered his name, Ellis Jones, and asked my secretary, Dorothy Watkins, to call my regular doctor and ask him to find Dr. Jones as soon as possible.

I arrived at The Cedars of Lebanon Hospital where they cut off my jodphurs and found one leg pushed up two inches shorter than the other. In spite of the fact that the hospital staff and attending physician were acting on studio orders, I refused to be put into traction and all other treatment until Dr. Jones could arrive. Stubbornly, I told my secretary that if I passed out, she was to see I wasn't touched until the specialist reached me. My intuition served me well, because when he did arrive he looked at the X-rays, waited until I was out of shock, then operated and set my hip the next morning. Although I was in bed for three months and didn't go back to work for six, I've never had any trouble resulting from the accident and didn't even have to go through physiotherapy.

As always in times of trouble, the family rallied. Father was close by, Mother and Barbara flew to my bedside from the East and Constance, who was vacationing in England, wanted to return at once, but I cabled her to stay in London since I had plenty of attention from the rest of the family.

Recuperating was a long and dull process, but there were many wonderful people who helped brighten the boring hospital routine. The studio sent a projectionist to run off movies for me several times a week. Mail poured in and that kept me busy and diverted. Among the notes from well-wishers, delightful ones began to arrive from Gene Markey, an exnewspaperman from Chicago's great journalistic days of Ben Hecht and Charles MacArthur. Gene was also a novelist and filmscript writer who listed among his film credits *As*

*You Desire Me* for Greta Garbo. I'd remembered meeting him at a party given by John Gilbert and his wife, Ina Claire. His notes were charming, witty, and reflected genuine concern over my illness.

By then the double-dealing John Considine, Jr., had complicated my life altogether, and I realized it was time to do something about it. He inundated me with flowers, phone calls and messages, most of them distressing, and Mother saw to it that he wasn't allowed in the hospital for a visit in person. I knew, too, that he'd been entertaining the other lady of his choice, and Mother urged me to cut off the relationship once and for all.

I'd been in the hospital about eight weeks with another month to go in the plaster cast when she decided I wasn't growing particularly robust on the hospital food. It's true I was getting alarmingly thin, so I was sent off to the Town House, a large apartment hotel on Wilshire Boulevard, complete with hospital bed and two nurses. Mother also felt it would be a safer haven from the insistent demands of an overwrought suitor. The Town House had a switchboard through which incoming calls were screened, and Mother made certain John's, in particular, were refused.

One evening Marge Kelley and her husband-to-be came to visit me, and as we sat there chatting, the doorbell rang. It was Mr. Considine, Jr., who'd come up, unseen, in the service elevator. He stuck his foot in the door and flung himself into the room with a dramatic declaration. "You may never walk again! I'll fly you to Yuma, Joan, and marry you at once!" I looked him right in the eye and said, "Let me think it over." I did, and decided the emotional demands were too burdensome to carry around any longer, and when he called the next day, I told him to forget it. Then I called the other encampment and said, "He's all yours!" There's no feeling so free as the release of torture, particularly when it's been self-inflicted.

Meanwhile, Gene Markey began to pay court, and his

funny, dear messages arrived in increasing numbers. Then one day he phoned and asked if he could come to call, and from then on he came to see me as often as his writing schedule at MGM permitted.

By the time Constance returned from her ten-week vacation in Europe, her romance with the Marquis de la Coudraye was flourishing, and the resulting feud with Gloria Swanson, by then Henri's exwife, was in full bloom. The feud between Constance and Gloria was an authentic one, not something contrived by the press, and once they'd competed in the battle of the title, they proceeded to compete in everything else. Constance had succeeded Gloria not only as the Marquise, but as one of the biggest box-office attractions of the thirties. The coolness between them turned into a genuine rivalry and Constance loved the game of one-upmanship.

She and Henri Falaise were married November 22, 1931, at the Beverly Hills home of our old family friend, director George Fitzmaurice. Father gave the bride away, and I was out of my plaster cast in time to attend as her maid of honor. There's no question that Constance loved the life of high society and the added piquancy of a titled husband. We all liked Henri immensely, for he was a charming and handsome man of great warmth and sweetness. Even Father liked him, though he couldn't resist the chance to reduce things to a proper perspective when he told Constance and her bridegroom, "I'll be damned if I'll curtsey!"

Constance considered matrimony the most important career a woman could have and declared she'd give up her film career for marriage any day. Unlike Philip Plant, however, Henri was extremely supportive of her career, and with her rise in movies in the early thirties, her ambitions began to accelerate, too.

As long as people responded at the box office, she was the most indifferent of actresses to what was said of her by the critics, and her declarations sounded like Father's: "If I depended on critics for popularity, I'd have been dead professionally a long time ago. Even Walter Winchell compares me to a Swedish servant girl on her day off. Since I have no doubt that Mr. Winchell is an authority in such matters, I'll let it go at that. I can imagine much worse things to be."

Because Constance was a feminine replica of Father, she had an outspoken aggressiveness and a nature that would suffer no nonsense and, like Father, it earned her the label of being "difficult." Restless and high-strung, she was given much more to causing scenes than I. Like Mother, I'm more passive by nature, though if pushed into a corner I'll hold my ground in the face of the enemy, but I've always hated scenes in which voices rise, nostrils flare, and there's a lot of heavy breathing. Constance, however, created controversy just for the sheer love of battle; it was simply her style.

By November of 1931, about the time of Constance's marriage to Falaise, I was limping along fairly well, recovering from my rude encounter with Gilda Grey, but I wouldn't be well enough to go back to work and finish the film with Spencer Tracy until January. Dr. Jones had advised me to take a leisurely trip, and I decided to go East by setting a slow pace through the Panama Canal. All during the weeks that I was gone, Gene Markey bombarded me with wires to remind me of his concern and affection, and almost daily he paid a visit to my four-year-old Ditty. It was love at first sight between them and they spent hours in solemn conversation at endless tea parties, addressing each other as "Mr. and Mrs. Grasshopper." To Ditty, Gene represented the father she'd never had, and their mutual affection is maintained to this day. He was the kindest of men with a gentle wit and a philosophical view of life, beloved by everyone who knew him.

When I returned from my trip to the East Coast, Gene asked me to marry him, much to Ditty's delight and mine. In January, I returned to Fox Studios to finish *She Wanted a Millionaire* which, despite all our efforts, turned out to be a reasonably bad movie.

Gene and I were married March 12, 1932, in a flower-decorated room at the Town House, the apartment hotel where I'd spent much of my convalescence. I was attended by Constance and Gene by his good friend, Captain Allan Clayton. Mother couldn't attend because my grandmother, Rose Wood, had died the week before in Tenafly, New Jersey, and she was distracted with the funeral arrangements. Nor could Father be with us, for despite his public attacks that the theater had fallen on evil days and was beyond repair, once more he'd answered its bewitching call.

For fifteen years, Father had eyed the role of Cyrano de Bergerac, Edmond Rostand's nosy, swashbuckling hero. Perhaps he'd coveted the part even longer than that, for he remembered seeing the great French actor, Benoit Coquelin, for whom it had been written in 1897. At last the opportunity presented itself when the San Francisco producing office of Belasco & Curran offered to star him in a revival.

Adapted by Father and director William Keighly, *Cyrano* was given a sumptuous production. It was a fine chance for any actor to pull out all the stops, and Father gave the role great vigor, youth, beauty and grandeur. He was nearing his sixtieth birthday, but to the audience, his rhyming, swaggering Gascon seemed half that age. By the time of the opening night in Santa Barbara, more than two years had passed since he'd stepped on a stage.

Then San Francisco welcomed him back to the Geary Theater with a rousing ovation. The Bay City's audience may have given it no thought, but it was the first opening night in nearly twenty years that Father did not make a curtain speech. The lapse was due to a sudden attack of laryngitis.

After the run in San Francisco, Los Angeles was treated to another Bennett battle when *Cyrano de Bergerac* moved into the Belasco Theater. Walter Hampden's national tour of the play was booked into the Biltmore Theater right on the heels of Father's production, and the newspapers promptly created a contest between the two. It was an unfortunate mixup in bookings, although the battle of the noses provided plenty of lively publicity, and both theaters were SRO throughout the runs. Comparison, of course, was inevitable.

Hampden's Cyrano was world-famous, and a role in which his career had reached its greatest height when, beginning in 1923, he'd played it in New York nearly seven hundred times. His version was uncut and played in the traditional manner with grandiose style. Father made what he felt were judicious cuts and, as usual, had made the play peculiarly his own.

The Bennett-Hampden contest ended in a draw, but Father had the satisfaction of knowing that one of the best performances of his career had been made in a classic, blank-verse drama, in his sixtieth year, and in the face of illness and a deteriorating marriage. "My version," he wrote later, "may not have been ideal for scholars and the purists, but it was a hell of a lot better theater! Still, the work on *Cyrano* sort of let me down. I had worked too hard and felt myself slipping again."

After a brief rest, he signed a contract with Paramount Pictures and returned to Hollywood. He lectured the Paramount executives and tried to bully them into developing a studio school to train young actors for the future. "If I were the head of a studio," he said, "I would organize a great stock company of guest stars. I would have the Barrymores and Arliss and all the other true artists of the theater who are in Hollywood. I would make these young punks who aspire to be actors work in support of these great stars, and I'd rub their noses in the drama until they liked it, or quit. I learned to act in the greatest of all schools—the theater itself! Hanging around stage doors as a young kid, getting the smell of the inside when somebody swung them open for a moment, looking up to actors, running errands for them, catching the honeyed wisdom that dripped from their lips when they recited, jumping in to fill a breach on the one-night stands, and my heart singing to high heaven for the chance. Now, with the stock companies dead and the decadence of Broadway, there is no place for a youngster to learn his trade. Maybe the Little Theater movement will take care of that. In the meantime, you movie people would do well to organize some sort of training program." Father was a little ahead of his time. Eventually, each studio did organize training classes for promising young contract players, and their talent departments were headed by some of the best coaches from the legitimate theater.

When I first arrived in Hollywood to begin work on *Bulldog Drummond,* Ditty, the nurse and I had moved into a small apartment in the new Beverly Wilshire Hotel. With only one bedroom for the nurse and Ditty, however, quarters were too cramped for any lengthy stay and we moved to a larger apartment, and finally to the Chateau de Fleur, where we stayed two years. During one of Mother's visits, she urged me to rent a house. I chose one in Coldwater Canyon, and when I married Gene he joined Ditty and me there. He was still writing for MGM; Ditty was happiness itself; I'd recovered completely from my accident of the previous July and went back to Fox Studios to begin the busiest schedule of films in my career. I made six in that single year of 1932. Most of them are unmemorable (except for *Me and My Gal* with Spencer Tracy) : *The Trial of Vivienne Ware, Careless Lady, Weekends Only, Wild Girl,* and *Arizona to Broadway.* I was beginning to think I'd be stuck in a run of lightweight material. In spite of it, however, the public's response to me seemed to grow with each release, and for much of my success at the time I have to thank a marvelous publicity woman at Fox, Frances Deaner, who took a great interest in my career and went out of her way to advance it.

Even though it was a busy time for me, there was something vaguely dissatisfying about it. I felt as if I were just treading in one spot. I must have discussed my dissatisfactions with Father, for I've kept a treasured letter he sent me at the time.

Always do I walk from your presence with a sigh of hope on my lips but behind it a sob of fear in my throat. You think in too small terms of yourself, my urchin. 'Tis a whale you are. Calculate on no less. Put the burden of your expectant smile to the world to fulfill; 'twill clutch you to its breast and paint your halo a double rainbow. Once cringe, you're a mist of the bog.

Father's letters were almost always things to treasure, even when he was lecturing. He wrote copiously and they came fluttering into our lives filled with pungency, wit, bombast and, often, great sweetness. Among his other eccentricities, he hated addressing envelopes. He loved to write letters, but always tried to get someone else to address them.

At last, 1933 brought the long-awaited film of merit, my twentieth feature movie in Hollywood, Louisa May Alcott's *Little Women*. To this day it remains one of the favorite films of my career. Everything conspired to make it everyone else's favorite, too. I played Amy, and included in RKO's splendid cast were Katharine Hepburn as Jo, Spring Byington as Marmee, Frances Dee as Meg, Jean Parker played Beth and Paul Lukas, the Professor. Douglass Montgomery, Henry Stephenson and Edna Mae Oliver rounded out the cast.

It was, indeed, a very special time for me and another thing made it so: I was pregnant. I remember there was one scene in which I had to fall off a chest of drawers, and I went to director George Cukor and explained why I couldn't risk it. The piece of business was changed to fit Jo instead of Amy, and the lot fell to Katharine Hepburn.

Under George Cukor's direction, each character in the film leapt into life. George had come to Hollywood from the New York theater about the time talkies arrived and became known in the business as a "woman's director," though that was an unfair label for he was equally skillful with men. Constance had worked with him twice before and I understood the reasons for her admiration. The year before, he'd directed her in *What Price Hollywood?*, based on a story by

Adela Rogers St. John, which later inspired *A Star Is Born*, and George had brought it in as a resounding hit. It remained one of my favorites of Constance's films, and she considered it her best. Then, in the same year as *Little Women*, they'd worked together again in *Our Betters,* an adaptation of Somerset Maugham's play, in which she worked with a young actor named Gilbert Roland for the first time. Under George's direction, both films had been milestones for Constance.

On my birthday, February 27, 1934, our daughter Melinda Markey was born. Gene was beside himself. He loved Ditty beyond measure, but when his very own daughter came into the world, he was ecstatic. Gene called me the "most baffling of the baffling Bennetts," I suppose because I seemed to be the most domestic one. There wasn't a detail about the house or the children that I missed, from counting laundry, to fairy tales and lullabies. But I saw no point in having babies and then turning them over to someone else to do the upbringing. I idolized them all, Ditty, Melinda and later, Stephanie and Shelley, but there were a few basic rules I tried to follow through the years regarding the children: praise them often, discipline them when it's called for (Ditty caught hell for shaving the dog's ears), see as much of them as possible, and treat them like adults. I thought it best to let them make their own decisions, even if they seemed like mistakes to me, and as soon as possible, I tried to teach them thrift and self-reliance.

If it ever came to the much-debated choice between a career and my children, I knew I'd never hesitate, but to combine the two careers, it became a matter of organization and timing. On a regular working schedule I was due at the studio at seven o'clock in the morning, and running a household and looking after the children took some juggling and systematic planning. Like a top sergeant, I wrote copious memos and posted "the orders of the day." I insisted on a six-o'clock "stop clause" in my contracts, and unless it was an emergency

I seldom worked beyond that hour. Now that I look back on it, I wonder that I was able to sustain both careers of home and acting, but I did and loved it.

In retrospect, it would have been much more difficult than it was had it not been for Scotty Leask, a trained nurse, who joined our household to help me with the children and became a member of the family. All told, she stuck it out for fourteen years, which netted her our eternal affection, as well as admiration for her endurance and forebearance. She loved the children dearly, but not in the possessive ways that some household guardians have in which they try to substitute themselves for a mother image, compete with her for the children's affection, or rule with an iron hand. There was never any question as to whom the reins belonged, though she'd tolerate no nonsense herself, and Ditty still has an apologetic letter she wrote to Scotty thirty years ago after indulging in a childish rudeness. With Scotty's loving aid, it was a household where mutual understanding, confidence and affection were everyday affairs.

# 14

When Father returned to movie-making after his triumph in *Cyrano de Bergerac,* he did a number of films for Paramount, then *Nana* for Sam Goldwyn, an adaptation of the Emile Zola story with Anna Sten. Sam was one of the few producers whom Father respected, and he wrote of him later, "Goldwyn's word is his bond, and he boosted the luminosity of many a star, including my own daughters. An honest and, therefore, rare man."

Father seemed dogged by illness during that period and withdrew from *The White Sister* with Helen Hayes and Clark Gable, then had to leave the cast of *Song of Songs* with Marlene Dietrich, due to a siege of double pneumonia. Gout and his emotional life didn't help matters, although he rallied slightly when Marlene sent him a mountain of flowers and a note expressing her regret at being unable to work with him.

No matter how much he protested, I knew his heart lay in New York, the stage and its people, but he'd fairly wrecked himself with a reputation for being untrustworthy by then, and offers from the East were simply not forthcoming. Often he wrote letters to check on the state of the theater, making subtle inquiries of his friends who were working in New York. George M. Cohan, appearing in Eugene O'Neill's *Ah, Wilderness!* in 1933, wrote in reply:

In the dressing room

My Dear Dick—
Thanks so much for your nice note to me. I'm happy to know that I have at least one friend left in Hollywood.

No indeed old pal life hasn't gone out of the old theater. Hit after hit coming in. People all theater minded again. Looks like the beginning of a new beginning.

This O'Neill play is very interesting. I call it a modern "Way Down East" without the snow. I still think however that "Beyond the Horizon" was his best. And boy, I'll never forget your performance in it.

Well old top once again let me thank you for your thought of me and remember me to the family.

Best Always—

Sincerely,
George M. Cohan

Often, too, Father tried to get his friends to join him in what he called "this noble experiment in the sun-drenched hills," and once arranged a contract for one of his Chicago cronies, the eminent lawyer, Clarence Darrow. The movie industry may have lost one of its most able actors when Mr. Darrow sent the following reply:

January 15, 1933

Dear Mr. Bennett:
Thank you ever so much for your fine letter. It is always so good to hear from you. I do wish we could go and see you, but doubt if I can get that far away from Chicago again. If I did, I should likely go to Europe, but I don't see much prospect of that. I often feel ashamed that I got you all "het up" to get me some money in Hollywood. After I got a good chance I felt that I should not do it. I think I had rather be a good actor than do most anything else (and I am some actor in my profession!) but the idea of accepting a contract to be an actor because I am a lawyer seemed too much for me. I really had no right on the stage just because I had gained some "notoriety" in my profession. Anyhow, that is the way it looked to me after you and your friends had found a good contract!

Anyhow, I wish I could see you again and hope you will
come this way soon.

> With Admiration and Affection,
> Your friend,
> Clarence Darrow

By the early months of 1934, Father's marriage to Aimee
had become untenable and their pitched battles, in private
and public, erupted with growing frequency. In May, Aimee
filed a separate maintenance suit in Los Angeles, demanded
a large sum of alimony and a division of property, and alleged that her husband "had called her opprobrious names,
spoken to her in a very disrespectful and scandalous manner,
threatened to shoot her with a gun and attempted to stab
her with a nail file." She then received the press, sporting a
flowered turban and a black eye, and confided to reporters
that Mr. Bennett was "a man of maniacal moods." Mr. Bennett came out of hiding long enough to make his own statement, and did so with princely dignity. "The allegations are
absurd. I couldn't do that, it's not my style. I love women, all
women, too much. That sort of thing is not in my heart. Besides, the only way one could kill a woman of that sort is not
with a gun or a nail file, but with a wooden stake!"

Then he disappeared, while process servers scoured his
haunts, trying to locate him. Father had agreed not to leave
California's jurisdiction until an amicable property settlement had been arranged, or a court order procured to rule on
the property rights of both parties, but instead he fled in fury
and vanished to escape "those rutting bloodhounds," the
process servers.

In five days he drove cross-country in his "reckless Ford"
to Barbara's home in Connecticut, stopping briefly in hotels
along the way and registering under false names. He relished
the melodrama of traveling incognito and used names of
characters he'd played on the stage: John Shand, George Dupont, Major Follonsby. Finally he arrived at the Downeys
at a painfully early hour of the morning and woke Barbara

from a sound sleep. "Will you be willing to harbor an aging fugitive from justice?" he asked. "Yes, indeed," she replied, "if the aging fugitive will please get the hell to bed!"

By then, Barbara and Morton had expanded their family to include two children, their adopted boy, Michael, and their first-born son, Sean. Father, never happier than with his grandchildren, romped and rested in Connecticut, and swore Barbara to secrecy.

A few days after his arrival, a man Father later described as "a slinky one" arrived at Barbara's door and announced himself as Mr. McNeil, a reporter from *The New York Times*. Barbara began to deny any knowledge of Father's whereabouts, when Father himself emerged from hiding, waved Barbara aside, and asked the slinky one if he was really from *The New York Times*. Indeed, he asserted, he was a representative of the newspaper. Then, asked to produce some identification, he reached into his pocket and handed Father a court summons. Just to show there were no hard feelings, Father punched his visitor right in the nose and laid him out, full length, at the Downeys's front door.

When he revived, Father apologized and laid on the charm, then helped him into the house where Barbara served them both an enormous breakfast, washed down with several bottles of wine. They spent a pleasant day together swapping anecdotes about their respective professions, and Father was particularly interested in the scheme of some dishonest process servers who purposely goaded their victims into violence, then accepted bribes to withdraw a charge of assault and battery against a servant of the law. Fortunately, Mr. McNeil assured him, he had nothing to fear on that score. To cement their new friendship, Father called for brandy and midafternoon found McNeil once more in oblivion, while his solicitous host tucked him into bed.

After making some hurried phone calls, Father woke his guest a couple of hours later with an eye-opening double scotch, helped him into the car and drove to the airport. Poor

McNeil thought he was going back to New York City, but he had several surprises in store before the odyssey ended. Father had booked two tickets to Montreal via Albany, New York, a stopover on the flight, slipped the summons back into Mc-Neil's pocket, borrowed twenty-five dollars from him, and given him a signed I.O.U. When they landed in Albany, he helped his lurching companion off the plane and deposited him in the men's room of the terminal, then continued on his merry way to Montreal, secure in the knowledge that he'd have no worries about an assault-and-battery charge with his I.O.U. in McNeil's pocket.

The process server was left in a strange town with seven dollars in cash, a slip of paper representing twenty-five dollars, an undelivered court summons, and what must have been a monumental hangover. But he proved himself a gentleman who didn't hold a grudge, and later, when the wild adventure was revealed in the newspapers, he told a reporter, "Mr. Bennett really is a most charming companion."

Father waited in Canada for two days, then sailed for England on *The Empress of Britain*. In London he proceeded to have a fine time, and capered in boozy comradeship with his old friend, Joe Coyne. He broke away from the dens of Limehouse long enough to do a film directed by Gregory Ratoff, *This Woman Is Mine,* and thoroughly enjoyed his freedom while Aimee fumed in Los Angeles.

On nothing more than an audacious whim, in November he decided to return to the United States to see Barbara, who was expecting her third baby. He arrived in New York on *The Bremen,* found Barbara at the Downey apartment in the Ritz Towers and for ten days came and went through the tradesmen's entrance, disguised in dark glasses and a beard. Then, on November 17, undisguised, he strolled on board *The Champlain,* having booked return passage to England under an assumed name. An enterprising reporter found him nonchalantly sipping a drink in his cabin just before departure, and feeling reasonably safe from the law, he chatted affably, then sailed off for England, missing his new grandchild by a month.

When the Downeys's third child, Lorelle Ann, was born in December, Barbara declared she was well on the way to establishing a baby farm and felt that nine children might be an adequate number. But privately, she had confided to Father that she wished Morton's career didn't take him away from the family so frequently. His career by then had skyrocketed through national radio programs, and he continued to make coast-to-coast personal appearances in the United States, as well as in Europe and England. Their home in Greenwich, Connecticut, was a forty-nine-acre farm complete with brook, a half-dozen dogs and a big flock of chickens, "Because," Barbara said, "the egg item in this house is terrific!" Her deepest, most abiding love was her children and her home, and there was a plaintive note in her wish that Morton could be home more often to enjoy them, too.

Three months after Father returned to his self-imposed exile in England, he was seriously injured in a horseback riding accident which occurred at the home of actor John Loder in Hertfordshire. While riding a spirited hunter, he was thrown from the horse and suffered a fractured shoulder, two broken ribs and a punctured lung. By the time we heard the news, doctors assured us he was off the critical list and since Constance and I were in the middle of filming, Barbara left for England at once. "Barbara," he wrote me later, "came to take my corpse home, got tired of waiting for it, and has returned to her brood of three. Do not measure me for a shroud as yet!"

The movie that prevented me from flying to Father's bedside was *The Man Who Reclaimed His Head,* with Claude Rains and Lionel Atwill. It was a weird, macabre story about a man who walked around with a head in a suitcase, and no wonder I can't remember anything else about it. The film that followed, however, was one I'll always remember, though no one else seems to, for it was the first American film to dramatize mental illness and the forerunner of a series of films which dealt with the subject later in the nineteen-forties, among them *The Snake Pit* and *Suspicion*.

It was the first really challenging and the most dramatic role I'd played up to that time, and from then on, ambitions for my own career began to grow more seriously. Adapted from a Phyllis Bottome novel, the cast of *Private Worlds* included Claudette Colbert, Charles Boyer, Helen Vincent and Joel McCrea, and was directed by Gregory LaCava and produced by Walter Wanger. Walter had read the book in England and was offered the rights to it, but he said, "No, I won't make a picture about a lunatic asylum." However, when he returned to the United States, he discovered the book was a persistent best seller, and it seemed to him every woman in the country had a copy tucked under her arm. He bought the film rights in a hurry, then had to sell the distributors and exhibitors on the idea. They were opposed to the idea of making a picture about insanity, but Walter was sold on the manuscript by then and proceeded to make it in the face of opposition.

I remember his opening remark when I first went to see him about the role in *Private Worlds,* one not designed to inflate an ego. "You've gotten awfully fat haven't you?" I'd just finished nursing a baby, though I've never weighed more than a hundred and ten pounds in my life, and I thought Mr. Wanger's exaggerations a trifle out of place. Apparently, however, he overcame his resistance to my "overweight," and we went into production shortly after. But when the movie was released in 1935, the critics felt the theme of mental illness was too "gloomy," and it was destined for failure at the box office. *Private Worlds* was simply ahead of its time.

Slowly, during that period, Father recovered from his accident in England. Though Aimee's divorce proceedings were still in the works, the threat of imprisonment was lifted and by the middle of 1935, he felt free enough to return home and "face the firing squad of wifely vengeance." When he landed in New York, he found vast changes in the theatrical scene.

Five years had passed since Father's last Broadway appearance in *Solid South,* and he was struck by the fact that many of his cronies were missing. "My God, it's almost impossible to cast a show on Broadway these days without first phoning for aid from MGM, Warner Brothers or Paramount. It seems all of my contemporaries have retired, gone to Hollywood, or passed away. No wonder I don't know a soul around the theater these days!"

He grumbled and moped around New York for several weeks, considering a return to the battle ground of the West Coast, when the dynamic young director, Guthrie McClintic, sent him the manuscript of a new play. Written by Maxwell Anderson under the working title of *The Bridge,* it was finally produced as *Winterset.* Inspired by the Sacco-Vanzetti trials, *Winterset* was the tragic account of a boy's efforts to clear his father's name of murder after he was unjustly executed. It was a strangely beautiful and evocative blank-verse drama, set in the shadows of an East River bridge. McClintic offered Father the role of Judge Gaunt, a man deranged by his condemnation of an innocent man, and immediately he was taken with the part and the play. Burgess Meredith played the boy, Mio, and a young actress named Margarita Bolado, his ill-fated sweetheart. Thereafter, she was known simply as Margo.

*Winterset* opened September 25, 1935, at the Martin Beck Theater, an outstanding success, and won for Maxwell Anderson a Pulitzer Prize for the 1935–36 season. Burgess Meredith was hailed as the brightest new star on Broadway, and Father came in for his fair share of superlatives. Percy Hammond wrote, "Mr. Bennett as the contrite and confused judge gives a distinguished characterization complete in study and execution. It belongs in the list of his honorable gifts to the theater."

The young people in the company adored my father, particularly Burgess and another young actor, St. John Terrell. They suffered his irascibility, roared at his wit, ran his errands, and admired him extravagantly as an actor. St. John was his especially willing slave, and they formed an affectionate friendship that lasted Father's lifetime.

During the run, Father was up to his old tricks, and one night when the audience seemed to be more pulmonary than usual, he stopped in the middle of a scene with Burgess and addressed them with a smile. "Now, listen folks. Buzzy here has just opened in this play and made a big success of it. He's got a very important speech coming up and if you keep coughing like that, you're going to miss it." Thoroughly intimidated, the audience sat in stunned silence, until the minute Father made his exit and they started to cough again.

For a time during that period, he shared an apartment with St. John in Beekman Place, where John Barrymore was a frequent guest. Barrymore was in the throes of a divorce from his third wife and frequently fled her wrath to the safe haven in Beekman Place. Father's litigations with Aimee by then had dragged on for months, and he and John often commiserated and reflected on the perfidy of women, over filled brandy glasses.

Rumors again circulated in the business that Mr. Bennett was having trouble with his lines, and his performances were increasingly inconsistent. Sometimes, he would play with extraordinary brilliance, at other times he mumbled through the scenes, barely able to get off the stage.

Though playing in *Winterset* gave him great pleasure, Father's personal problems, his private capers and high living, and the fact that he'd not recovered fully from his accident of the previous February, all contributed to undermine his health and affect his performances. Four months after the opening, he was stricken with double pneumonia; again it looked really serious and he was forced to withdraw from the play. It was the last time he would appear on a Broadway stage.

Barbara, who was just recovering from the birth of her fourth baby, Anthony Patrick Downey, called Constance and me, and we flew from Hollywood to New York at once. I left right from the set of *Thirteen Hours by Air,* wearing the wardrobe I used in the picture. But Barbara was always something of an alarmist, and we found, to our relief, that Father's condition was not so serious as we'd anticipated. He snapped back, eventually, but with less aplomb and energy.

The weeks of his illness had taken a heavy toll, both emotionally and physically. He went to a Miami resort for a rest of several weeks while his understudy continued the run of *Winterset,* then he prepared himself to join the company for the road tour scheduled to begin in Boston. He wrote to Stanley Gilkey, the company manager, to lay at rest any anxieties he might have had about his condition:

> If you could see me you would know what they mean when they talk about going to Florida to recuperate. I could play tomorrow, if necessary, but would much rather play down here in the Florida sunshine.

And aware of his shaky memory, he added,

> I wish there were some means of sending me a copy of Judge Gaunt, one that has been used and has all the notes and stage directions. I would like to be up and easy in the part again when I get there.

When the road tour opened, he was content and happy for a few weeks, but once again he was plagued by ill health and in May he left the company for an extended trip to South America, to rest and to put as much distance between himself and Aimee as possible. Their financial differences had been settled out of court and required Father to pay her a lump sum in settlement. But his illnesses of the past few years and only intermittent jobs had drained him financially.

On May 1, 1936, he boarded a freighter in Hoboken and after a month at sea, arrived in Rio de Janeiro. The night before docking in Rio, he heisted a number of drinks in the bar and had to be helped to his cabin where he passed out, fully dressed in a white Palm Beach suit. Unconscious all night, he unknowingly relieved himself where he sat and was finally awakened the following morning by the steward. The ship was already pulling into the dock. He was horrified at the condition of his white suit, particularly because he knew he'd be met by a welcoming committee of friends and local dignitaries. There was no time to change his clothes, and leaving the steward to wrestle with his luggage, he walked to the gangway that led to the dock. Suddenly, he thought of a brilliant solution to the embarrassing stains. It was a stroke of genius. He simply tripped himself and fell into the water. The welcoming committee rushed forward and pulled him up on the dock, dripping wet. Everyone was very solicitous about the unfortunate "accident" suffered by the dignified Mr. Bennett, and reporters were charmed by his good sportsmanship when he waved the incident aside.

He stayed four relaxing, if lonely months in Rio, much of the time spent in writing his memoirs and editing his poems. I knew very little of his childhood and the early developments of his career until, in the process of writing this book, by sheer accident I discovered the only existing copy of the unpublished memoirs which, fortunately, had been kept through the years by one of his closest friends, Susan Palmer.

It seems an odd whim that he should have chosen the theatrical profession. There was nothing in his background to recommend a life in the theater, and his family was the least likely to produce an actor. By contrast, Mother's family had been in the theater for four generations when Father was born.

While my maternal grandparents were closing their second season with Edwin Booth at the Walnut Street Theater in Philadelphia and the Vokes family was making its debut in the United States, Charles Clarence William Henry Richard Bennett was born May 21, 1872, at Bennett's Switch, Indiana. He used to brag that his name took up a line and a half in

the family bible, and later, for the sake of brevity and marquee space, shortened it to Richard Bennett. Located near
Kokomo and Logansport on the banks of the Wabash River,
Bennett's Switch was named for the whistle-stop junction of a
short railroad spur that ran to the Bennett sawmill and home-
stead.

For generations the Bennetts had been lumbermill operators, first pioneering the frontiers of New Jersey, and then
migrating to Indiana. In the early eighteen-hundreds, Father's
great-grandfather, Moses, settled Bennett's Mills, New Jersey,
near Tom's River. There, he ran a sawmill and a flour mill
and occupied himself with "agricultural and mercantile pursuits," which is another way of saying he was a farmer and
shopkeeper. He became one of the class of unordained, lay
preachers known as community circuit riders, who traveled
the surrounding country on horseback and, without fee,
preached for the glory of God and the salvation of men. The
driving tradesman merged with the religious itinerant and
was the custom with the following generations of Bennetts
up until my father's.

It was Richard's grandfather who moved from New Jersey
to Indiana and founded the home and sawmill at Bennett's
Switch, where he brought forth seventeen children and sent
nine sons to the Civil War, only three of whom came back.
One of those three sons was my paternal grandfather, George
Washington Bennett, self-ordained preacher, sawmill operator, and three times Sheriff of Howard County.

Perhaps the link with the theater wasn't so obscure after
all, for all of the Bennetts were powerful speakers and given
to histrionics in the pulpit. In those days of old-time religion,
hell-fire and brimstone, a good preacher also had to be a good
actor. The Bennetts were never known for their "soft sell"
of the gospel, and they licked anyone in sight who didn't believe that Jesus, Moses and Noah Webster were the smartest
men in history.

I don't know what first prompted Father to entertain

thoughts of a life in the theater, but in his memoirs there's a hint that the dreams began early. The Bennetts's religious home life didn't prevent them from taking part occasionally in civic or church theatricals, and Father's Uncle Henry, in fact, was known as a very good amateur actor. Although nearby Kokomo was perhaps a tenth of its present size, it boasted an Opera House that was visited frequently by such attractions as the circus and professional traveling stock companies. Occasionally, Father passed out handbills for the visiting attractions and was given a ticket in return.

He seemed to take naturally to the charades in grade school and Sunday school. In his words,

> They broadened into a very bad dramatic society called The Carlton Club. Later we did light opera, melodramas and comedies, anything we could get hold of on which there were no royalties. . . . My first experience onstage was at the age of eight—in the hayloft along toward Spring, when the hay was nearly gone. My uncle, an amateur actor of much local note, was playing in the City Hall in a romantic drama, and hearing him constantly rehearse, I learned all his lines by heart. Some of the other boys learned the other roles, and we did our own production. Mother's sheets were utilized for a drop curtain and a couple of pieces of carpet from the waste heap during Spring cleaning made the side drops. An old four-legged kitchen table turned upside down with its legs in the air was a ship where the action took place. Price of admission was two marbles. The best seats, chairs without backs, soap boxes and a bench, cost three marbles. When we couldn't remember all the speeches from the play we interpolated some of our own, and I can assure you that I have never played since, before such an enthusiastic and appreciative audience, as at those performances.

For a short period in his twelfth year, Father was somewhat sickly, "spindly" his Grandmother Bennett called him, and his father urged him to take up boxing and other athletics.

George Washington Bennett's friend, a farmer named Sam Carson, was an exprizefighter, and for Richard and some of the other local boys, Sam rigged up a training center in his woodshed, which included a trapeze, horizontal bars and a punching bag.

Sam also gave Father some common sense advice to rid his senses of thoughts about girls. According to Sam, one only had to keep the bloodstream clear and filled with oxygen by breathing deeply. Clearing the mind of the opposite sex, and thereby preventing loss of appetite, was easy enough if he would only breathe to the very bottom of his lungs. Father flunked that part of the course.

It was clear from the start that young Dick Bennett was handy with his fists, and Sam Carson was proud that "his boy" could swear like a pirate and lick anybody twice his size. In addition to those abilities, Father picked up some facility for the guitar. His voice was clear and had a good range, and he was drafted to sing first tenor and play second guitar in a local quartet. The surrounding towns may have boasted a brass band, but Kokomo at the time bragged of a singing quartet made up of native sons which played weddings, barn-raisings and country fairs.

My father had plenty of opportunity to witness real-life melodrama as the son of the Sheriff of Howard County, though it was difficult for him to reconcile his father's authority as an elected law officer with his religious scruples. Richard once asked his father what Jesus did before he ran for Savior.

One of his most vivid childhood recollections revolved around the capture of the Monahan gang, a group of hoodlums who robbed freight trains and was also credited with the deaths of four or five commercial travelers. In his official capacity as Sheriff, Grandfather Bennett had been responsible for rounding up and jailing most of the suspects, and the final shoot-out with the gang's ringleader, Doc Kole, came at an abandoned shed near the Bennetts's mill. The single one of the gang left uncaptured, Sheriff Bennett had lured Kole to the shed on a fake pretext, using an exconvict as bait. In true theatrical style, the villain was blasted from several directions and fell dying on the spot. Grandfather walked over to him and said, "I guess we've got you, Doc."

"Yes, you bible-thumping Hoosier bastard!" he answered, and died. Father always thought it one of the best exit lines in real or imagined melodramas.

Gradually, it became apparent that his theatrical ambitions were reaching beyond the harmless stage. He took to hanging around the stage door of the Opera House, and once his father caught him in clandestine rehearsals in the barn, working on an impolite song-and-dance act. Reprisal was swift. It was perfectly acceptable to appear in church and school plays, but the raffish nonsense he was entertaining had to be stifled once and for all. At fourteen, Grandfather sent him to Indianapolis to run errands in Packet's Dry Goods Store, but the results were disastrous. Mr. and Mrs. Packet took him to New York on a buying trip, and there Father bought a ticket to see Edwin Booth's Hamlet. He was staggered by the experience. Many years later, he would remember it as "the performance that created the profoundest impression on me. I have seen many Hamlets since, most of which are as memorable as high school performances. But Booth's acting had design and form and sensibility, just as great paintings have."

His job at the dry goods store didn't last long, since it was clear that Mrs. Packet had taken a not altogether motherly interest in the new errand boy. Mr. Packet sent him packing. Father returned to Bennett's Switch, puzzled by unrequited love and profoundly moved by the experience of seeing Booth's Hamlet. The mold was cast on both counts.

Next, his father gave him a job as nightwatchman at the lumber mill with the intention of teaching him the business. Although his mother was somewhat supportive of his acting ambitions, since at one time she'd entertained a secret longing for the stage, his father would brook nothing of the sort.

The resulting breach was one that took a long time to heal. Years later, with Father's name blazing on a theater marquee, Grandfather Bennett crossed to the other side of the street, rather than pass by the spot where his son was performing. Eventually, my Bennett grandparents separated, and Father even alienated himself from his mother, Eliza. Years later my mother was responsible for their reconciliation, and I remember once she came to live with us for a time when I was five or six, although Grandmother incurred his displeasure when she ran off to marry a dentist named Tipton. Father thought it reprehensible behavior for a woman of "her age."

His rebelliousness at the age of fifteen set in motion one of a long series of Bennett revolutions. The solitary job of night-watchman at the sawmill held little charm when compared to his dreams of theatrical glory, and his solution was simple. He left home. That began a period when he was buffeted from one city to another, taking any job that presented itself and working whenever possible as a performer. They were grinding, lonely years in which the man and the actor would merge to form his character traits and hone his talents to a fine edge. He'd carry the hostile imprint of those rebellious years for the rest of his life.

First, he made his way to St. Paul, where he got a job as a waiter in a hotel. That didn't last long, not because he was an inattentive waiter, but when a minor misunderstanding arose over an order, he promptly belted the offending patron in the eye. Finding that his popularity in St. Paul had diminished somewhat, he hopped a train for Duluth. The next morning he awoke to find a brakeman glaring down at him. He was yanked out of the freight car, threatened with jail, and relieved of the three dollars and twenty-six cents in his pocket. Father poured on the histrionics, and by the time he had finished the sad history of his life, he was released, his money intact and an extra dollar added to his meager bankroll.

In Duluth, he shipped aboard a Great Lakes Steamer again

as a waiter, a job that required a little singing entertainment on the side. The dining patrons may have been charmed by his songs and guitar playing, but a junior officer on board seemed something less than enchanted by the performance and made it clear in round tones. Father laid him out horizontally with a wooden two-by-four. Needless to say, his career as a singing waiter came to an abrupt end, and by the time the steamer docked in Buffalo, he was jobless again.

The night he landed, he slept in a park. A dishwashing job provided breakfast and dinner, and that evening the flare of gasoline torches attracted him to a traveling medicine show which sold "Hamlin's Wizard Oil." Father talked himself into a job as singer and barker with the show and traveled with it as far as Toledo. There, one of the crowd gathered around the medicine wagon turned out to be his Uncle Henry, and he was taken back to his family in disgrace.

However, he'd promised to sing and dance at the opening of a five-and-ten-cent store in Columbia, Indiana, and he ran away again to fulfill that engagement. During that period, he also tried his luck as a professional boxer and managed to get a few minor professional bouts, events for which he changed his name. But his attempt at anonymity failed, and he was brought back home to Bennett's Switch once again. George Washington Bennett was doubly offended. It was a sensible thing to learn the manly art of self-defense but to be paid for it was unthinkable. Respectable people knew that both prizefighters and actors consorted with the devil, and neither profession was acceptable to a reputable family. Decent hotels even had signs on their registry desks that read, "No dogs, prizefighters or actors allowed in this hotel." To add to the insult, actors were billed last. There were few who defended the acting profession in polite society, except for the maiden aunt of an actress of the time who kept a collection of clippings to prove that clergymen were in the police courts far more frequently than actors.

Undoubtedly, at that point, Grandfather Bennett's powers

of persuasion were very strong, and he caught his young son at a particularly vulnerable moment, for Father, then about seventeen, agreed to give up his theatrical ambitions to learn the tailoring trade. Of course, it was a promise he couldn't keep. Grandfather apprenticed him to a tailor in Frankfort, Indiana, and he stuck with it for several months. Although he learned his trade, he spent his spare time secretly hanging around stage doors.

Then an English performer named Joe Coyne came through Frankfort in a melodramatic thriller called *The Limited Mail*. Father approached him, begged for an audition, and Coyne graciously sat through the Bennett bag of tricks. But there was no place in his company at the time, and he advised the young hopeful to go to New York where opportunities were greater. Encouragement from a professional was all he needed, although the flame of his desire didn't need much fuel. The urge to act had become an all-consuming passion.

Soon after his meeting with Joe Coyne, a "ten-twent-thirt" rep show* passed through town, and Father got a job as a musician and sometime actor. That kind of company was called a "rag" show because it played under canvas and, usually, stayed a week in each town. Actors were required to do a specialty act and play an instrument in the band, which gave concerts before each performance. The salary was minimal but room and board were paid by the management.

In Wheeling, West Virginia, the trails of Father's troupe and the Barlow Brothers's Minstrels crossed. He switched companies and played five or six weeks of one-night stands with the blackface minstrels. Keokuk, Iowa, found the outfit broke and stranded, and Father was forced to return to the tailoring trade. He stitched away three months and finally saved enough money to go to Chicago, but theater jobs were few and instead, he found work as a card dealer in a gam-

---

* Term refers to admission price of ten, twenty and thirty cents. Usually it was a repertory company of second-rate caliber which played stereotyped melodramas.

bling house. There, he met Joe Coyne again who gave him a job as a property man, doubling in two small roles, and a salary of twenty dollars a week. Coyne was still playing *The Limited Mail*, and Father made his professional debut at the Standard Theater in Chicago, May 10, 1891. He was nineteen.

He recalled it later as "a god-awful performance in a god-awful play," but it netted him a degree of personal success and eventually he was elevated to the leading juvenile role of Tombstone Jake and given a raise in salary to twenty-two dollars a week. He played *The Limited Mail* for fifty-four weeks, mostly one-night stands, in almost every whistle-stop village, town and city in the country from coast to coast. By the end of the run, he'd played every male role in the cast and once, in an emergency, the part of an elderly maiden aunt. Near the end of the tour, Father made his first New York appearance at Niblo's Garden, the same theater where my maternal great-grandfather, William F. Wood, had appeared in the eighteen-forties.

His first year in the professional theater was a grueling and demanding one, made at the cost of alienating himself from his family. But for Father, it was also a time filled with growth and excitement, and later he confided to his memoirs,

> I had spent fifty-four weeks with *The Limited Mail* and felt I had passed through my baptism of fire in the theater. But, oh, how mistaken I was! From the time you first cast your lot with Thespis to the moment when the curtain goes down on your final performance, you are under a baptism, and your illusions are in a constant state of flux. You find new ones today, which are shattered tomorrow. Yet I know of few who would depart from its romance. Its fascination holds as nothing else and no other profession can.

At the close of the tour, he went to see his beloved sister, Blanche, who was happily married and living in Logansport, Indiana, near their birthplace of Bennett's Switch. Except for

Blanche and a new nephew, there was little to keep him there for long. Through her, his father sent him a message to give up what he termed "a tramp's life," and again offered him a chance to take over the lumbermill business which by then had been moved to Frankfort. Father would have none of it, and he left for Chicago, where he arrived in time to see the opening of The Columbian Exposition, the World's Fair of 1893.

In Chicago, Father found another engagement with a touring company that took him to Oklahoma, where almost immediately he found himself in disagreement with the management. Insults were exchanged, then blows, and he may have won the battle, but he lost the war and almost at once rejoined the army of unemployed actors. It was the first of a long series of lively battles with the managerial side of the theater.

Two seasons of stock followed of sixteen and twenty weeks each, with a change of play every week, then a touring company in a repertory of seven plays which were alternated each night. It was in that company that he had his one and only brush with Shakespeare, though he'd never admit the roles he played, and wrote of it later, "I was practically forced in my earlier experiences to essay two of the bard's earlier tragedies. How graceless I emerged will never be mentioned by me. As for the customers who came to see, I hope and pray the dust of time has kindly obliterated it from their memories. I'm sure my prayers have been answered, for I do not recollect any disquieting references to the disgusting spectacle!" Later, as a fine and skillful actor, he had all the equipment to play Shakespeare and was often asked why he never rose to the supreme challenge, but he dismissed it with an explosive answer: "Why in the name of God actors all get an itch for the classics at some time in their careers, I cannot understand. If not cured, it is an itch which carries them into the realms of atrophied hams!"

Gradually Father's career expanded and the caliber of both

parts and companies improved. Engagements followed under the more successful managements of Klaw and Erlanger and Augustin Daly, and after that, more stock experience in Richmond, Virginia, and Milwaukee.

Until then, Father had used Chicago as a base of operations, since many of the Midwestern companies were booked from there, though sometimes there were long uncomfortable periods between jobs. In one of the slack periods, he worked as a night clerk at the Palace Hotel and, after several months, met Gustave Frohman, the Chicago representative of the Frohman theatrical empire. Gus hired him for the leading role in a touring company of *Charlie's Aunt*, for which Anita Loos's father was the advance agent.

Gus Frohman liked his work and after the *Charlie's Aunt* tour engaged him again for Haddon Chambers's melodrama, *The Fatal Card*, which opened in Detroit in September of 1895. Father made special note in a letter to his father that the great English actor, Henry Irving, had recently added new honors to the acting profession when he became the first actor in history to be knighted. "The theater is slowly reverting to respectability," he wrote, "at least for the enlightened few who understand that if actors are a distinct tribe, they are no less respectable than the rest of society."

By the following year, at the age of twenty-four, he had established an acceptable reputation for versatility and went from one job to another with increasing regularity. Finally, the day approached when he would ally himself with Charles Frohman, in an association that eventually hurtled him into the front ranks of American actors.

After finishing his memoirs, he wrote me from Rio,

I have no fear, no dread. My work is finished. I am exiled from my vocation and familiar haunts. I retain but scant belief in human nature. Ideals flit back and forth across weary eyes—truant rays of sunshine pass to new shadows. Not one moment's surcease from a grief that will not let me recapture lost belief. Still I can giggle as one demented, living in translucent memories. Yesterday, I finished 100,000 of them. The end. Today they are my idiot's dream rehashed to edify my vanity. What damned liars we all are. My poems are ready assembled. I shall call in the stray street dogs tomorrow for tea and cookies, and read my doggerel to them. How they will wag their tails and bark. A script conference in Hollywood? God bless you and yours, darling. To hell with the sadistic members of my loin.

The last line refers to Constance who, apparently, was out of favor at the moment. She and Father were forever differing about something. Once it was over a story he'd given to the press about her childhood stubbornness, which made her furious, and they didn't speak for months over that.

Occasionally he indulged himself in the feeling that he was victimized and left alone to struggle with his problems, deceived by the world and betrayed by his family. His offstage histrionics at those moments were beautiful to behold. Once, he strode along the beach at Santa Monica with his young friend, St. John Terrell, wearing a black cape that billowed out behind him in the wind, and in tragic tones he wailed, "My children have deserted me!" playing King Lear to the last balcony. At one time or another, either Constance or Barbara was reduced to the role of Lear's wicked daughter, although for some reason I almost always managed to escape being cast. At one point in Rio he became so overwrought with his plight, he declared his acting days were over and claimed he would stay in Brazil to mine for gold.

While Father was in Rio considering a change of profession, I was in Hollywood considering a change of name. Not for myself but for my older daughter. Ditty had already renamed herself on one occasion—from Adrienne to Ditty; then one day I was asked about my daughter "Diana." I knew perfectly well, or thought I did, that I had a child named Ditty, and one named Melinda. We called Melinda "Mims," a diminutive of her name and also because the character of Mimsy in *Peter Ibbetson* had particularly appealed to her, although she referred to herself as "Me, Markey!" But in Ditty's case I couldn't figure out the "Diana" until she simply began telling people that was her name, for reasons unknown to anyone but her, and they weren't really clear. From then on, she was known officially as Diana. However, I was much more concerned about her surname of Fox. I wanted the girls to grow up as sisters and to share in everything, including the last name of Markey. Also, it had occurred to me at the time of my accident that if anything ever happened to me, Jack Fox might appear to claim her, and since she adored Gene anyway, it seemed a logical step. In August of 1936, I went to court on a petition to change Ditty's surname, and it was granted after some minor difficulty, when Jack appeared to oppose it.

Father gave up all thoughts of becoming a goldminer and returned from Rio to face the death rattle of his marriage to Aimee, and to file bankruptcy. To free himself of her once and for all, he'd depleted his bank account and property holdings until there was nothing left. When, mercifully, the divorce became final in October of 1937, he made a solemn vow: "Never again will I embroil myself in the strangling coils of matrimony. I would rather be hung from a gibbet. The cost to my health, sanity and finances has been immeasurable. Besides, one must do something to relieve the monogamy. It is a most unnatural state."

# 15

When Constance completed her RKO-Pathe contract in 1933, she made four films as a free-lance player: *Moulin Rouge, Affairs of Cellini, Outcast Lady* and *After Office Hours,* all of them failures. Thoroughly dissatisfied and infuriated by the scripts offered to her, she slammed the door on the industry and she, Henri and seven-year-old Peter Plant retreated to Europe, where they lived for almost a year. In England, she did one film for Gaumont-British, then returned in mid-1936 when Darryl Zanuck cast her in *Ladies in Love* with Loretta Young and Janet Gaynor. The story of three girls searching for husbands, *Ladies in Love* was later reworked into a number of pictures, including *Three Coins in the Fountain* and *The Pleasure Seekers.* It led to Hal Roach's *Topper,* the film in which many people now remember Constance at her best. She and Cary Grant played a high-living couple killed in an auto accident who reappear on earth and decide they should do one good deed before offering themselves to a higher judgment. They proceed to brighten the life of Cosmo Topper (Roland Young), an intimidated bank president who becomes a swinging man about town. Constance and Grant were ideal as Thorne Smith's irrepressible ghosts, and *Topper* made her "box office" again, when it became the most popular comedy of 1937. The following year, she made a sequel, *Topper Takes a Trip,* which was equally successful.

How she ever made a film during the thirties was beyond me, for during those years she spent much of her time in the law courts, either suing someone or being sued. Sometimes she won and sometimes she lost, but she loved a good battle and would go to court at the drop of a summons. She sued Jimmie Fidler, a Hollywood columnist and radio commentator, for libel, and because he wrote an unpleasant item about her, filed a suit for two hundred and fifty thousand dollars, alleging that he defamed her character and made such statements "maliciously and with intent to injure her in her career." Suing a Hollywood columnist, some people felt, was treading dangerous ground, and although she lost that particular battle, it made its mark on California libel laws when a Superior Judge ruled that motion picture stars fell in the same class as public officials. His ruling held that "certain remarks directed against a public character are privileged, even though false, if made without malice."

Just to keep things in motion, Constance sued Gaumont-British Studios for breach of contract and won; then sued the writing team of Ben Hecht and Charles MacArthur for the same thing and lost. She was sued by a Hollywood taxi company for refusing to pay a fare of four dollars. "He took the long way around," she said. "It's a point of honor." Another lively brush with the courts involved a painting. She'd commissioned artist Willie Pogany to do her portrait, but when she saw herself in oils, she declared, "That woman is an Amazon! I look like a sack of Portland cement with a rope tied in the middle!" She refused to pay the artist's fee, Mr. Pogany refused to compromise his artistic conscience and they saw each other next in court. The judge ruled in favor of the artist and, for the benefit of reporters, Constance showed her views of the matter by kicking a hole in the canvas.

She hated losing at anything, but most especially at cards. She once termed herself "the best femme poker player in the country." Certainly, she was one of the sharpest poker players in Hollywood and often was allowed at gaming tables which ordinarily excluded women. A game with Constance was likely to go on all night, by the end of which she'd cleaned out every opponent who was still vertical.

I remember some years later when I joined Hollywood's lively poker-playing set, she and I were playing one night at the home of producer-director Mervyn Leroy. By five or six in the morning, everyone had dropped out except the two Bennett sisters. I had a great hand and so did she. We kept raising each other, and I kept thinking I'd beat her if it was my last act on earth, so I waited her out and finally she folded. It was a delicious moment of triumph for me, and a rare one of loss for Constance.

Except for the frequent forays into the law courts, those were reasonably calm years for the Bennetts. Almost too calm for me. Professionally I wasn't particularly dissatisfied, although the films I did during that period had little to distinguish them. Personally it was another matter. I had no apparent reasons for dissatisfaction in that area either and, outwardly, it seemed quite perfect. My career was swinging along at a fast rate and steadily rising; Ditty and Mims were healthy and growing; Gene was a devoted husband. Inwardly, I was feeling something else. I couldn't account for my discontent, though I thought some of it could be laid to the fact that Gene's life and mine had settled into a kind of dull, lusterless routine. Little by little some sort of erosion set in and steadily and quietly wore away our relationship. There was nothing tempestuous about our break; it was probably the warmest and most amicable parting in Hollywood history.

I look back on those years of marriage to Gene Markey with the greatest warmth. He was a gentleman to the core, and the divorce presented no difficulties for either of us. There was never any question of my having Mims's custody, and he saw her whenever he pleased. There was only one sticky moment a few years later when he married Hedy Lamarr, and she came to the house alone to see Mims when I wasn't there. I was resentful of that and said so. The rumor brigade worked overtime and spread reports that Hedy and I were feuding and that I wouldn't allow Gene to see his own child. Nothing was further from the truth. My only stipulation had been that Gene visit Mims in my home so she wouldn't be confused over two households. Always my thought had been to raise the children away from anything that smacked of Hollywood artificiality. I wanted them to grow up as normal children with a home life as free as possible from the difficult external problems that were neither natural nor necessary to childhood.

In any case, Gene and I have remained the best of friends to this day, and throughout the years we've discussed mutual problems, heeded advice from each other, and given aid when trouble arose. To me, he will always remain an altogether remarkable friend.

After our divorce in 1937, I was restless and ill at ease, and I looked around for something that would take me away from Hollywood for a time. My contractual arrangement with Walter Wanger allowed me a breathing spell of several months, fortunately timed with an offer to do a road tour of the George S. Kaufman-Edna Ferber comedy, *Stage Door,* produced by Sam Harris. Since Margaret Sullavan was expecting a baby, her husband, Leland Hayward, asked me if I'd replace her in the role of Terry.

With the exception of the brief production at the Biltmore Theater in Los Angeles in 1931, it was my first experience in the theater since *Jarnegan,* nine years before. It scared me half to death, but I loved every minute of it. For me, there was another important factor, a factor that most Hollywood actors had to cope with, and that was the strong desire to make good in a medium from which they'd been absent for a long time or had never tried. Both Mother and Father, of course, were delighted.

Rehearsals were hectic, since I'd joined the company less than two weeks before the opening in Hartford, Connecticut. I'd been so used to keeping within the confining limits of a movie set that I kept all movements and gestures down to a minimum. I remember George Kaufman stopped me at one point, and said, "Now, Joan, you're not in front of the cameras. You have the whole stage to work in, so take it, it's all yours!" From then on, I enjoyed working in the larger framework of the stage and the new freedom it gave me.

The tour lasted six months, and the stand in Cleveland brought a feud with one of the critics, Windsor French, of *The Cleveland Press*. Instead of reviewing the play, he printed a column that was filled with trivia and a personal attack, ending with the patent lie that I'd demanded a private elevator each time I entered my hotel. I opened my big guns and sent him a blazing wire, which it pleased me to read in his column the next day, and accompanied the wire with a huge bowl of pansies. *Variety* reported, "Scrap reminded playgoers with long memories of the tiffs carried on with reviewers by Richard Bennett, father of the actress." It wasn't the last time I "pulled a Dick Bennett" and battled with newspaper columnists.

Some years later, I had a widely publicized beef with Hedda Hopper in Hollywood. Several sniping items had appeared in her column about me. One was a criticism of changing Ditty's name from Fox to Markey, a private matter which I felt didn't warrant her attention. Then, during the war, when Ditty was graduating from school, as a present, I ordered a new car from Bill Hopper, Hedda's son, who owned an auto agency. She printed the information as an item and promptly spoiled the surprise I'd intended. To top it off, she inferred in her column that a prominent actress, a friend of mine, was drunk at a party I'd also attended, and I knew it wasn't true. Harry Crocker, another columnist, took exception to the lie as well and wrote a harsh article about "responsible reporting," but without mentioning Hedda by name. I followed it up and took out a full-page ad in the trade papers, *The Hollywood Reporter* and *Variety*, which reprinted Hedda's and Crocker's columns side by side.

Since it was close to Valentine's Day, I had both columns outlined in hearts, and the whole page headlined: "CAN THIS BE YOU, HEDDA?" For a topper, I had a live, descented skunk delivered to her door. Friends predicted that I'd endangered my career, which was ridiculous.

The closing four-week run of *Stage Door* in Chicago was a source of satisfaction on two counts. First, it meant I'd be in one spot for a whole month and could take my clothes out of a suitcase for a change, and second, the play broke records at the box office. The management asked me to extend the run, but there were some professional and personal reasons that called me home.

To begin with, I was about to become one of the landed gentry. I'd lived in a number of apartments and rented houses since my arrival in Hollywood, but for some time, I'd wanted a home of my own and had chosen a lot on Mapleton Drive in Holmby Hills on which to build a fourteen-room French Provincial house. It was a project that demanded a lot of attention, and I'd involved myself with builders, contractors, decorators, and all the attendant labors and pleasures of building a dream house. Construction had begun before Gene Markey and I separated, and by the time I prepared to leave the *Stage Door* tour, it was near completion.

And then, there was Walter Wanger. I'd done a number of films produced by Walter for Paramount, and frequently he appeared on the set of whatever film I was working on at the time. It was Claudette Colbert who first enlightened me and told me that Walter never came on the set when I wasn't working. "But when you are, he's always around." Occasionally, during the tour of *Stage Door,* he'd fly on to see me on some pretext or other, but when Sam Harris asked me to extend the run in Chicago, Walter resisted the idea and I packed my bags and returned to Hollywood.

At that point in his career, Walter was one of the most distinguished and respected producers in the industry, with a long history of theatrical and film experience behind him. His interest in the theater had been stimulated at an early age by his mother's scrapbooks of old theater programs. A native San Franciscan, he was born in 1894 to Sigmund and Stella Feuchtwanger. When her husband died in 1905, Mrs. Feuchtwanger brought her four children East and streamlined the family name to Wanger. Later, Walter sentimentally adopted the "F" as his middle initial. In New York he attended the Ethical Culture School and supplemented his education one summer at a school for boys in Vevey, Switzerland. He entered Dartmouth College, where his classmates and closest friends included Gene Markey and Arthur Hornblow, Jr. It was there, as a member of the college drama society, that he introduced Broadway hits at Dartmouth, simultaneously with their New York runs. He approached my father for permission to produce *Damaged Goods,* and although he was refused, their meeting resulted in Walter's lifelong admiration for Richard Bennett.

When the United States entered the war, he abandoned Dartmouth in his junior year to enlist as a recruiting officer. Turning to propaganda, he produced the original "I Want You" posters painted by James Montgomery Flagg and turned out the first million copies, examples of which are preserved in the Hoover Museum in California. Then he joined the Signal Corps, the forerunner of the United States Air Force, attended ground school and was sent to France, where he was assigned to a captain named Fiorello LaGuardia, the future Right Honorable Mayor of New York City. The group was sent to Italy where Walter cracked up the first five planes assigned to him and earned the nickname of "The Austrian Ace," since anyone who destroyed five planes or more, regardless of the method, was considered an expert. Not surprisingly, he was transferred to the intelligence service at the Italo-Austrian front, and it was there he first became impressed with the potential power of motion pictures. In Italy, people didn't believe that the United States was really in the war, and Walter asked his propaganda chief if he could make a film showing American war preparations. The film had a great effect on the Italians, and he made up his mind that he'd go into the motion picture business some day.

After the Armistice he was demobilized in Paris and spent a few months as an attaché with President Wilson's Peace Mission. By the time he returned home, he contemplated entering the diplomatic service, but back in the provocative climate of Broadway he allied himself with the New York Theater Guild and took out a road company of its first big success, St. John Ervine's *John Ferguson.* The next season found him producing on his own when he leased the Princess Theater in New York and launched the Russian star, Alla Nazimova, in a big hit, *'Ception Shoals.*

In 1919 Walter married Justine Johnson, a Ziegfeld show-girl, and after a year spent with Famous-Players-Lasky as Jesse Lasky's chief aide he went to England, where he temporarily converted Covent Garden into a motion picture theater and produced several plays at other London theaters, in association with Frederick Londsdale. In partnership with Arch Selwyn, his next most important theatrical step was to bring to Broadway *Charlot's Revue,* the production from which I'd borrowed liberally for my own revue at St. Margaret's School for Girls.

Reengaged by Jesse Lasky for the production company which eventually became Paramount Pictures, he stunned moviemakers by suggesting a story about a love affair between an Arab and a Western woman, but the phenomenal success of Rudolph Valentino in *The Sheik* proved his uncanny knack for selecting properties and his talent as a star-maker. Walter introduced many actors to film stardom, including Jeanne Eagels, Walter Houston, Claudette Colbert, Miriam Hopkins, Kay Francis and the Marx Brothers. As general manager of Lasky's Astoria Studios, he arranged for and rejected the screen test I made when I was appearing in *Jarnegan,* predicting that "she'll never photograph."

After a policy dispute at Paramount he moved to Columbia

Studios for eighteen months, then to Metro-Goldwyn-Mayer, where he produced Greta Garbo's *Queen Christina,* and *Gabriel Over the White House.* The latter, one of Walter's all-time favorites, was called "timely, interesting and original" by one reviewer, and "the most important bad film of 1933" by another. It was one of the first attempts to introduce political ideas into films. Another movie with political overtones followed in *The President Vanishes.* To mark him further as "unconventional," in 1935 he introduced the serious treatment of psychiatry to the screen in *Private Worlds,* in which I was offered my first challenging dramatic role and the glorious chance to go insane—on film.

Frequently, Walter was the articulate spokesman in the industry who fought for better writing, acting, production techniques and distribution methods. In the areas of publicity, he raised a cry against innocuous and misleading advertising, and one of his favorite examples was the phrase used to publicize *Private Worlds*: "She loved him so much she couldn't help it!" which had nothing whatever to do with the film or its theme of mental illness.

Misleading advertising happens to be one of my favorite subjects, too, and in 1939 I raised a public issue over the advertising for a film I made called *The Housekeeper's Daughter,* with Adolph Menjou and John Howard, produced by Hal Roach for United Artists. "She couldn't cook, she couldn't sew, but oh, how she could so-and-so!" I hated the line, the twenty-four-sheet billboards, and the title which suggested something more like The Farmer's Daughter and traveling salesmen jokes. The ads implied a vulgarity that simply wasn't there and had nothing to do with the film, which was a bland comedy, and not a very good one at that. I wrote protesting letters to over twenty-six hundred women's clubs throughout the country, asking them to boycott the movie. I didn't win the battle with Hal Roach, but I have an idea he knew he had a worthy adversary by the time I was through.

Despite the astronomical costs of Walter's final film, *Cleo-*

*patra,* in 1963, in the earlier stages of his career he generally used an economical approach to movie-making that disarmed critics of his daring subject matter and high-handed methods. As one observer declared, "Wanger inherited the banker's attitude that when the books show red, there is something wrong." That fact didn't escape the notice of an advisor in Paramount's financial affairs, Joseph P. Kennedy, who named Walter as one of the two or three Hollywood producers who could keep the studio in the black.

When color posed another challenge to the industry in the thirties, Walter ignored the warnings that natural, outdoor light could never be controlled and made *Trail of the Lonesome Pine* with Henry Fonda and Fred MacMurray in 1936, the first color spectacular filmed outdoors. "I give black-and-white pictures two more years," he said. "I'm fighting for color now, just as I fought for sound. It's like a recurring dream. I seem to be listening to the same old arguments."

His greatest battles were waged against censorship. At the time I was touring in *Stage Door,* Walter had moved to United Artists and was deep in a controversy involving his film *Blockade,* an espionage story with a Spanish Civil War background that was intended as a preachment against war. Authoritative sources in Europe reported that Spain's Generalissimo Franco bitterly resented the film and would retaliate by banning it in his country, along with future United Artists releases. Gossip was rampant that Hollywood was a hotbed of political adventurers bent on stirring up international trouble, to which Walter replied with a sulphurous blast against censorship and intimidation, as well as political witch-hunting.

Eventually, *Blockade* was banned in Spain, Italy, Germany, all of the Balkan countries and several in South America, but the attendant publicity in the United States was enough to make up for the financial losses abroad. In 1939, a similar attack arose over another Wanger production, *Foreign Affairs.* Pointing out that "the shadow of increasing censorship at home and abroad has bred a fear complex among Hollywood producers," he wired Secretary of State Cordell Hull and urged legal protection for freedom of speech on the American screen as well as retaliatory boycott measures against those countries that banned American film companies.

Walter was a man of immense personal charm and attractiveness, erudite, urbane and witty, and he pursued me with the same attention that he lavished on his other productions. But, during that period, I think we were both marriage-shy, and although we were free of previous marriages, I, for one, wanted to wait until I was sure of my emotional ground.

For me, 1938 was a year to remember on several accounts. I'd made a successful, if nervous, return to the legitimate theater, and I returned to Hollywood and filmmaking to join in a little boycotting of my own. Along with fifty-six other members of the motion picture industry, I signed a "1938 Declaration of Independence" to help spur a nationwide protest against Germany's treatment of the Jews and, in a formal petition to President Roosevelt and the United States Congress, urged a move to break off trade relations with Nazi Germany.

In retrospect, it was probably during that period that I became more politically aware, and I've never lost my taste for the arena of politics. As a good, practicing Bennett, I have an intense hatred for bullies or anything that smacks of discrimination, and in election campaigns I've backed the candidate of my choice, vehemently and publicly. Many people feel that actors should not air their views in times of political crisis. I disagree and will continue to stand up to be counted on the issues whenever possible.

Constance, too, was always geared to the political scene, often violently, and when election time rolled around, it was sure to produce some first-rate arguments between us. She almost always outshouted me, but she never changed my mind, which irritated and delighted her at the same time.

Nineteen-thirty-nine was also a time of complete transition

for my career. That was the year my hair turned prematurely brown. I was scheduled to do another film produced by Walter and directed by Tay Garnett. Tay, who had just viewed Walter's film *Algiers,* with Hedy Lamarr and Charles Boyer, insisted that Hedy was a brunette edition of me, and he and Walter thought it would be a great joke if they put me in a dark wig for *Trade Winds.*

For ten years, with the exception of *Little Women* and *Private Worlds,* I'd played the insipid blonde ingenue, short on brains, long on bank accounts, the victim in a love triangle, and, for some reason that now escapes me, I was often English. Suddenly, I found myself filming *Trade Winds* in a dark wig, and with eyes at half-mast and voice lowered an octave, I positively smouldered all over the South Seas.

No one anticipated the reaction, least of all me, but the resulting publicity went wild. An avalanche of mail poured into the studio; later, one of the national magazines did a cover story on the three lookalikes: Hedy, Vivien Leigh and me. A national hairdresser's association expressed its wholehearted approval and predicted a new trend of brunette-ism would sweep the country. Always the comments noted the striking resemblance between Hedy Lamarr and me. I could never see it myself. To me I just looked like Joan Bennett with dark hair, but there must have been something to it because often after *Trade Winds* was released, in dimly lit restaurants I was greeted as Miss Lamarr. Personally, I liked the idea of escaping from all that bland, blonde innocence and thought the whole thing was very funny, but I don't think Hedy found the comparisons very amusing.

Had it not been for my new darker image, I'd never have been considered for the role of Scarlett O'Hara in *Gone With the Wind.* David Selznick had ransacked the world to test actresses and nonactresses to fill the role of the brash belle of Atlanta, and near the end of his search, he called and asked if I'd make a test for Scarlett. In those days, it was rare to ask an established actress to test for a specific part, but because it was such a plum role I agreed at once. For several weeks I worked on the Southern accent with Bill Price, a dialog director, and the test was filmed in three scenes. About that time, Vivien Leigh came to Hollywood from England to visit Laurence Olivier while he was filming *Wuthering Heights,* and agent Myron Selznick urged his brother, David, to test her for the coveted role. The choice finally settled down to the two of us; then I received a letter from David, accompanied by a large bowl of orchids.

Friday—the Thirteenth!

Dear Joan,

The Scarlett hour has arrived; and the decision, unfortunately, is against our Joanie.

I am more grateful than I can say for your effort, which was magnificent. That it may perhaps point the path to great things for you is the sincere and affectionate hope of

David

At a time when I was vamping my way into a new phase of my career in 1938, Morton and Barbara welcomed their fifth child, another boy, Kevin Peter Downey, and it looked as if she'd get her wish to have enough children to fill out a baseball team. But all was not as happy for Barbara as it might have seemed on the surface, although she adored the children, and more and more her life became tied up in them alone. By then Morton had left the radio business, but he continued to entertain in nightclubs, almost exclusively outside of New York. "We say three things in this house," she said. "Hello, I'm pregnant, and goodbye." After Kevin was born, she began to feel left out of Morton's life and increasingly alone.

Meanwhile, Father was wrestling with some problems of his own. Once he'd returned from Brazil late in 1936 almost two years went by before he was presented with another offer in the theater. Rumors continued to circulate that he was untrustworthy, his drinking was more prolonged, and he had difficulty in retaining his lines. Producers had less patience with the cantankerous Bennett who gloried in striding before his audiences to tell them what he thought of them, or anything else that moved him. Once, when he was at a loss for subject matter for a curtain speech, he'd waited for the inspiration of the moment and delivered a fifteen-minute denunciation of the new electric razors, the social evils they would induce and the passing of the venerable institutions surrounding the masculine art of shaving. Fine and versatile actor though he was, as time passed his parts grew fewer and less secure, and his health less certain.

He still roared his displeasure and struck out at the Philistines, but he was an older lion now, the handsome shaggy head snow white, his eyesight beginning to dim. He fumed and fretted while he waited for a play and continued to level his critical broadsides. "The New York theater today is suffering from delusions of mediocrity!"

Fortunately, in July of 1938, St. John Terrell, his young friend from the *Winterset* company, gave him the opportunity to revive *What Every Woman Knows*. A brief run of the Barrie play was given at The Players Theater in Clinton, Connecticut, then under St. John's management.

At last, in the fall of the year, he was offered a new play bound for Broadway that excited his enthusiasm and brought back the old energies. Paul Osborn's *On Borrowed Time,* based on a novel by Lawrence Watkin, concerned an old man and his grandson who cornered Death in a tree. The play was directed by the distinguished Joshua Logan and was one of his first big successes.

But in rehearsals, the old ghosts returned. The difficulty in remembering lines was heightened by the similarity of wording in various scenes, and Father had great trouble recalling which scene followed which. The memory blocks hampered his performance, and although he wouldn't admit it, he was deeply humiliated by his lapses and used a variety of excuses for his confusion. Suddenly, the pleasure of acting was destroyed by the terror of forgetting.

On the opening night in New Haven, Joshua Logan stationed prompters on either side of the stage to help him when the need arose, but he got so confused by the barrage of prompting from both stage right and left that suddenly he roared, "One at a time, for Chrissake, one at a time!"

It couldn't have been easy for the rest of the company either but Peter Miner, the small boy who played his grandson, weathered it like a veteran. One evening in particular, when Father forgot his lines, Peter climbed into his lap and prompted him in a cautious whisper so the audience wouldn't be aware of his difficulty. Father thanked him gravely and repeated the line.

Years later, Peter shared with me his favorite Richard Bennett story. At one point late in the play, Father crossed the stage through a small garden gate, and one night it got stuck, which caused him to forget another line. His anger at himself was so great, he stopped and said, "Just a minute while I join the stagehands' union and fix this goddamned gate!" Coincidentally, Peter Miner is now the producer of *Dark Shadows,* the daytime television show in which I'm currently involved at the American Broadcasting Company. His mother, Frances Fuller, now the executive director of The American Academy of Dramatic Arts, was the actress whom Father replaced in *Jarnegan* in order to give me my first professional job in the theater.

Soon, it was apparent that Father could never get through the show without stumbling, though when his memory permitted he played with the old brilliance and power. Regretfully, producer Dwight Deere Wiman had to replace him with Dudley Digges for the New York opening. *On Borrowed Time* would be his last play.

Father went into orbit and occupied himself immediately with a law suit against the Westover Hotel, his residence in New York on West Seventy-second Street. A carpenter at the hotel, he claimed, had closed an elevator door on his thumb and incapacitated him so completely that it forced him to withdraw from his newest production, *On Borrowed Time*. He even tried to convince me that he was in such physical pain he simply couldn't remember his lines. The case was dismissed when it went to court in January of 1939.

Once again, St. John Terrell came to the rescue. In mid-1939, he opened the Bucks County Playhouse in New Hope, Pennsylvania, a theater that would become one of the best known in the country on the summer circuit. In connection with the new theater, St. John organized a school for apprentices and asked Father to direct its activities and curriculum, an invitation which he accepted eagerly and with his old verve. At the formal opening of the Bucks County Playhouse on July 1, he gave a curtain speech to dedicate the new theater, after promising St. John that his address would be "terrifyingly brief," and therefore unprecedented.

Father moved to New Hope to take up his new duties at the apprentices' school but he found during his lectures that his attention wandered to the pretty girls in his classes and, instead, St. John suggested he confine himself to readings of his most prominent roles from plays of the past. All told, he spent several years in Bucks County and for him it was an enjoyable and peaceful time. He directed productions of *What Every Woman Knows* and *They Knew What They Wanted* for the theater and loved working with the young apprentices in school. New Hope was surrounded by a colony of writers, artists and actors, and Father enjoyed the company of many of his friends and was seldom seen without his pet monkey, Aimee Semple McPherson, or his dog named Mr. Bennett.

One of Father's closest friends in New Hope was restaurant owner Susan Palmer, who stimulated interest and aid for the theater by giving parties at her place of business, to which she invited many of the influential people in the arts and entertainment world. Miss Palmer provided Father with one of the most meaningful and affectionate relationships of the last years of his life, and I'll always be grateful for her many kindnesses not only to him, but to me at the time of his death.

Though both Father and Mother frequently encouraged Constance and me to address ourselves to the legitimate theater, Constance had never really wanted to make the attempt. She kept putting it off for a specific reason, an abject fear of live audiences. "The very thought," she said, "of that great seething monster out there in the dark, breathing fire, terrifies me!" On a few occasions, she'd allowed herself to be talked into a stage production but had withdrawn at the last minute. Finally, she decided the time had come to face the dark monster, and on New Year's Eve of 1940, she made her stage debut in Noel Coward's comedy, *Easy Virtue,* in Wilmington, Delaware. Originally scheduled for Broadway, the out-of-town performances were greeted with appallingly rude notices, but business held at the box office and the management decided to arrange a national tour instead of subjecting it to the wrecking crew in New York. In her words, "It's a bomb, but people keep coming to see it and I'll play it as long as they insist on buying tickets."

She may have had an inordinate fear of live audiences, but she had little fear for the other dangers of touring. In *Easy Virtue* Constance wore a lot of jewelry that received a good deal of publicity in the newspapers, and during the Chicago run, she showed her steel when she was robbed by a masked gang of four men. She and her leading man, Richard Ainley, and Anita Louise, who was playing in another production in Chicago, were returning to their hotel after a charity performance. When their car stopped for a traffic light, the thugs approached, held a gun on the driver and directed him to park in a nearby alley. They relieved Constance and Anita Louise of their jewelry, which totaled a sizable sum in value. Then, one of the men tried to take Constance's mink coat, but she folded her arms and looked him right in the eye. He suggested he'd take her with the coat, if necessary, to which she replied, "Then you'll have to hurry, there's someone coming!" One of them said, "Thanks, Connie," and they all fled, though in their haste they'd overlooked a pair of diamond earrings and a brooch which she'd concealed with her coat collar. The thief who called her "Connie" probably incurred her wrath as much as the loss of her jewelry. She hated any abbreviation of her name, and anyone who knew her well never called her anything but Constance, or else.

In Columbus, Ohio, one performance of *Easy Virtue* was canceled at the Hartman Theater due to a fire department violation, and Constance objected when the management, relying on the old "act of God" clause, threatened to dock the company a day's pay. "Don't blame God," she said. "Blame the negligence of the theater's manager," and she took a petition to Actor's Equity, won her point and a day's pay for the company, and added to her reputation for temperament.

She was always much better at it than I. The only time I can remember throwing a temperamental scene was during the filming of *Man in the Iron Mask,* produced by Edward Small in 1939. Edward and I had a disagreement on the set about releasing me from work early that day to attend Gene's mother's funeral. I told him I'd work late and continue to work after I got back to make up the time, but he had extras on the set and he didn't want to keep them beyond a certain hour because it would mean overtime. The argument went back and forth for a few minutes, when finally I rose in what I thought was righteous wrath and stamped into my dressing room, with Mr. Small close at my heels. To punctuate my point, I picked up the nearest cold cream jar and threw it at him. He thought it was all very funny and later exaggerated the story by telling everyone I'd thrown a chair at him. But it wasn't a chair, it was nothing but a small, lethal jar of cold cream. In any case, we became the best of friends after that. My aim was bad.

# 16

After twelve flourishing years of prosperity, 1939 was the year
of catastrophe for the Pinker-Morrison Literary Agency.
Throughout those years, Mother had represented some of the
most important theatrical literature of the nineteen-thirties,
and had helped develop many of the young playwrights of
the period. Some of the plays she negotiated for production
were *Death Takes a Holiday,* Rose Franken's *Another Language, Victoria Regina* with Helen Hayes, five plays for The
Group Theater, *If This Be Treason* for the New York
Theater Guild, *Scarlet Sister Mary* with Ethel Barrymore,
*The Gay Divorcee* by Dwight Taylor, and St. John Ervine's
*The First Mrs. Frazier.* Early 1939 found another of her
properties running on Broadway, *Family Portrait,* starring
Judith Anderson.

Eric's department of the agency enjoyed great success, too,
with a number of celebrated fiction writers on his client list,
including Aldous Huxley and Louis Bromfield. He also represented Joseph Conrad's literary estate. All seemed to be
going so well with the agency that no one, particularly
Mother, had the slightest premonition of disaster. It came
with shocking swiftness on March 11, when Eric was indicted
for the theft of ten thousand dollars from one of his clients,
E. Phillips Oppenheim, an extremely successful writer of
mystery stories. Oppenheim cabled New York's District At-

torney, Thomas E. Dewey, from his home in Monte Carlo, charged that Eric had withheld his royalties from the Crown Publishing Company for a magazine serial, and demanded an investigation. Detectives made the arrest at the Pinker apartment and took Eric to jail. Since he was still a British subject, he was held without bail and remanded for a hearing on March 17.

The investigation turned up other irregularities in Eric's dealings with his authors and listed thefts of up to thirty-seven thousand dollars from Oppenheim alone. Although he was indicted only on the Oppenheim charge, probation reports alleged thefts exceeding a hundred thousand dollars.

For Mother, it was a horrifying nightmare, an incomprehensible turn of events. Constance, Barbara and I had always maintained a low temperature where Eric was concerned, and his affection for us was no less cool. Naturally, my feelings of dislike were heightened by the ultimate cost to my mother. Still, there had never been cause to doubt his honesty or an unimpeachable background, and a thing so reckless as embezzlement was simply not his style. He'd been educated at private schools in Surrey and London, then enlisted at the outbreak of World War I, and was decorated with the Military Cross for gallantry in action. The Pinker-Morrison Agency had earned him an impeccable reputation in the United States, and it thrived under his direction for twelve years. Calamity destroyed it overnight, with nothing left but the scarred and tragic wreckage.

Certainly it was cold comfort, but it wasn't uncommon practice, among literary agents at the time, to juggle fees collected for their clients. Eventually authors were paid their rightful due, but occasionally an agent would mingle the money with his own to pay current expenses or smaller, less affluent authors, and make up the difference later. Since then, the practice has been declared illegal.

Eric's first act was to exonerate Mother completely. She had known nothing of debits and credits, books or figures, which were handled by him alone, and it was a part of the business in which she had no interest. He put up no defense or excuse to the grand larceny indictment, pleaded guilty in General Sessions court and was sentenced to two and a half years in Sing-Sing Prison.

Typical of her style, although the strain was excruciating, Mother never wavered. She stood by him loyally through the hearing, the sentence, and his imprisonment. But her life, too, was in shambles. The agency was dissolved immediately, the clients scattered, a dozen years of hard work were destroyed, she was ruined financially, and there seemed no way to escape the horrors that were left behind.

We didn't know the full extent of her agony at the time. She never showed her wounds. Among the friends who were closest to her in New York, playwright Chester Erskine retains the image of that slender, gallant figure to this day. "Every Friday she departed by train for Ossining with books, newspapers and gifts and most of all herself, to spend the weekly visiting hours with him. I used to see her go off cheerful, courageous and determined, and my admiration for her steadfastness was without stint."

Fortunately, Mother's friends rallied to help solve some of the insurmountable problems that confronted her. Another close friend at the time was Virginia Carrick, an astute agent in her own right who had worked with the Pinker-Morrison Agency previously. Virginia called Mary Leonard Pritchett, another prominent New York literary agent, and asked if she would consider including Mother in her office. Mary had known Mother only slightly before that but, after giving it some thought, decided she would indeed invite her to join the Pritchett Agency.

Publishers and others in the literary world were horrified. There were questions from many quarters and wonder that she would involve herself with the existing situation. But Mary Pritchett was, and is, a lady of irrepressible spirit, and she formed the union in the face of protest. Still, criticism of the partnership was in the air, and although Mary was convinced that Mother was blameless, she was also certain that the practical thing to do was to arm herself with a legal opinion. She made an appointment with the District Attorney's office and there the representative who'd handled the Pinker case gave her just the ammunition she needed to silence criticism. "Do you think if there was the shadow of a doubt about Mrs. Pinker's integrity she would have been exonerated and not made a party to the suit? She was not implicated in any way."

The association was a most fortunate one for Mother and unquestionably a circumstance that saved her pride and peace of mind. Also, it was a happy one for Mary, and she told me recently that the eighteen months she shared her labors with Mother were among the most favored of her life.

Always extremely circumspect, Mother seldom spoke of her problems, and she carried her burdens with simple and endearing grace. But in a rare revealing moment, she told her associate, "You and I are very fortunate, Mary. We both have wonderful husbands. You may think that's a strange thing to say now, but Eric has given me more understanding and affection than anyone else in my life. I just don't believe he is a thief. I have the strongest feeling that he is not. He just got himself involved in his own gullibility." Mary also shared her feeling that he'd become involved in trying to help his brother, who was head of the London branch of the agency.

She worked very hard during that period, and because she was loved and respected by everyone in the theater, was accepted wholeheartedly in the business of negotiating plays with the Pritchett Agency. One of her clients was Brian Doherty, who wrote the delightful play, *Father Malachy's Miracle*. For awhile she seemed to be the only one who had faith in it, but she kept pursuing producers to give it a production. It was called "Adrienne's Miracle" when it was finally produced and sold to Paramount for a motion picture.

·   ·   ·

By early January, 1940, I decided once more on domesticity. By then I knew I was in love with Walter and felt I could give him, at last, the settled domestic life he'd never had. Since we'd worked together on numerous films, combining both careers with marriage seemed eminently desirable and sensible. Most important of all, he loved Ditty and Mims.

He called me one evening and, in the midst of our chat, asked me to marry him. I thought there was no time like the present moment. Since Constance was touring on the road, I stopped only long enough to pick up my good friend Maggie Ettinger, and the three of us took a train to Phoenix. Walter and I were married there by a Justice of the Peace, January 12, 1940, and we returned to take up our lives together in the house on Mapleton Drive.

The only thing that marred my happiness was Jack Fox's public fuss over my marriage to Walter. Two days later, in Los Angeles, he produced some headlines when he swallowed a handful of sleeping pills and immediately summoned an ambulance. "I didn't like the idea of Joan being married to that other guy," he told the police. I thought that a trifle high-handed. He was one husband late, since he'd passed over my marriage to Gene Markey and picked Walter instead. Furthermore, he'd been married twice since our divorce twelve years before and had had one child by each wife. In any case, Walter was very permissive when I arranged for Jack to be taken from the police receiving hospital to a private one and engaged a private physician. We didn't hear much from him after that.

My life with Walter was lived in something of a rarefied air, often among people who were fascinating, accomplished, and vitally involved in the world that went on around them. An erudite man, Walter was interested in a world that went beyond the sometimes superficial and insular one of Hollywood. He served not only as an industry spokesman but in the community, and was informed and interested in national and international affairs as well. From 1939 to 1945 he was president of the Academy of Motion Picture Arts and Sciences; president of the Motion Picture Society for the Americas, which was Hollywood's liaison with the Office of Coordinator for Inter-American Affairs; a trustee of the Motion Picture Relief Fund; a board member of the American Red Cross, the American Council of Race Relations and The National Tuberculosis Association; trustee of Antioch College; president of the Dartmouth Alumnae Association. In 1936, The American Legion created a Motion Picture Division of its Americanism Committee, with Walter as its chairman. When the Hollywood for Roosevelt Committee conducted a radio campaign in behalf of the President's third term, both Walter and I joined the ranks of other industry members in the crusade. Also, Walter was one of Hollywood's most enthusiastic polo players.

He was proud of his remarkably varied library, read incessantly, and subscribed to an alarming number of periodicals which dealt with current politics and international affairs. Curiously, he didn't object to movie magazines in the house, although I deplored them because of Ditty and Mims. But later when his own two daughters came along, the magazines were banished from the premises on Mapleton Drive.

Though I've defended Hollywood passionately on many occasions, I have to admit that some of its habitués seemed superficial, occupied with the "low-down" from the gossip columns and other trivia, and not overly concerned with what went on outside of that shallow and limited circle. Through Walter and his varied interests, I met many fascinating people I doubtless wouldn't have met otherwise, people like Jan Masaryk, Carl Sandburg, Wendell Willkie, President and Mrs. Roosevelt, and President and Mrs. Truman.


About the time I was acquiring a new husband, Constance was rejecting one. Her marriage to Henri Falaise had deteriorated during the previous few years, and Henri's absences became more and more frequent. She seemed dissatisfied for no apparent reason, but like some beautiful, fitful moth, darted from one emotion to another and never lit long enough to find out if she was happy or not. Her relentless energy couldn't have been altogether easy to cope with for Henri either. They parted company; Constance established residence in Reno late in 1940 and received a divorce for "desertion."

Earlier in the year, Mother had been persuaded to return to the theater for the first time since 1927. Her last appearance on Broadway had been in Basil Sydney's modern-dress *Hamlet,* and she was delighted to be returning to the stage after thirteen years of retirement as an actress. She'd negotiated the play, *Grey Farm* by Terence Rattigan and Hector Bolitho, through the Pritchett Agency and was consulted by the producers in matters of casting. Oscar Homolka was engaged for the leading role in his American stage debut, and Mother submitted a list of actresses, none of whom seemed suitable. One of the producers asked her to play the role herself, and she agreed. It amused her when she had to reinstate her Actor's Equity membership, for she'd been a charter member when the union was formed twenty-seven years before.

*Grey Farm,* a mystery drama, opened early in May of 1940 at New York's Hudson Theater, but unfortunately Mother's return to the stage was short-lived. Despite sensitive direction and a fine cast which included Oscar Homolka, Evelyn Varden and John Cromwell, the play was greeted with thumbs-down reviews. It closed in three weeks, the scenery was retired to Caine's Warehouse, and Mother returned to the security of Mary Pritchett's literary agency.

After that, the months went by in a seemingly endless chain of routine events. Her activities at the agency kept her busy, and each week, with the regularity born of love and loyalty, she visited Eric at the prison in Ossining, New York.

He was scheduled for release in April of the following year. The summer passed into September . . . October . . . November. Thanksgiving approached, and on the morning of November 20, she arose to prepare for a visit to Eric for the holiday. Sometime during those early morning preparations, without warning, she collapsed in the bathroom of her apartment, her makeup half applied, a nearby suitcase half packed with Thanksgiving delicacies. At eleven-thirty, a maid entered the apartment and found her, but too late to be of any help. My mother was dead of a sudden heart attack. Although she'd been plagued with high blood pressure, she'd had no history of heart trouble and had only the one attack that took her life. She was fifty-seven years old.

Mother's good friends Virginia Carrick and Mary Pritchett were summoned at once to the East Sixty-sixth Street apartment. I was notified first and, in turn, called Constance and Barbara to tell them the news that struck us all with terrifying suddenness and shock. Immediately we flew to New York, accompanied by Walter, and after services there, Mother was buried in the Morrison family plot in Old Lyme, Connecticut.

Father, in Hollywood and unable to attend the services because of illness, was inconsolable with grief and wept in anguish. For the fifteen years since their divorce, he'd worn his love for her like a secret talisman, a cherished image examined lovingly in the private moments of his regret and he knew, since then, that his life had been diminished without her.

In all of my lifetime, my mother had been the one fixed point in a changing world, a selfless presence of compassion and sweetness. The maternal instinct in her was stronger than any other, and she willingly deserted the activities of her own life when she was needed in ours. Babies, ours or anyone else's, reduced her to a state of complete helplessness. She cooed over them in elevators, clucked over them in carriages, and was forever raiding the wardrobes of her grandchildren, or adding to them. Naturally, the children responded in kind. Ditty and Mims, Constance's Peter Plant and the five Downeys adored her. She wrote grownup letters to them and made them feel they belonged to the adult world, at the same time she spoiled them in her own adroit and loving way. One of the most satisfying periods of her life had been the development of The Children's Players, which occupied her for several years before scandal destroyed it.

She had a deep and abiding love for the theater, its people and traditions. To her, it was a profession of dignity, nobility and purpose, to be regarded with pride, and she served it with passionate loyalty in two capacities for forty-three years. "The theater," she said once, "is a bewitching lady. She should be treated like one!"

She had unlimited recesses of love which left an indelible mark on everything and everyone whose life she touched. Her inner personal resources were immense, tempered with steel and whetted by an impudent sense of humor. She was a gentlewoman who believed that the great business of life was to fill it with laughter, love and generosity, and in those things she was eminently successful. She gave to us that elegant legacy and a world of gentle humanities that made life fine.

Early in January of 1941, Barbara announced her separation from Morton Downey after twelve years of marriage. It didn't come as a surprise, for her dissatisfaction had grown to unbearable proportions. Morton's career had taken him away from home so frequently that she felt like an isolated stranger. Her excessive drinking had become a serious problem, one that plagued her throughout her life, and in her loneliness, she had sought companionship in a group of people whose tastes also ran to heavy drinking. Morton's seeming indifference to her pleas for attention at home hadn't helped matters, and she had formed an ill-advised attachment to a Western movie actor named Addison Randall. In Addison, she sought an answer to her loneliness and the companionship she felt had been denied her at home.

With that last development, Morton made a cruel bargain: he'd grant her a divorce if she would give him custody of the children: Michael, Sean, Lorelle Ann, Anthony and Kevin. In a weak moment and an alcoholic welter of despair, she agreed. For Barbara, it was a disastrous move. I knew the loss of the children would be a mortal blow and begged her not to let him start divorce proceedings. Morton's demand seemed brutally unfair, for what Barbara needed at the time was understanding and professional help, not punishment. Very like Mother in nature, she was a sweet and gentle person with wide latitudes of love, but the old Bennett stubbornness could and did assert itself. It was almost as if she willed her own destruction, and emotional stability had never been her strong point.

Morton's divorce decree, finalized in June of 1941, charged "intolerable cruelty," and awarded him the custody of the five children. Under the divorce terms, she was prevented from visiting the children unless she was in "a condition of complete sobriety," unaccompanied, and "conducts herself with propriety becoming a good mother." Morton was to be the sole judge of her compliance to "propriety," and his judgment seldom strained the quality of mercy.

Three days after the divorce was final in Connecticut, in a gesture of defiance, Barbara married Addison Randall in Ensenada, Mexico. Forever after, she bitterly maintained she'd been coerced and forced to yield to Morton's demands, but whether she was pressured into the circumstances or not, the cost to her emotional health was unaccountable, and the ache of losing her children followed her like a hateful shadow for the rest of her life.

As time went on, there were a long series of unhappy incidents, both public and private, which indicated the extent of her despair. Once she disappeared for three days and no one could find her. Addison finally called the police, and she reappeared of her own volition, saying merely that she'd been in "seclusion" and couldn't understand what all the fuss was about. On other occasions, she was found unconscious after an overdose of sleeping pills, which gave the authorities more than a suspicion of attempted suicide. At times, however, she managed to pull herself out of her deep melancholy, and there were long periods when she seemed to have made peace with her lot.

In the summer of 1951, she spirited her son Anthony away from a Maine summer camp because he was ill. Barbara didn't think he was getting the right care and held him in the apartment of a friend in New York City. In mid-October of that year, ten years after the divorce, I gave Barbara the money for a legal attempt to regain custody of the children, or at the very least, to modify her visiting rights. It did little to endear me to Morton, but I wasn't engaged in a popularity contest. She was my sister—I loved her and felt I had every right to help in the matter, if it was at all possible.

However, Morton's legal representative maintained she'd given up the children "voluntarily," and the Connecticut court turned down the plea that she be allowed to share in their custody. Magnanimously, the judge qualified the harshness of his decision by adding the remark that she had done "an excellent and commendable job of personal rehabilitation" since 1941, when she was adjudged an unfit mother. He hoped the Downey children would "always respect Barbara as their natural mother and that they will share with her the pleasure of their company. This result, however, must be accomplished through the free choice of the children rather than by judicious decree."

It was obvious that "free choice" for the Downey children wasn't altogether easy to obtain. In the same decision, the judge denied Morton's petition that Barbara be held in contempt of court for kidnaping Anthony from the Maine summer camp two months before, in violation of the original decree which placed the children in the sole care of their father.

While Barbara was being put through the agonies of Morton's divorce, Constance took another fling at marriage, her fourth. In April, 1941, she eloped to Yuma with Gilbert Roland. She'd know Gilbert since 1932 when they had worked together for George Cukor in *Our Betters,* and he'd traveled in the same social circles with Constance and Henri Falaise. I liked Gilbert immensely. He's a man of great flair and colorful background. The son of a Spanish bullfighter, he was born in Juarez, Mexico, and during the Mexican Revolution, the family fled across the border to El Paso, Texas, where he was raised and educated. In his teens, he left home bound for Hollywood, with less than three dollars in his pocket, to embark on a long and successful film career. Since his first silent movie, *The Plastic Age* with Clara Bow, to date, he's made over a hundred films.

In the following years of their marriage, the Rolands expanded their family to include two daughters: Lorinda, who is now a brilliant young sculptress with a growing reputation, and Christina Consuelo, known as "Gyl," who may be the only one of the generation that followed ours to pursue a theatrical career.

With the gathering threat of war in Europe and, ultimately, the United States, both Constance and I threw ourselves into various activities of the war effort. Hollywood went all out, and there were few actors who didn't make a contribution. As chairman of the International Committee for Refugees in England, Constance was a tireless fundraiser, speechmaker and organizer. She also entertained servicemen at military installations, and organized industry-wide studio tours for men in uniform. I involved myself in The American Women's Volunteer Service and headed a committee in charge of recreation for servicemen, participated in a reception given by David Selznick to welcome Madame Chiang Kai-Shek at the Hollywood Bowl and joined the Hollywood Caravan, which was a nationwide train tour of film actors to sell war bonds. It was a wild and woolly trip of two weeks that I'll never forget. It included, among others, Cary Grant,

Bing Crosby, Claudette Colbert, Olivia deHaviland, James Cagney, Joan Blondell, Charlotte Greenwood, Pat O'Brien, Rise Stevens, Merle Oberon, Bert Lahr and Groucho Marx, and gave us all a riotous taste of trouping one-night stands across the country. Having nothing to do between pictures and war bond rallies, I wrote a book called *How To Be Attractive*,* a beauty book geared to busy women in wartime.

One of the most interesting characters to emerge on the national scene of the time was Wendell Willkie, a big, hearty man of great charm. We became good friends, despite our political differences, and when he came to Los Angeles on his speaking engagements, he frequently paid us a visit at home. Mims and Ditty sometimes addressed Walter by the affectionate name of "Bossy," and it amused Wendell enough to mention it in a note after one of his visits.

July 29, '42

Dear Joan & Walter,

Just a note to tell you that I never visited in a home where I enjoyed myself more. Those children I fell in love with—and although that "Bossy" was an ironical mocking title compared with the actuality of Mumsey's set will, never-the-less, it made such a delightful picture and atmosphere that I developed a real resistance to leaving. My thanks and great appreciation to both of you and please kiss those lovely children for me.

Affectionately,
Wendell

How any of us made films during the war years is beyond me, but it was a busier time for film production in Hollywood than ever before in its history, and the demand for movies was doubled as people sought escape in theaters.

After the outbreak in Europe, the industry turned to the war for its principal themes, and one of the most successful of those was Walter's production of *Foreign Correspondent*, a Hitchcock thriller adapted from Vincent Sheean's *Personal*

* New York: Alfred A. Knopf, 1943.

*History.* Released in 1940, it was a grim story of American newsmen in Europe and provided a timely look at political chaos and terror. One of Walter's finest contributions to creative filmmaking also came in that year, when he produced *The Long Voyage Home,* an adaptation of four one-act sea plays by Eugene O'Neill. Though not a box-office success, it received a great critical reception and today is regarded as a film classic.

When the United States entered the war in 1941, Walter's films dealt more often with war themes, and among them were *Gung Ho, Eagle Squadrons, We've Never Been Licked* and *Ladies Courageous.* At the request of the United States Public Health Service and the California State Department of Public Health, he made an educational film on venereal disease which was shown to the public as well as the armed forces, despite vigorous opposition from The National Legion of Decency.

Constance made half a dozen films during the early war years, among them Garbo's last, *Two Faced Woman,* in 1941, and managed to combine her career with a frantic round of other duties. Already occupied with movie-making, fundraising, a home and three children, she started her own cosmetic company, nursed it along by setting policy and judging products, then sold out on a royalty basis. Fashion Frocks was her next project, for which she designed the dresses and collected royalty fees. Then she tackled a New York Theater Guild road tour of Philip Barry's play, *Without Love,* opening in Chicago in October of 1943. Live audiences seemed not quite so monstrous to her by then, and she was beginning to like the feel of a legitimate stage. Critics declared her "patrician" and "a cool, delightful comedienne," but her own view was much more blunt. "I'm a lot more sartorial than thespian. They come to see me and go out humming the costumes."

Certainly she wore clothes like few others in the business and frequently was chosen as the screen's best-dressed woman, a title she disliked thoroughly.

Like Barbara and me, she was always whiplash thin, although she ate like a boa constrictor. She could stow away a dinner that would make a truckdriver blanch, then top it off with her favorite dessert, a hot fudge sundae. But as much as she loved to eat, she never learned to cook and often pointed me out as the best chef in the family.

Early in 1941, I made my first film with the incomparable director, Fritz Lang, a circumstance that would be an important boost for me as an actress. The film was *Man Hunt* for Twentieth Century Fox. I played a Cockney, and for weeks before the shooting began I worked on the accent with Queenie Leonard, an English music hall performer. It was the only movie I ever made in which I knew the entire script, like a play, beforehand. Conquering the dialect was tricky enough, but the real challenge came in working with Fritz Lang.

In the twenties and thirties, Fritz had been one of Germany's most distinguished film directors. Three years after the Nazis rose to power, he was called into Hitler's presence and asked to head the Third Reich's propaganda film production. But the growing horrors of Europe and the terrors to come were already frighteningly apparent, and Fritz fled Germany the very day after his personal interview with Adolph Hitler. His reputation and many friends had preceded him in Hollywood, and it wasn't long after his arrival in 1936 that he became one of the industry's busiest directors. Later, I remember, Darryl Zanuck gave him a Western movie to direct, and I asked him how on earth he could allow a middle European to do an American Western. "Because he'll see things that we don't," Darryl replied. And he was right.

Fritz was terribly exacting and demanding and working with him was sometimes abrasive, but he commanded great respect, and I performed better under his direction than at any other time in my career. Almost always I did what I was told, and we developed a great working rapport.

After *Man Hunt,* the opportunity to work with Fritz came

again, later in the same year, in *Confirm or Deny* with Don Ameche. But Fritz was at sword's point with the studio heads at Twentieth Century Fox, and he walked out one week after the film had started. The studio assigned Archie Mayo, a big, jovial man who endeared himself forever his first day on the set with his first greeting, "Well, I'm not Fritz Lang, but I'll do my best."

Four more films went by before I worked with Fritz again, none of them very exciting, though I do have cause to remember *The Wife Takes a Flyer* directed by Richard Wallace in 1942. I found out I had a good pair of legs. For years, Father had told me my legs were my only unattractive feature, but that was years before, when I was still a teen-ager and hadn't lost all the baby fat.

Still, I'd never gotten over the thought that I was deformed until Dick Wallace got the idea for the opening shot of *The Wife Takes a Flyer,* a scene with Franchot Tone. The idea was to have the camera follow my legs down the street and up to a door. I told him my legs were not my best feature, Father had drummed that into me all of my life, and to forget it, but Dick insisted and I found out I wasn't unsightly after all. Later, I played a chorus girl in something-or-other and wore a brief, revealing costume, and as I remember, there were no complaints, even from Father.

I had only one film released in 1943, *Margin for Error,* directed by Otto Preminger. There was a good reason for my inactivity. I was pregnant again. Part of the time before the baby was born in June I spent organizing a record of my career up to that point. There had been bits and pieces of clippings, publicity articles and photos hanging around for fourteen years, and I decided to put them all together in one collection of bound volumes, in chronological order. It seemed a good chance to get it off my mind and into the basement once and for all.

Early in May, on a Mother's Day to remember, the house caught fire. The fire started in the basement with faulty wiring in the water-heater equipment and went up through the walls after smoldering for awhile. It went unnoticed by anyone until I awoke and saw a few wisps of smoke. I told Walter the house was on fire and he said that was nonsense. I went to Scotty, who was with the children, and told her the house was on fire. She didn't believe it either. Then I mentioned it to two maids and had no luck there. In fact, I found it very difficult to convince anyone that something was going on in that house and we'd better get the hell out. I discovered there was no water coming from the taps, and finally it was obvious even to the halt and the blind that, indeed, the house was ablaze. Ditty found the crisis an excellent opportunity to get rid of her teeth retainer. She promptly threw it in a wastebasket and ran, and found out later it was a detail that did not go unnoticed by me. Scotty carried Mims to safety, and everyone else made it outside without any difficulty.

Always at my best in an emergency, I found a carafe of water, poured it on a washcloth to protect myself from smoke inhalation and made sure that it didn't drip on the carpeting, most of which was destroyed by water from the fire hoses. A good portion of the house was badly damaged, mainly by smoke and water, and the next morning it looked like Wuthering Heights after a blitz. As a Mother's Day present, Walter had had the solarium completely enclosed in glass, and the firemen cheerfully hacked their way through it in high style. Much of Walter's library was destroyed, and all of the memorabilia of fourteen years of my career. From that day to this, I've never collected so much as a scrap of a clipping or a photo. The few things I possess in the way of a record have been sent to me by others.

It was a first-class heartbreaker. One of my life's greatest pleasures had been in building a dream house on Mapleton Drive, and there it lay in shambles. With the shortage of building materials due to the war, it took us over a year to rebuild it. We couldn't even get a permit to haul away the debris, and the neighbors were treated to the spectacle of a blackened ruin for months, while the Wangers moved into a rented house.

Six weeks later, on June 26, our daughter Stephanie was born. Walter always said he really didn't want children of his own, but he was the proudest of fathers.

Then it was back to work and a steady round of movie-making. The next most significant film I made was again directed by Fritz Lang: *Woman in the Window* with Edward G. Robinson. Its success equaled that of *Man Hunt,* and ours seemed a most fortuitous working relationship. I did a couple of films after that, neither of which pleased me very much, and it was then Walter, Fritz and I formed an independent producing company and arranged to distribute through Universal. As a namesake for Ditty, we called the company Diana Productions, and our first film as an organization was *Scarlett Street,* with a cast headed by Edward G. Robinson and me. It was another hit and a good omen for the newly formed company.

All the proceeds from the successful *Scarlett Street* went into the next Wanger-Bennett-Lang film, *Secret Beyond the Door* with Michael Redgrave, in 1948. But Fritz was a real Jekyll-and-Hyde character, calm and purposeful one moment, and off on a tirade the next. At script conferences he was rebellious, on the set he was outrageous and demanding. I remember he wouldn't use doubles for Michael Redgrave and me for a sequence in a burning house. We fled, terrified, through scorching flames, time and again, and it wasn't a fire for toasting marshmallows.

Fritz and I had some thrilling arguments during the filming. When he was in a successful period, he was impossible and Darryl Zanuck told me, "Let him have one good resounding flop and he'll be adorable." He got it in *Secret Beyond the Door.* It flopped and Fritz was adorable at once. By then, however, it was too late. I showed what I thought about it all by getting pregnant again. Walter, Fritz and I dissolved the company, and Lang and the Wangers parted friends.

To me, Fritz Lang remains one of the great directors in the history of the business, and working with him was a fascinating exercise in the art of making motion pictures. On occasion, whenever he makes a trip to New York from his home in California, we still get together for a delightful evening of do-you-remember-when, and the-trouble-with-you-was.

# 17

Early in 1942, Father came to the West Coast again to do a film with Orson Welles, *The Magnificent Ambersons*. His momentum had slowed considerably since his unhappy withdrawal from *On Borrowed Time* three years before. His general health was poor, and there had been a few ominous signs of heart trouble, though nothing to cause serious alarm assuming he stayed on his good behavior, which he did not. He puffed incessantly at his deadly little cigars, and there always seemed opportunity to hang a few over the yardarm.

Orson Welles was one of his greatest admirers, and I'll never forget his solicitous treatment of Father during the filming of *The Magnificent Ambersons*. There was a long flight of stairs in one scene that might have given him trouble, but Orson arranged the shots to make things comfortable and easy and treated him with the utmost deference and kindness. But it was a lonely time for Father. The theater, he felt, had deserted him, and with the exception of Orson Welles, the movies seemed to echo the theater's indifference. The following year he made *Journey Into Fear*, again with Orson. It was his last acting assignment.

For a time he lived with our old family friend, Molly Anderson (Aunt Molly to us), at her home in Beverly Hills, but even her durable patience was fractured when, as often happened, his arrogance was intolerable. He was a most trying guest and took over the household like some aging Oriental prince, scattering fearful servants, dipping into Aunt Molly's private stock of liquor whenever it pleased him, and hiding bottles in improbable places. Finally, I bought him a house in Westwood and engaged a housekeeper to look after him. He romped with his grandchildren, visited old cronies, ruminated on the evil days that had brought the theater to the brink of ruin, and wrote copious letters to Washington with advice on how to conduct the war.

Above all things, he hated the limitations of his failing eyesight and was too proud to acknowledge it. When Constance played *Without Love* at the Los Angeles Biltmore Theater, I planned to take him to a performance, but he refused. "No! I'm not going to walk down that aisle with somebody leading me."

In mid-September of 1944, he was stricken with a heart attack, one serious enough to send him to bed. He refused to go into a hospital and I engaged private nurses to take care of him at home. Predictably, he was an impossible patient and refused to be confined. In one of his more obstreperous moments, he insisted he wasn't sick at all, lurched to his feet, knocked the containing bars off his bed and fell with a crash into an oxygen tank. After that winsome scene, the doctors ordered that he be removed to The Good Samaritan Hospital, which fell immediately under his singular domination. "This damn place has every modern medical inconvenience!" he snorted. He proceeded to make life intolerable for the nurses who were chosen for their quick reflexes and acrobatic ability. In some heart cases, doctors recommended an occasional drink for their patients. "But not in your father's case, Miss Bennett," they told me. "The nurses aren't safe!"

He fretted under the hospital confinement and, to pass the time, shot memorandums to his doctors and the hospital staff and smoked the forbidden cigars that were smuggled in by his friends. Even those pleasures were denied him at last, and on October 22, 1944, he was stricken with another attack and died in a coma. He was seventy-two. After memorial services at All Saints' Episcopal Church in Beverly Hills, I later made arrangements for his burial next to Mother in the Morrison family plot in Old Lyme, Connecticut.

A consummate actor in a career that spanned fifty-three years, indeed, his life had been "a voluntary dream, a studied madness." His passion for the theater led him to a pinnacle of success and, at times, plunged him into the despair of a perishable dream, but he followed that dream, as he said, "To look for the truth in the company of poets."

Father was one of Nature's originals. As the theater's foremost gentleman hell-raiser, he became a legend in his own lifetime and often contributed generously to the legend himself, though certainly his antics needed no embellishment. He once said that he counted the day lost when he didn't add a new line to his current play; his favorite sport was frightening Boy Scouts; he never promised a manager he'd appear for more than one act; and his favorite sleeping attire was a green smock. Some of the stories about him were apocryphal, but most of them were not.

The contradictions that made up his complicated chemistry were eternally fascinating. By nature, he was inquisitive, with a wide range of interests which embraced everything from women's suffrage to combustible engines. However, his amorous proclivities and glandular adventures were the areas which gave him the most pain and pleasure. As an active amorist his life, at times, was hopelessly complex. His marvelous looks had made him an alluring target for feminine susceptibilities, against which he put up little or no defense, though in the final sum of things only his love for my mother had been really meaningful and abiding. Despite his own excesses, Father had a thoroughly mid-Victorian view of home and family, of "proper" conduct and "demure" deportment, and at times he was as militant as Carrie Nation.

To him, rhetoric was not just a pleasant pastime but a way of life, whether he poured it forth before a large audience or in small groups, or confined it to paper. A brilliant raconteur and extemporaneous speaker, his use of the language was articulate, pungent and witty. He quite fancied himself as a poet, wrote poems by the score and spouted them endlessly, given the slightest encouragement. Most of his poems are still in my possession, and they reveal not only his humor, but a deeply sensitive, restless man who sought answers to the perplexities of life and death, a glimpse that showed that for all his bluster and bombast, he was extremely vulnerable.

To me, he was an altogether adorable, intimidating, loving and fascinating parent, a stormy wind who blew hot and cold and came home to mete out discipline in the same way he lavished curtain speeches on his audiences—motivated by love, but with little regard for consistency. For someone who loved to make speeches as much as he, who mounted a pulpit all of his life, it seemed to me a proper salute to his memory to donate a new pulpit to our parish church, All Saint's Episcopal in Beverly Hills, with an inscription plate that reads: "To the Glory of God and in Loving Memory of Richard Bennett." But the most fitting tribute I might pay to my father is one Hamlet paid to his: "This was a man, take him for all in all, I shall not look upon his like again."

The years that followed Father's death brought a number of transitions to the Bennett sisters. Late in 1944, Constance separated from Gilbert Roland after three stormy years of marriage. Gilbert's Latin temperament and Constance's own fireworks often met in opposition, and they were divorced soon after their separation.

To keep pace with her considerable energies, she started her own radio show, a fifteen-minute, five-day-a-week program on which she dispensed fashion hints and women's news, and interviewed Hollywood celebrities. One of her broadcast announcements was a decision to produce her own movie, *Paris Underground,* directed by Gregory Ratoff and released in 1946. It was a disastrous venture from the start, her first and last attempt at film production.

That year she married Colonel John Coulter of the United States Air Force, the beginning of the happiest nineteen years of her life. She'd met John during the war years when he was a technical advisor for a series of Air Force training films made in Hollywood, at a time when they worked on adjoining sound stages. They were separated until John's return to the United States after the war and were married June 22, 1946, in Riverside, California. They had a wedding with a military air, and she was given in marriage by her son, seventeen-year-old Peter Plant, and attended by Lorinda and Gyl. From then on, the Coulters lived the nomadic life of the military and Constance, at last, was a deeply contented woman.

John was extremely fond of the children, and they returned his affection wholeheartedly. In all, during their marriage, they moved twenty-eight times. Asked during that period how she managed to stay so young, she answered, "By being happy, interested and having a great husband with whom I have to keep moving around—so I move!"

Fassberg, Germany, was their first foreign destination, where John was stationed as Commander of the airlift base. A pall of war gloom still hung over the city, and there was little to relieve the grim, monotonous routine of the GI's who were stationed at that allied outpost. My indomitable sister took over at once and launched a one-woman campaign to provide entertainment in the area. She flew to the United States and organized professional companies of three comedies, *Over Twenty-One, Dear Ruth* and *John Loves Mary,* to play Fassberg and other allied military bases in Europe. She shuttled between the United States and Germany half a dozen times to induce actors to contribute their time, arranged Air Force transportation for the companies, scheduled the tours in Europe, and generally busied herself with the details of being a producer, business manager and complaint department.

During the years that followed, she was much happier as an Army Air Force wife than a film actress, though John always supported her career. Occasionally she went back to Hollywood to do a film, but she left it willingly. whenever his duties called them beyond its reach. At last, she'd met her match in a perfect husband who adored her but would not suffer temperamental nonsense.

In the summer of 1945, Barbara was struck by fresh heartache and tragedy when her husband, Addison Randall, was killed on a movie set. Addison was the brother of Robert Livingston, "The Lone Ranger" of Western movies, but his own career hadn't been a particularly thriving one at any time. That summer, Walter had arranged a job for him in a Western at Universal Studios. The Randalls were living compatibly in San Fernando Valley, and things looked more hopeful for them than at any time since their marriage.

The first day of shooting on the Universal film, the company was on location for outdoor action shots. Addison, for one scene, galloped his horse under a tree; his head struck an overhanging branch and he was killed instantly. For a time, Barbara came to stay with me and lived quietly with her anguish; then she returned to New York to work for CBS in the renewed hope of being near her children. "I couldn't have lived without the kindness and understanding of you and Walter behind me," she wrote. "First I had you and Walter and your children with me, then suddenly emptiness stared me in the face and I realized I couldn't rush into your dressing room and talk with you just to get over a sinking spell. But I've snapped out of it now, and you've helped me to go on at an unhysterical pace. . . ."

Barbara's defenses against despair were not very strong at

best, and a series of incidents in the years that followed showed the index of her unhappiness: "mistaken" overdoses of sleeping pills, public skirmishes in nightclubs, nightmarish drinking bouts, and occasional brushes with the police. All duly reported in the newspapers.

I've never met anyone who knew Barbara who didn't recall her sweetness, gentleness and warmth, but there were two faces to her nature and sometimes the abandon exploded in hostility, particularly when she drank. Those periods were followed by complete composure when she would visit the children, the image of the dutiful mother she so desperately wanted to be. There was no contrition more endearing than hers. But it became a cruel, unending circle, for a visit with the children was followed by new waves of suffering and further doses of alcohol.

Constance had no patience whatever with her behavior. She simply had no time for the weaknesses of others. Strong and defiant herself, it was merely her nature to be dictatorial and high-handed, and she and Barbara were often at odds over something. "I wish," Barbara once told me, "I were as sure about anything as Constance is about everything!" I must admit, however, that Barbara's antics sometimes strained things beyond endurance, even for me.

At a time when she was living with me in the Mapleton Drive house, she disappeared after a drinking spree, then reappeared on the front pages a few days later in an encounter with the law. It was a messy, if minor incident, and I'd about given up when Walter arranged a job for Barbara with CBS in San Francisco, and tranquility was restored to the household. I didn't see much of her after that, nor did she correspond often in the years that followed. In 1954, she married Laurent Surprenant, a Canadian journalist, and went to live in Montreal. I remember meeting him only once, but apparently he was another disaster in her life and she married him, in her words, "only out of loneliness."

·  ·  ·

The years after the war are simply a kaleidoscope of films: *Nob Hill, Colonel Effingham's Raid, Scarlett Street,* with Fritz Lang, *The Macomber Affair, Woman on the Beach,* directed by Jean Renoir, *Secret Beyond the Door,* my last film with Fritz and the dissolution of our partnership.

On July 4, 1948, my fourth daughter, Shelley Wanger, was born. Less than a year later, Shelley became an aunt and I became a thirty-nine-year-old grandmother when Ditty's first daughter was born. Marlene Dietrich, who'd already been labeled "Hollywood's Most Glamorous Grandmother," sent me a wire which read:

THANKS FOR TAKING THE HEAT OFF.

Something akin to a giddy nightmare haunted me from then on, the thought of the day when I'd be known as a glamorous great-grandmother.

Then disaster approached with Walter's production of *Joan of Arc,* starring Ingrid Bergman. I'd always thought Walter functioned best with low-budget films. He was a very creative idea man, but when he got into the big extravaganzas they spelled failure, and I sensed calamity from the very beginning of *Joan of Arc*'s costly negotiations. One evening he came home and into the room where I was sitting, pasting scrapbooks with the children. Triumphantly, he waved a fountain pen over his head and said, "This is the pen that closed the deal with Ingrid Bergman!" I don't know why, but at that moment I had a strange premonition. I looked around the room and thought, "Yes, and this is the house that Joan built. A lot of effort and money and love have gone into this house and we've been a happy family here. I'd better enjoy it while I may."

From then on I wouldn't go near the film and didn't even see it in a rough cut. It was released in November of 1948, a critical and box-office failure. I did, finally, see *Joan of Arc* at its premiere in New York's Victoria Theater, and forever after Walter maintained that I squirmed in my seat and at the scenes of Joan at the stake kept muttering, "Burn, damn you, burn!" I can't vouch for the truth of that anecdote, but it does reflect my opposition to the entire production. He insisted the failure of the film was due to Bergman's ill-timed romance with Roberto Rossellini—that her offstage image did not equate with the saintly Maid of Orleans. But closer to the truth was the fact that it was simply a very costly and massively dull movie. For Walter it was financially disastrous. From the time of its release, his fortunes went downhill and he had great difficulty in finding backing, or even another property that was suitable for production. We spent much of the following year in Rome with the children, waiting for Greta Garbo to make a decision on a proposed film, but the deal fell through and we returned home after a lot of sightseeing, a surfeit of pasta, and an audience with the Pope. Walter faced a long, dry period when every project failed or was abandoned.

In the preceding years I'd made *Hollow Triumph, The Reckless Moment,* and *Father of the Bride,* a comedy sleeper with Elizabeth Taylor and Spencer Tracy. (So it was mother roles now, was it?) Then *For Heaven's Sake* and *The Guy Who Came Back.* I returned from Italy to make a sequel to *Father of the Bride* called *Father's Little Dividend.* Suddenly it was 1951. I don't know where the years went but the films went to *The Late Show.*

As the monster of television approached, the postwar decade in Hollywood held a combination of hope and apprehension, and at first, the film industry tried to ignore the menace of home entertainment. For a time, there was panic in the ranks, but television, which got most of its early talent from radio, had to turn to the film industry for much of the necessary equipment. As the new industry advanced, however, the demand for more material to fill the hungry home screens became greater, and television offered large sums for the use of movies which had already played in theaters. At first, most of the major studios refused to release their films, but finally they were forced to surrender and sell the television rights to all but their newest movies. There's no denying that television drastically cut down movie attendance. Many theaters closed and several production companies folded. The movie industry tried to stimulate a dying box office with the technical devices of wide screen processes and the promise of new visual thrills. Eventually, of course, moviemakers went into the full-time business of producing for television. The first few ominous years were only a period of adjustment, and since have proved that there's plenty of room in the world for both mediums.

For years I'd worked not only in films but in network radio, both in Hollywood and New York, and appeared on many coast-to-coast dramatic programs. But I must admit I looked askance at the new medium of television. It loomed, however, and couldn't be ignored, and in March of 1951, I did my first show. Then in its infancy, television was a miracle of inefficiency and disorganization. I remember it was an NBC *Show of Shows*, a variety program with a lot of big names and little else to recommend it. I thought at first I'd walked into Bellevue. In early discussions of the program in New York with the producer and Jerry Lester, the master of ceremonies, Jerry kept saying, "That's George, that's real George!" and I kept asking, "George who?" Half a dozen people advised me on what to wear; one color was good, another should be avoided at all costs. Finally I decided that the only answer was to go on heavily veiled, regardless of color. Show time arrived, and in the final chaotic moments of the program, Pat O'Brien and I were summoned before the cameras. That's all I can remember except that, so help me, we sang a song about a beanbag. It was not a particularly shining hour.

By the following summer, Mims had shown a marked ambition to go into the theater. I promised her that when she graduated from school, I'd do a play with her, as my father had done to introduce me into the business. We did a production of *Susan and God* on the summer theater circuit, and it was great fun for us to work together and to find Joan Bennett and Melinda Markey on the same playbill. Later, Mims went to New York and did a number of television commercials, some modeling, then a revival with Victor Moore of *On Borrowed Time*, Father's theatrical swan-song. For a while I thought she'd be one of the sixth generation to carry on the traditions, but her ambitions waned and today she's married with a family of her own, quite content to be a devoted mother and compulsive housekeeper, traits that Ditty swears she got from me.

Over the preceding three years my relationship with Walter had become filled with untenable problems. Actually, the decline of our marriage had begun much earlier than his professional decline. I learned too late that he was not essentially a family man, and although he cherished Ditty and Mims, he'd never been overly enthusiastic about fatherhood until after his own two daughters were born.

There was added distress and pain in the not too subtle evidences of his wanderings in other directions beyond the family hearth. On that score, the marriage had been extremely rocky from the beginning. I was on the point of divorcing him for a romantic dereliction only three months after we were married, but through a gently remonstrating letter from Mother, which arrived just after her death, and my own deep attachment to him, I was reluctant to force a break at the time. Throughout the years that followed, there were any number of other amorous misdemeanors, and finally I couldn't overlook them any longer.

About that time I was stricken with a sudden illness. Walter was out of town and it was Jennings Lang, my agent of several years, who helped make some of the necessary arrangements for medical attention in Walter's absence. Suddenly I was offered the sympathy and gentleness I found lacking at home, and I turned to Jennings more often after that with feelings that went beyond our business relationship.

Added to our personal differences were the mounting financial troubles surrounding Walter's career. Remarkably successful in the past, he'd gambled everything on his massive production of *Joan of Arc* and, to produce it, had gone deeply into debt to the Bank of America. Though long on expectation, the film was short on box office, and the bank instituted a court action to recover its losses in January of 1951, an action which nearly forced him into involuntary bankruptcy. Walter fought that move and narrowly escaped bankruptcy, involuntary or otherwise, but there were some shaky moments when the bank eyed the property on Mapleton Drive. For a time, the threat of losing it was a real one, but fortunately, that didn't happen until later.

To my embarrassment, Walter made no secret of the fact that he hated the thought of his wife as sole breadwinner and resented the "walking-around" money in his pocket, subjects not designed for happy moments at the breakfast table. Finally, when none of his production plans materialized, he was forced to take a job with Monogram Pictures, a company which featured Class B films. The damage to his ego and pride was enormous. With the memory of past success, he recoiled violently from present failure. His fear of failing became an obsession, and I tried to fill his desperate need for security and continued reassurance. The more despondent he became, the more I tried to help with finances and moral support, but both were insupportable and filled him with resentment. Daily, the circle of discontent widened between us. Of such stuff is tragedy made, although the seeds of melodrama had been sown earlier in that year of 1951.

In January, Walter and I went to New York to discuss the possibility of a TV series for me. The trip had been arranged by Jennings, who at the time was television coordinator for Music Corporation of America, an agency known simply as MCA. There was then no cross-country coaxial cable and the proposed TV series would have had to originate from New York. Aware of my waning affections, Walter saw it as a conspiracy between Jennings and me and uttered a threat to "kill anyone who threatened to break up my home." His work, he reasoned, was located in Hollywood, and a series based in the East would be unthinkable. Instead, I did a few dramatic shows and specials in New York, and later, when Jennings and I discussed a series that was to emanate from Hollywood, Walter reacted violently to that idea, too, finding in it again a challenge to his position as head of the household. Jennings represented a conscious, positive threat to Walter, and he said to me, more than once, "If you see any more of Jennings, I'll kill him."

Jennings and his wife, Pam, Walter and I had been friends for several years; they were often guests in our home or we in theirs; and on more than one occasion, Jennings had shown the sincerity of his friendship to both of us. By then, because the Wangers were in dire financial straits, I was taking anything and everything that came up in the way of work: stock, television, radio, films—it didn't matter to me. In other circumstances, it probably wouldn't have occurred to me to accept television assignments, for TV was still in swaddling clothes, but Jennings knew we were in financial trouble and did everything possible to help and negotiate any offer. Due to his constant efforts in my behalf, it was impossible not to see or talk to him. But I knew Walter's hostility toward Jennings was merely a symptom of a greater rage, launched at an industry that had shunned him and rendered him professionally impotent.

Suddenly, it was a world convulsed by catastrophe. The horrors erupted on December 13, 1951. On that day, Jennings and I had been discussing a business deal at lunch and drove back to the MCA parking lot in Beverly Hills, opposite the City Hall and police station. Jennings, who had been driving, got out of the car to help me around to the driver's seat. We'd just finished our chat when I looked up and saw Walter standing not more than a dozen feet away with a gun in his hand. I heard Jennings say, "Don't be silly, Walter, don't be silly," and he threw up his hands as if to ward off a blow. Then there were two shots. The first bullet went wild, the second ricocheted off the pavement, struck Jennings in the groin, and he crumpled to the ground next to my car.

Some memories of that horrifying day are crystal clear, but with others, thankfully, time has made some welcome erasures. I do remember that Walter dropped the gun, a thirty-eight automatic, and I picked it up from the pavement and threw it in the back of my car. I don't know why or even how I did it, because I've always been extremely gun-shy.

As I look back, it's a curious thing to me that it was my father who always waved firearms around and threatened people with them, but it was Walter, a controlled and rational human being who'd never threatened anyone, who finally brought himself to the extreme of violence. But what even Walter didn't realize was that he wasn't shooting at Jennings so much as he was shooting at the entire motion picture industry. To this day I think he never meant to do anything but frighten us, that the gun fired involuntarily, and the fact that there were bullets remaining in the gun seems to prove the theory.

From the first moment of terror, a series of bizarre events took place that would reverberate in the chambers of my mind for some time to come. When the shots were fired, a parking lot attendant rushed to the scene, and since I was in no condition to drive, we helped Jennings into the car and the attendant drove us to a doctor's office. The doctor then sent us to the Midway Hospital, located in nearby Los Angeles County. There doctors performed an emergency operation on Jennings, and although his condition was serious, it was not grave enough to place him on the critical list. Meanwhile, Walter waited for the police in the MCA parking lot and was taken immediately to the police station across the street. He was calm, detached, perfectly cool. "I've just shot the sonofabitch who tried to break up my home," he told the arresting officers.

I called Jane Wyman, who was expecting Jennings and Pam as dinner guests, to get the news to Pam as quickly as possible. By then, what I needed more than anything was a strong shoulder, and I called one of my best friends in Hollywood, Maggie Ettinger. As I expected, she came at once to Midway Hospital. Beverly Hills police chief C. H. Anderson sent two detectives to the hospital, and with Maggie trailing loyally behind, they took me to the police station. I was told not to worry about the press, who had congregated at the station, that we'd be able to avoid them by going into the building through the fire department.

I was detained as a material witness and went through a period of questioning that was something less than polite. In fact, in the best fictional traditions of law enforcement, I was "grilled," and the examination was rude and tough. Chief Anderson dismissed Maggie, and midway through our conversation, he said, "You're pretty cool about all this, aren't you?" I don't know where he got that idea. I may have given the impression of coolness, but I felt as if I were sitting in the middle of a blast furnace. I told him, however, that if he thought I was going to break into hysterics for his benefit, he was very much mistaken. I was barbecued on both sides for what seemed an interminable period and then was informed that Assistant District Attorney Ernest Rolls wanted to see me before I was free to leave. Instead of arranging a meeting with Mr. Rolls in a quiet, removed office, Chief Anderson led me directly into the jaws of the press, through a gamut of photographers and reporters, and thereby gathered no little publicity for himself in a number of photographs at my side, looking stern, official and properly important.

When I'd finished my interview with Mr. Rolls, I was released, which again presented another athletic confrontation with the press. I went first to Maggie's to collect myself and try to put all the incredible pieces together. Gene Markey, who'd remained a loyal and cherished friend to both Walter and me, came at once with Ed Maltby, Marge Kelley's husband, and they took me home where I could simmer down in private.

David Selznick called me that night from New York to advise that I might need a lawyer. David suggested three names and, at random, I picked Grant Cooper, who eighteen years later was head of the defense team for Sirhan Sirhan.

Meanwhile, Walter spent the night in jail, booked on a charge of suspected "assault with a deadly weapon with intent to commit murder," a charge that could have jailed him for fourteen years. Whenever trouble arose in Hollywood, the first cry for legal help that went up was, "Get Giesler!" and, indeed, the legendary Jerry Giesler had already been retained for Walter. The next morning he was released on bail, pending the arraignment and indictment for which the sentence would come the following April. Walter was detached enough to call the house on the evening he was arrested to suggest ridding the premises of all radios, "so the children won't know about this." His precaution seemed a little late in coming and I wondered why he hadn't thought of that before the gun went off. I was out at dawn, gathering up newspapers from the front lawn, and made a daily collection for weeks afterward. Shelley was then three, but Stephanie was eight years old and aware enough to know something of what had occurred. I tried to keep it out of the children's lives as much as possible. Ditty and Mims, however, were both grown young women: Ditty with a two-year-old daughter and Mims in New York pursuing a career of her own.

I reeled under the staggering news coverage. Every problem, it seems to me, is more difficult to meet when it must be met in a glass house. Things are made more conspicuous and vivid in Hollywood than in Ashtabula or Omaha. Plumbers, apparently, make poor news copy and insurance salesmen aren't very glamorous to the public, but a community populated by theatrical people is an attractive target. Some of the news was larded with a flagrant disregard for the facts, truth was deformed, conjecture was rampant. Other reporters were kind and sympathetic, among them Louella Parsons, who wrote a supportive article that appeared on front pages throughout the country. Clamor from reporters reached an hysterical pitch almost at once and my lawyer, Grant Cooper, advised me to give a statement to the press. On the afternoon that followed the shooting, bolstered by Grant, I faced a battery of photographers and reporters at my home with a statement as clear as I could make it.

I hope that Walter will not be blamed too much. He has been very unhappy and upset for many months because of money worries and because of his present bankruptcy proceedings which threaten to wipe out every penny he ever made during his long and successful career as a producer.

We have lived together in my Holmby Hills home for some eleven years, with our children who love Walter dearly. Jennings Lang has been my agent and close friend for a long time. Walter and I have been close friends of Jennings and his wife, Pam, and saw them often.

I feel confident that Walter would never have given voice to the suspicions expressed by him in the newspapers were it not for the fact that he has been so mentally upset with the complexities of the financial burden he has been carrying for such a long time.

Knowing Hollywood as I do, knowing how good, wholesome and sincere by far and away a majority of motion picture people are, I want to express my deep regret that this incident will add to the opinions entertained by so many.

Fortunately, Jennings's recovery had never been in doubt, and within a few days he made a statement that must place him among history's most forgiving victims. "I'm bewildered by the unfortunate and unprovoked event that has occurred. I've represented Miss Bennett for many years as her agent and can only state that Walter Wanger misconstrued what was solely a business relationship. Since there are families and children concerned, I hope this whole regrettable incident can be forgotten as quickly as possible."

Meanwhile, Jerry Giesler prepared Walter's defense and, in his inimitable style, presented his case with a flair that any scriptwriter would envy. "When all the facts are developed upon the trial, we are satisfied that it will be obvious to anyone that the act charged against Mr. Wanger was the climax of many unfortunate facts and circumstances over a period of time . . . culminating in a bluish flash through a violet haze, in the shadows of early evening in the parking lot where his wife's car was parked. The fact that this defendant fired low and that the gun contained other unused bullets, with ample opportunity on the defendant's part to fire, clearly demonstrated that the defendant was at the moment restored to full competency and normalcy. . . ."

Despite Mr. Giesler's bluish flashes, violet hazes and purple prose, there was an element of premeditation in the fact that Walter had been waiting in the parking lot for over an hour before we returned, and his repeated threats to Jennings had occurred over a period of eleven months. However, I kept silent and refrained from any reference to premeditation. Mr. Giesler had enough trouble on his hands.

January 7, 1952, Walter entered a plea of "not guilty by reasons of temporary insanity," and a trial date was fixed. April 15, on Giesler's advice, he waived trial on a reduced charge of "assault with a deadly weapon," and was sentenced to four months in prison.

On June 4, after winding up his personal affairs, he entered Wayside Honor Farm at Castaic, California, fifty miles from Los Angeles, and served three months and nine days, mostly as a librarian. September 13, dapper and suave as ever, he walked out a free man. The press was on hand to greet him and asked him for a statement. Immediately, he launched into an attack on the United States penal system. "It's the nation's number one scandal! I want to do a film about it," he said and walked away.

# 18

Without question, the shooting scandal and resulting publicity destroyed my career in the motion picture industry. Within a short time, it was painfully clear that I was a professional outcast in Hollywood, one of the "untouchables." I was excommunicated, and evidence lies in the fact that before December 13, 1951, I'd made sixty-five films in twenty-three years, while in the decade that followed I made five. Suddenly I was the villain of the piece, the apex of a triangle that had driven my husband to a shocking act of violence. I might just as well have pulled the trigger myself. The movie business was still bound by an inviolable code of behavior. One simply didn't act like "that," though like "what" is still not clear. Had the incident occurred in the present day, I'd be quite fashionable, but then it was a different matter.

In the weeks that followed the shooting, I found myself sitting in the middle of a fourteen-room French Provincial house, facing professional and financial ruin with two small daughters still to be raised. Above all things, I needed moral support, and I received it in abundance from such friends as James and Pamela Mason, Lauren Bacall and Humphrey Bogart. I'll never forget their kindness and warmth which was everpresent in one of the most crucial periods of my life.

In April, I replaced Rosalind Russell in a national tour of *Bell, Book and Candle* with Zachary Scott and was on the road almost a full year. After that I did a film called *Highway Dragnet*, which may be judged by its title; then the indomitable Humphrey Bogart stood up to be counted as one of my staunchest supporters. Paramount was planning *We're No Angels* starring Bogart, and in the face of vigorous opposition, he told the studio heads he wouldn't do the film unless I played the principal female role. In Hollywood, he fought not only his own battles but everyone else's, and he made the stand to show what he thought of the underground movement to stamp out Joan Bennett. Producer Y. Frank Freeman had no choice but to relent in the face of Bogart's formidable arsenal. *We're No Angels* was released in 1955. The following year I made *There's Always Tomorrow* and *Navy Wife;* in 1960, *Desire in the Dust.* And that was it, the end of thirty-two years in the industry.

Walter fared somewhat better. The Hollywood producers had rallied behind him and, though personally they were very critical of his act, stuck by him and protected him within their exalted circle. He was one of their clan and therefore tied to their public image. Many powerful figures in the industry, among them reportedly Spyros Skouras, Walt Disney, Sam Goldwyn and Joe Schenck, bought shares in his defense costs ranging up to a thousand dollars each.

When he was released from prison in September of 1952, it was almost as if he'd been out for a long lunch. Soon he was filming *Riot in Cell Block 11*, his plea to reform the prison system. The film had impact and proved to be successful at the box office. As long as he stayed within the bounds of low-budget films, his ventures met with success. *Riot in Cell Block 11* and *The Invasion of the Body Snatchers,* which followed, have become minor classics of their kind. He proved it again a few years later when he produced a powerful indictment of capital punishment, *I Want to Live,* which won an Academy Award for Susan Hayward.

However, in 1958 he began negotiations on what film critic Judith Crist called "The Monumental Mouse," *Cleopatra,* and he proceeded to repeat the mistakes of *Joan of Arc,* but on a much more magnificent scale. By the time *Cleopatra* was released in 1963, it had almost wrecked Twentieth Century Fox, forced the retirement of its president, Spyros Skouras, and made its stars, Elizabeth Taylor and Richard Burton, the hottest box office in movie history. Walter sued Fox for having dismissed him during the last days of the film's production, and Spyros Skouras sued Walter for having libeled him in his book, *My Life With Cleopatra,** coauthored with Joe Hyams. The suits were settled out of court. Until his death in November of 1968, Walter never produced another film.

While Walter was serving his sentence in the Castaic prison farm, I was on tour with *Bell, Book and Candle,* and had taken Stephanie and Shelley with me, but as the tour wore on and we worked our way West, the one-night stands took over and touring with the children became increasingly difficult. I arrived in Los Angeles, still on tour, almost simultaneously with the day he was released. I left Shelley at the house with the nurse, arranged to put Stephanie in school in Arizona, then continued North with the company. Although by then I'd made it clear to Walter that our relationship was ended, he was in bad shape for money and I couldn't very well let him shift for himself, so I allowed him to stay at the house with Shelley until the tour closed. When *Bell, Book and Candle* ended in March of 1953, he moved out and I returned to home base. But it was obvious the children missed him and not long after my return, my nine-year-old Stephanie asked me to let him come back home. The children were far more important than any personal feelings and I knew Walter was adrift and without money, so I let him move back to Mapleton Drive. From then on, our lives were separate, and we preserved the amenities only for the sake of the girls.

Within a year after my return from the road tour, it was apparent that I'd have to sell the house. I didn't relish the

* New York: Bantam Books, 1965.

idea, but it was a financial reality to be faced, and I sold it to Louise Fazenda. About then, too, Walter had his first heart attack, and I bought a smaller house in Stone Canyon that had no stairs to aggravate his heart condition.

I didn't divorce Walter until many years later. Because of sheer perverseness, he wouldn't grant it without a fight, even though his personal interests lay elsewhere, and I wanted no more stunning controversies in public for the sake of the children. But the years passed, and finally he consented. When I went to Juarez, Mexico, in 1965 to obtain the divorce, *Time* Magazine noted the transition. "Joan Bennett and Walter Wanger after twenty-five years of marriage. Grounds: incompatibility." Yes, I suppose one could say that.


From time to time during her nomadic life as an Air Force wife, Constance flew back to Hollywood to do an occasional film, but when the Coulters were stationed more permanently in the United States in 1953, she decided on another fling at the theater. About the time I closed in *Bell, Book and Candle,* she went into rehearsals for *A Date With April,* which opened at the Royale Theater in April. It was Constance's Broadway debut, but there was little else attractive about it. Woolcott Gibbs called it "a calamity," and Richard Watts labeled it "the worst play of the season."

Unperturbed by its failure, she threw herself into a project in Washington, D.C., where the Coulters were stationed. In the international atmosphere of the capitol, her idea was to show the foreign visitors something of Americana in the form of its most representative musicals. She negotiated with the Department of the Interior to use the three-thousand-seat Carter Barron Amphitheater in Rock Creek Park and produced a thirteen-week season which included *Kiss Me Kate, Showboat, Carousel* and *Of Thee I Sing.*

Not content to rest on those laurels, she began a double

assault on other fields of entertainment. First, a series of readings from the works of John Steinbeck on a college and service club tour of forty cities; then a foray into the nightclub circuit as a singer. Developed by Bert Bacharach, the mentor of many a variety performer, Constance opened her nightclub act in Miami Beach, then moved to The Cotillion Room of New York's Hotel Pierre. Eventually she played Las Vegas and the Cafe de Paris in London, singing everything from French lullabies in a Balenciaga gown, to rock numbers as a hip teen-ager, wearing jeans and bobby-socks. Reviewers dubbed her "the most glamorous basso profundo around."

The following year she opened a national road company of *Auntie Mame,* a huge success throughout the country for eighteen months. Constance loved touring and seemed to thrive on the rigors of the road, as did Prudence, her eleven-year-old poodle. Constance was an absolute fanatic about dogs, and once refused to allow her agent, Geoffrey Barr, to have a pet of his own. "No," she said, "you're not ready to accept the responsibilities!" Just before one matinee performance, Prudence somehow sneaked out of her dressing room and fled through the theater into the front lobby. Constance roared like a banshee and tore around to the front of the house, where the matinee ladies were treated to the sight of my deranged sister flapping about in haircurlers and a wrapper, without makeup. It was a rare sight, since she never appeared in anything but an impeccable state, with all the trappings of her sophistication.

She worked like a demon on the *Auntie Mame* tour and demanded the same intensity from the rest of the company. Some people thought her difficult and temperamental, and at times she was, but above all, she was a professional and recognized her responsibility to "give the audience its money's worth." Like most actors, she was very superstitious: the left shoe had to go on first or she detonated. There were eighteen Travis Banton costume changes in *Auntie Mame,* sometimes made with only seconds to spare, and one night her dresser inadvertently put on the right shoe first. Constance hit her over the head with it, and yelled, "Lita Lopez, why aren't you in *West Side Story?*"

About the time she was making her nightclub debut in September of 1956, I began an eleven-month national tour of Carolyn Green's comedy, *Janus.* Producer Alfred de Liagre was looking for a leading man, and since I was given cast approval, I suggested the distinguished actor, Donald Cook. I'd seen him in his greatest successes, *Skylark, Claudia* and *The Moon Is Blue,* and thought him a superb actor. We met during preparations of *Janus,* and because I felt I knew him, I said, "Hello, Donald," to which he replied, formally, "How do you do, Miss Bennett?" It was the beginning of one of the most important relationships of my life.

It was during the tour we discovered that we'd actually worked together before, although neither of us had remembered it. A chance acquaintance declared the playbill of *Janus* was mistaken when it noted Joan Bennett and Donald Cook had never appeared together in a film. He assured us both that he'd seen us together the night before on television in *The Trial of Vivienne Ware,* a film made in 1932. "Oh, yes," Donald said, "I was in that, but you weren't, it was Fay Wray." And I replied, "I was in that, but you weren't, it was John Boles!" But, indeed, we had worked together twenty-five years before. No such memory lapse about Donald Cook would ever occur again, and I consider the four years we worked together among the most charmed of my life. It was a four-year acting lesson. An actor who was the very opposite of the introspective performer, his offhand charm and ease with a laugh line were incomparable. Endowed with impeccable timing, he knew exactly when to drop the bomb, and his technique was accurately described as "playing with a steady glib absurdity."

At the time I worked with him, Donald's career had spanned almost thirty-five years in the theater, beginning with community theaters and vaudeville, and his first professional stage experience came in a road tour of *The Rivals* with Minnie Maddern Fiske. The flame-haired Mrs. Fiske, a passionate lover of animals and militant member of the ASPCA, found that her new juvenile shared her enthusiasms, and immediately he was swept into the duties of confidante, general nursemaid and dog-sitter for her traveling rescue mission. His basic theater training and disciplines came from the great lady herself. The callboard of every theater they played, he recalled, bore the notice: "Please uphold the dignity of the company at all times!"

He made his New York debut in 1927 in *Seed of the Brute,* which brought him an invitation from Hollywood to appear opposite Ruth Chatterton in *Unfaithful.* In all, he appeared in some forty-five films, but was never far from the theater where, eventually, he became the most sought-after leading man in the business, playing to perfection the sardonic, world-weary "man of distinction."

Some time after the *Janus* tour closed, I sold the house in Stone Canyon and moved to New York City. Most of my work by then was centered in the East, and I've made it my permanent residence ever since. The following spring, Donald and I opened in John Fuller's first play, *Love Me Little,* produced by Alexander Cohen and directed by Alfred Drake. Bound for Broadway, it was to be my first appearance on a New York stage since *Jarnegan* thirty years before. I thought it was doomed from the start, although out-of-town previews in Philadelphia and Boston seemed to indicate otherwise. Audiences flocked and reviews were better than we anticipated. New York was something else. *Love Me Little* opened April 14, 1958, at the Helen Hayes Theater, and despite great personal reviews, closed after a mercifully brief run.

Early the following August, I received a brief letter from Barbara, the first news I'd had from her in a long time. She'd been living in Montreal for the past two years, still married to Laurent Surprenant, the Canadian journalist, though her life with him had been anything but jolly. She was suffering from an asthmatic condition, had lost an alarming amount of weight, and had been under a doctor's care for some time. She asked me to get her back to California, but before I even had a chance to answer her letter, she was found dead in her apartment, August 9, 1958, and was buried at Lacolle, Quebec, forty miles south of Montreal near the United States border. She was fifty-two.

For me, there was a touching sadness in her death. It seemed to me she had some of the qualities of a figure in a Greek tragedy. Whatever the private demons that drove her, there was something inexorable about the disasters in her life, almost as if she'd been singled out by a caprice of the gods.

Of our childhood together, I remember her as a wonderful and imaginative playmate, full of affection and innocent of guile, although even then she suffered from emotional extremes. At times, she was a profound enigma. One never knew from her gentle exterior what was going on inside, and her eruptions always came as a surprise.

Her spiritual yearnings to join a convent as a young girl were intense and sincere, and I'm sure that if Father hadn't interfered so vehemently, she would have led a perfectly peaceful and happy life. But his opposition to her joining an order was so violent, it sent her into opposite directions of hostility and protest. She was forced into a worldly life that she really didn't want and, as an adult, went to opposing extremes and sought escape from those dissatisfactions in alcohol.

There was another factor in the makeup of her nature: she was a classic case of the "middle" child. Early, life had handed her opportunities that were originally intended for Constance, like an outgrown jacket passed on to the next in line. In Father's production of *The Dancers,* the role Barbara played was offered to Constance first, and the opportunity to dance with Maurice Mouvet fell to Barbara only because Constance refused it. There were several other examples of what, in Barbara's mind, was second best. Though she never had any driving ambition for a career in the entertainment world, it produced an unconscious feeling of having to "compete" with an older sister who dazzled the world with little or no effort. Constance was the gilded Glad Girl, out there swinging away at life, and I think that's the reason Barbara hung back with me in childhood, although she was closer to Constance's age than mine. I was the youngest, probably more indulged than the other two, and Barbara fell somewhere in the middle between two chairs.

Her capacity for love was nothing short of miraculous, and rather than directing it toward the ethereal world of which she'd been deprived, she lavished it on the people around her; her children, her family, friends, even chance acquaintances felt the effect of her sweet and affectionate grace. She gathered hearts like flowers, including mine.

Despite my frenetic introduction to television on NBC's *Show of Shows* in 1951, and memories of the beanbag song, between stock engagements and national tours, I did quite a bit of television in the following years: *Playhouse 90, Climax, Junior Miss* with Don Ameche, and others I can't even remember. I was beginning to think TV wasn't so monstrous after all. In 1959, Donald Cook and I starred in a nighttime series for David Susskind, called *Too Young to Go Steady*. The series lasted about six weeks, and doing one show a week was something of a grind, although it was a tea party compared to what was in store for my future in television.

In November, Donald and I began a tour of Samuel Taylor's comedy, *The Pleasure of His Company*, in a "Bus and Truck" production. It was barnstorming with a vengeance, and as a mechanized strolling player, I got a taste of what my eighteenth-century English ancestors must have gone through. Donald and I replaced Cornelia Otis Skinner and Cyril

Ritchard for their vacation break and played a month in Toronto. Then producers Guber, Gross and Ford bought the Bus and Truck rights, and a few months later we hit the road.

The road, as my parents and grandparents knew it, had all but disappeared before the start of World War II. The touring company that played one-night stands and split-weeks was as close to extinction as vaudeville. Railroads had closed their stations in many smaller towns, and transportation costs to the larger cities were prohibitive. The movies dealt another mortal blow and television, the automobile and other diversions of an affluent, postwar society finished the job. Producers had to decide to either quit the road altogether or find some new way to conquer it. The Bus and Truck system was the answer, and since its beginnings in 1955, it has revolutionized the road and brought professional Broadway theater to both the large and smaller communities throughout the country, many of which hadn't been touched by live theater in years.

The great advantage of the system lies in its utter mobility. Stage crew, electrical equipment and scenery are transported by trailer-truck, actors by chartered bus, and the company covers longer distances more quickly than by rail, at much less cost. Scenery is specially constructed in sections to erect or dismantle quickly and to fit into limited truck space. Since each theater presents different problems of stage space, lighting and acoustics, nightly the company is faced with a test of ingenuity. In each city, extra union stagehands are hired to help "hang" the show and "pack out" after the performance, and the truck moves on at once to the next stand.

The first rule of etiquette to be learned in these highway-hopping companies is that the bus driver is not a bus driver, but a "Motor Coach Operator." Secondly, an actor learns why, after rattling through the countryside all day, the system is called a "Truss and Buck" company within the profession.

Since Donald and I headed the company, we were privileged on tour, and for most of the nine months we flew to each destination on chartered or commercial flights. But regardless of the mode of travel, it was a tough grind. A new city almost every night, a new hotel, a new theater. Sometimes I had to make up on the plane before a performance. We played towns I never knew existed, and the company moved so fast, we were often confused about location. Once, after a performance, someone asked Donald where we were booked next and with cheery conviction, he replied, "Salt Lake City!" It so happened we were in Salt Lake City.

I look back on that experience as a very rewarding one in spite of its rigors and frenzied pace, and *The Pleasure of His Company* now seems an apt description of the time.

In the fall of 1961, Donald went into rehearsals of a new Broadway play with Julie Harris, *Shot in the Dark*. During the out-of-town tryout in New Haven in October, he was stricken with a heart attack and died the following evening. It was a stunning blow to all of us in the business who knew and loved him and seemed an irreparable loss for the theater. I was heartbroken and at a loss myself, not only personally but professionally. Working with Donald, I understood what "ensemble" playing meant for the first time and felt I never wanted to set foot on a stage again without him.

His death was so unexpected, I went around in a state of shock for weeks afterward. Eventually, however, the manager of the Drury Lane Theater in Chicago called with an offer to work with a new leading man, a great friend of Donald's, John Emery. Producer Tony De Santis told me that I'd like John, he was a fine actor, and I'd be comfortable working with him. Somewhat hesitantly, I went into rehearsals in Chicago for *The Reluctant Debutante,* but found Tony's prophecy to be right. From a feeling of mutual loss in Donald's death, John Emery and I were friends from the start. A tall and handsome man, he often was described as a member of the "profile" school of acting, although he was far more accomplished as an actor than his good looks might have indicated. He belonged to a theater family whose members had appeared on British and American stages since the early eighteenth century, and he carried the family traditions into a seventh generation. In a career begun in 1925, he'd played everything from Shakespeare to bedroom farce and had a sizable list of film credits as well.

In the middle of 1963, an offer came for me to do *Never Too Late* at the Cocoanut Grove Playhouse in Miami, Florida. The company was to play a two-week run, and if that proved to be successful, the producers hoped to take the play to London with as many of the Miami cast members as possible. Happily, the Cocoanut Grove performances warranted plans for a London company and, in the break between, I spent the time preparing for Stephanie's wedding to Frederick Guest on August 21, 1963. The next day I flew to London to prepare for the opening of *Never Too Late*. Fred Clarke and I opened September 28 at The Prince of Wales Theater, the same theater where Father had made his London debut in *The Lion and the Mouse* fifty-seven years before.

It's a thrill for any American actor to play London. I loved England and the English and was happy in the play, which enjoyed a successful run. The only blight, if a minor one, was that I found the British press no more responsible in its reporting than its American counterpart. The press, it seems to me, has an extraordinary talent for exaggerating the most casual remark into ridiculous proportions, until it bears not the slightest relationship to the original. During an interview with an English reporter, he asked me my age and I told him, although it's always seemed strange that a reporter can be so cheerfully rude to an actress and ask questions he wouldn't think of asking in any other social situation. Then he asked me if I drank and I said occasionally; queried me on smoking and I answered, yes, I smoked; asked if I was on a diet and I said, no, I'd never had to count calories. The next day in the newspaper I was greeted with the following statement: "I drink whiskey, smoke thirty cigarettes a day, never diet, am fifty-three years old and don't care who knows it!" It gave the impression of a real swinger in her middle years, chain-smoking and lushing her way through life in total abandon.

The accent on trivia and the minutiae of life in the press never ceases to amaze me. The facts, for example, that I was born in 1910; am mad about peanut butter; knock wood for luck; make a perfect hollandaise sauce; love fresh flowers; hate turnips; sleep in a nightgown; and favor shocking pink and green, all seem far less interesting than the soap opera phenomenon; the current long-hair, four-letter revolution; current pornography; today's movies; yesterday's movies; or Senator Eugene McCarthy's and Mayor John Lindsay's election campaigns in which I willingly worked myself to a frazzle.

As an actress, I'm not at all unaware of the values of publicity or the importance of promoting a movie, play or television show. In those areas I've never been uncooperative, but trivialities, especially when they're deformed, can only stimulate boredom in the reader and irritation in the subject. Press and public relations have become big business. Newspapers and magazines, of course, must have publicity to exist, but in a world almost totally influenced by news media, the public is likely to take for gospel what it reads, when in reality much of it is only grubby gossip or fan magazine hokum.

For the most part throughout my career, except for a few notable exceptions, I've enjoyed a satisfying rapport with the ladies and gentlemen of the press, and I've had cause to be grateful for their favors on more than one occasion. On the other hand, I've earned the rancor of a few columnists, whose enmity I consider a sincere compliment. In any case, because I happen to be an actress, I see no reason to forfeit every claim to plain old garden-variety intelligence and common sense.

Be all that as it may, I enjoyed my stay in London and played contentedly until January of 1964, then had to leave the company to continue the run for another month without me, when heartbreaking news called me home. Unknown to anyone, John Emery had been stricken with cancer, probably before we'd even met, and by the early weeks of the year, the disease had developed into a terminal case.

I was deeply attached to John. I knew he depended on me wholeheartedly as a friend, and I came home to be near him through the long, agonizing months ahead. Until his death the following November, I accepted no offers of work in order to go about the privileged duties of meeting his daily needs. I wasn't going to let anyone I loved die with his face to the wall, and if it sounds grim and anguished, to be in his company was anything but that. We never discussed his illness, we entertained close friends, we enjoyed endless discussions of mutual interest, and if the implacable face of death was everpresent, it was never apparent to the eye. The agony ended for John in mid-November of 1964, but he left me with many cherished memories of warmth and trust, laughter and goodness, and I carry them with me still. Our good friend, John Steinbeck, wrote John's eulogy, which expresses his gentlemanly humanities with greater incisiveness than mine.

> He was an actor, a member of that incorrigible peerage against which, along with gypsies and vagabonds, laws once were made lest they cause living to be attractive, fear unthinkable, and death dignified, thereby robbing church and state of their taxes on unhappiness.
> . . . Because of his profession, his life was exposed, downstage, lighted, but none but the stupid, the vain, or the vengeful could charge him with ungentleness.

# 19

At the end of her eighteen-month tour of *Auntie Mame* in January of 1959, Constance occupied the next years of her life with the usual well-ordered frenzy. She completed a couple of TV specials and, in between her other varied activities, toured and played in a number of stock productions that included *Marriage Go Round* and Daphne du Maurier's *September Tide*.

Occasionally, during her last few years in the theater, middle-aged ladies would approach her after a performance and say, "Oh, Miss Bennett, you were my favorite actress when I was a child!" and she would moan, "Dear God, I guess no adults ever saw my films!" She hated being identified with older generations, probably because she was so perennially youthful herself. Referring to her children at a time when Lorinda and Gyl were teen-agers and Peter was in his early twenties, she observed, "At their ages, I don't know whether I find it harder to keep up with them, or they find it tougher to keep up with me." The fact was the children found it tougher.

Like many women, she fiddled with her age and as time went by, she even confused herself. Once I remember being interviewed by a newspaperman when she was present, and when he asked my age, I told him. "You're a fool to tell your age," she said later. "You know perfectly well they automatically tack ten years onto an actress, anyway!" With all of her juggling of dates through the years, I started out as the youngest, then became her twin, and wound up as the oldest sister.

Early in 1962, she began a public controversy involving a fifteen-week run of Lillian Hellman's play, *Toys in the Attic.* While appearing in Chicago, Constance was interviewed on television by Irv Kupcinet, and asked what she thought of the play, she launched a scalding attack. "There's too much sickness and unhappiness in the world for anyone to want to see *Toys in the Attic.* This is a very unpleasant play. It's merely an acting exercise for me. My forte is really comedy. My agent, Geoffrey Barr, thought this might change my image. Wait until I get back to New York, I'll change his image!"

Newspapers picked up the blast and producer Kermit Bloomgarden was moved to counterattack in *Variety.*

> . . . Miss Bennett's sharp words were obviously made with an eye to her own future. Frankness in ladies is now considered both daring and amusing, and television interviewers enjoy leading them on. While Miss Bennett's critical opinions are hard for me to take seriously, they have reached a larger audience through television and newspapers and, therefore, I consider them damaging to my play and reserve the right to take whatever action my lawyers advise.

Constance charged into the fray and fired a few salvos of her own. "If all this nitpicking will help sell tickets for *Toys in the Attic,* I am pleased to be able to be of service. Bloomgarden's attack on me seems to be an announcement to the trade that I 'hurt' 'his' play. *Toys in the Attic* opened in Los Angeles recently without me and the reviews were less than enthusiastic. Whom will he blame now?"

To Constance, speaking her mind was as natural as breathing and the slightest irritation was enough to shake the rafters. I remember the time we were to meet in Chicago for the opening of the newly decorated Drury Lane Theater in nearby Evergreen Park. We arrived at O'Hare Field on different flights and met in the terminal, when someone informed me that my suitcase was missing. Constance thought it was roaringly funny until we discovered it was her luggage that was lost, not mine, and I fled to a waiting car, knowing the air would turn blue. It did.

Soon after the *Toys in the Attic* fracas, she and John spent some time in Switzerland. She was an excellent skier, and even then, in her mature years, she flew down the slopes with all the zip of a twenty-year-old. One day, in making a descent, she'd already gone past a difficult run and pulled out on the flat surface, when she fell and broke her leg. It was a bad one, a triple fracture, and doctors predicted she wouldn't walk for eighteen months, but she was walking in six without aid. For all of her energy and perpetual movement, she was a very good sport about her confinement and couldn't wait for the next skiing trip.

Late in 1964, film producer Ross Hunter sent her the manuscript of a scheduled remake of *Madam X* with Lana Turner, John Forsythe, Ricardo Montalban and Burgess Meredith, to be directed by David Rich for Universal. Twelve years had passed since her last film appearance. Ross threw a party to welcome her back to Hollywood, and it was like Old Home Week. Asked to make a comparison between contemporary films and those of the past, Constance declared, "Back in the thirties, there were more pictures about women. The roles were glamorous and the clothes divine. They weren't dramatic roles, they were more synthetic. But they were exciting and the actresses acted like movie queens. Pictures have certainly changed today!" And I couldn't agree more.

When Constance returned East after filming *Madam X*, her fifty-fifth film and her last, once more she threw herself into a round of activities. She looked radiant and felt it, but one morning she suddenly awoke with a spell of dizziness. After a series of tests, the doctors decided the trouble stemmed from a middle ear infection and recommended an operation.

The surgery was successful and she recovered with her usual briskness. I called her one day from Chicago, where I was appearing in a play, just after her release from Walter Reed Army Hospital. She sounded like her energetic self, and I remember she called me the pet name she'd used through the years.

"Joanicah! Are you still smoking?"

"Yes, Constance."

"Well, you're going to stop at once, do you understand?"

"Yes, Constance."

"I stopped smoking four months ago and if I can stop, anyone can. Now, you're going to quit that habit at once!"

"Yes, Constance," and I hung up and lit a cigarette.

In mid-July of 1965, she was stricken again very suddenly with an undetermined illness and John rushed her to the hospital again. An attendant noted down the necessary information from John, while Constance lay nearby, under sedation and not very alert. But when the question of age came up on the hospital entrance form, before John could answer, she took over. "I was born in 1914," she replied, knocking off ten years.

She seemed so vibrant and alive, and seemingly invincible, that her death of a cerebral hemorrhage on July 26 came with breathtaking shock. I was in Philadelphia in a summer-stock production of *Never Too Late* when Stephanie called me during the performance. Since I knew Constance would expect it of me, I finished the show that night, then flew to Laconia, New Hampshire, for the opening there the following evening. Getting from New Hampshire to New York for the services presented time and transportation problems the next day, however, and I'll never forget the kindness and gallantry of a total stranger, James Tyler, a local resident, who offered his private plane and flew me to La Guardia Field, waited while I attended the services and flew me back to Laconia in time for the performance that evening. On July 28, Constance was buried in Arlington National Cemetery.

A few months before her death, author Gene Ringgold was

preparing a career article and a list of her films for the magazine, *Films in Review,* and she sent him a note, saying,

> . . . I'm flattered that you want to write about me. But if you do, keep it light. And be truthful about my film work. After all, I was no Sarah Bernhardt. Good luck.

And she added a postscript,

> Did I really make a film called *Bed of Roses?*

It was a typically direct, no-nonsense attitude she reflected all of her life. A woman of winged intelligence, Constance had a flair for logic that could be irritating, and it earned her a good deal of enmity in the business. Hollywood, particularly, found it difficult to reconcile itself to an actress who reduced absurdity to a proper level with all the delicacy of a bulldozer.

Of her fifty-five films, there were only five she considered worthy and she made no pretenses otherwise: *Common Clay, The Common Law, What Price Hollywood?, Our Betters* and *Topper.* Now that I stop to think of it, there are only a scant half-dozen of my own total of seventy films that were acceptable to me and they include *Little Women, Private Worlds, Trade Winds, Man Hunt, The Woman in the Window,* and *Scarlett Street.*

That beautiful sister of mine was an overwhelming and volatile mixture. One had the feeling she'd been shot from a cannon and showered her sparks over an incredulous world, with no thought or care where they fell. To some people, John Coulter among them, she was demure, at times even shy, though I must admit that was a side of her that escaped me. Others stressed her arrogance and emotional outbursts, ruthless business deals, and bullying to get what she wanted. She was capable of the most extreme selfishness and the most extravagant generosities.

It was true that Constance was egocentric to her elegant bones, given to theatrics and wild exaggeration, and not above guile, but shrewd enough to leave herself with more than one exit. By nature she was quixotic, turbulent, stubborn, and aggressive, a veritable carbon copy of Father, but the giddy whirlpools of her life were often created for the sheer love of conflict. She was like some silvery comet who streaked through life with daring speed, the wellspring of which was an inner confidence that I deeply admired. At times, particularly in childhood, I was intimidated by her, but she dictated from an aura of affection for me that was never threatening.

Constance often forced her will on others with little thought of the consequences. The least domestic of women, she ruled her children with an iron hand, a cause for controversy at times, but she earned their respect and was proud of their accomplishments.

Though even late in her life she appeared ageless, she lied passionately about her age to the very end; the marker at her gravesite in Arlington National Cemetery lists only her name and the date of her death. And once she remarked to young actor James Coco, "What a pity we weren't old enough to have seen my father onstage!" But youth is a viewpoint, a matter of being active, enthusiastic and not bored with life, and in those things she was eternally youthful.

She was fanatically loyal to her friends and implacable in the hatred of her enemies. There's no doubt that she was a strong and vital personality, a woman of indomitable will who sprinted through life as if it were an obstacle course, but to me, Constance will always be an iridescent memory that arouses my affection and admiration.

At the time of John Emery's death in November of 1964, I'd been out of the running in the entertainment world for almost a full year. I accepted a number of stock engagements and then began looking around for a play in New York again. Nothing of interest presented itself and it was then that my agent, Tom Korman, came up with an offer for a daytime television series, *Dark Shadows,* for the American Broadcasting Company. At first I shuddered at the idea of a daytime "soap opera," never realizing that I'd be shuddering for the next four years in a far different way than I'd imagined. I'd worked in a good deal of television by then, but I'd never even seen a daytime soap opera, and had no idea of what went on in its sudsy world, except that actors had to cry a lot because everything was intensely sad. Furthermore, I had some vague notion that the actors who worked in them were second-raters. I must admit I was forewarned about the work schedule when ABC's Dan Curtis asked me if I really wanted to put up with a daily routine that was so demanding. Well, I thought, I've worked hard all of my life and a tough schedule certainly never intimidated me. Besides, my agent told me he could always get me released if I found the pace too difficult.

At first, I was slated to do only a couple of shows a week, then it was extended to four and five, Monday through Friday, and I began to meet myself coming back. *Dark Shadows* went on the air in June of 1966, and after the first thirteen weeks, I thought I'd have to take a rest cure. On a typical day, I reported at the ABC studios at eight in the morning, worked until six-thirty, and at night learned as much as twenty-four pages of dialog, when I had cause to be grateful for my photographic memory. Of course that schedule doesn't prevail all of the time, but when it does it keeps life frenzied. In movies, it would have taken a week to get that much material on film. In filming *Little Women,* one scene I remember was repeated twenty-two times before George Cukor got the "take" he wanted.

I found television an infinitely more spontaneous medium. As our executive producer Dan Curtis says, altogether too cheerfully, "We work the hell out of them! It's death in the afternoon and panic in the streets every day on the set. If somebody blows a line, that's too bad." Although the show is taped ahead of time, it's a "live" tape technique, there's no way of going back to correct mistakes and, occasionally, there's a really spectacular lapse.

Of all the entertainment mediums, television is surely the most demanding for actors, and technically the most complex. There are a dozen things to distract an actor and fracture his concentration besides the lights, miles of snaky cable, hand signals and constant movement of cameras. Crewmen stand around just out of camera range, but always within the sightline of the actor; they stretch, yawn, walk around, scratch and mutter, and once I thought I was getting a cue to elongate a scene when a technician gave out with a splendid yawn and stretched his arms in a wide arc. The floor of a set is a patchwork of colored tape marks to keep the actor within the confining limits of the cameras. There's very little freedom of movement and I'm inclined to think that hitting the tape mark is far more important than giving a performance. There's little chance for anything but instant acting amid all the technical devices; most of it is completely spontaneous and issues from an actor on the spur of the moment. No wonder, within the business, it's called "summer stock in an iron lung."

For a time, I thought I'd have to give up the ghost of *Dark Shadows*, and when I found the series was going to be extended beyond the first thirteen weeks, I hinted to Tom Korman that perhaps I wasn't geared to life as a galley slave after all, but four years later, I'm still pulling the oars. By now, of course, I've made my peace with the schedule, although I admit I'd find it sheer misery if it weren't for a great and compatible company, from which I've made some enduring friendships. Also, the production heads are extremely generous and often make allowances and rearrange schedules for vacations or activities in other entertainment fields. The entire company works smoothly together, and I'm sure we couldn't survive otherwise.

I've certainly revised my original view of the acting caliber on daytime television, having found many fine actors who manage to do other things in the business, from Broadway or off-Broadway shows to television or radio commercials and summer stock.

I suppose it might be said that *Dark Shadows* is not typical of Detergent Land Drama, but rather it's a Gothic tale of intrigue, filled with somber apparitions, ghosts, murder and vampires, and set in an old mansion near a Maine fishing village. The Collins mansion is not the most ideal spot for suburban living; there are a great many rusty hinges, and a good deal of candlelight, moving draperies, and eavesdropping. Thunder and lightning aren't infrequent occurrences, to say nothing of ectoplasm. The impulse is to invite a visitor to lie down, rather than sit, since the house has more coffins than chairs. Everyone frowns a lot, which is perfectly natural after a long night of terror. I've also gathered a good deal of information about vampirism and witchcraft during my work on the show, though I can't say it's been particularly useful, as yet, in everyday life. For example, I know that witches cannot whistle, vampires won't cross a running stream and will call your name only once when they knock at the door. Wolfbane is wonderfully effective for repulsing werewolves, penicillin is no cure at all for the bite of a vampire, and a Christian cross is still infallible protection against all creatures of the netherworld.

Anything can happen and does, with harrowing frequency. First of all, I murdered my husband and buried him in the basement. Then, a very sinister character moved into the house and tried to blackmail me into marrying him. I looked on his proposal as a fate worse than death, rushed to the nearest cliff to hurl myself into the surf below, changed my mind and, like an utter fool, confessed to the murder. But when the police investigated and came to search the basement, my husband's body had disappeared. Apparently, I hadn't killed him after all, I'd made an untidy job of it, and he's still lurking around somewhere out there in the world. As Elizabeth Collins, mistress of the mansion, I seldom leave it unless I need a vacation and then the writers conveniently arrange for me to have a splendid nervous breakdown or they keep me in a deathlike trance, until it's time to go back to work again.

Most people can boast of some sort of skeleton in the family closet, but I have a cousin who's a two-hundred-and-thirty-five-year-old vampire, though somewhat more benign than Count Dracula. Now, take the average vampire. Usually, he's highly infectious, in sore need of orthodontia, disorderly, and a thing to be avoided at all costs. However, my distant vampirish cousin, Barnabas, is quite a sympathetic character and Jonathan Frid, the actor who plays the role, has become everybody's favorite vampire.

And so it goes. The plot is so complex I'm certain the good and faithful people who watch it daily have a better grip on the threads of it than I. From coast to coast, somewhere out there, they drop whatever they're doing in midafternoon, Monday through Friday, to watch *Dark Shadows,* and their rapt attention has given the show a top rating over any other daytime TV program. In one day, I appear before more people than my strolling player ancestors did in their lifetimes. Sometimes we marvel at its impact on the public, but the desire to "find out what happens next" is a strong one in all of us, especially when it's pleasantly macabre and nicely agonizing.

Off-camera, too, the company history has all the fascinating elements of a full-time soap opera within itself; friendships of a lifetime have been formed, and marriages, births, divorces and illnesses produce enough real drama and variety for a sequel.

For a time, the fate of *Dark Shadows* was threatened with union troubles when, shortly after it went on the air, The American Federation of Radio and Television Artists struck against the networks. Fortunately, there were enough shows taped ahead to fill the thirteen days of the dispute, and we went back to work and once more settled into the well-ordered panic of a regular routine. Then, in October, 1967, new trouble brewed when NABET, the technicians' union, went out on strike, and in a sympathetic gesture, AFTRA members were asked to respect its picket lines. The American Broadcasting Company was the only network in trouble; CBS was never in doubt, and NBC settled with the technicians' union before the strike began.

Dutifully, all actors and newscasters at ABC observed the request for about a week, until a rumble began when AFTRA sent a wire to its members "forbidding" us to cross the NABET picket lines. It was an irreversible order; there was no vote; we had no choice in the matter. Tapes for *Dark Shadows* were running out, and time became a desperate factor. The future of not only our show, but a great many others, was in serious jeopardy. I suppose I could have suffered it all gladly, had it not been for the intractable order from the actors' union, but it was the kind of rigid dictatorship and bullying that makes a Bennett voice rise, as well as a Bennett gorge. I thought it was altogether autocratic, especially since we were deprived of a vote on the issue, and I joined the ranks of dissenters, of whom there were many, and went back to work.

Charges and countercharges, endless meetings and rhetoric, flew thick and fast. The technicians' strike was settled in twenty-one days, and those of us who had returned to ABC before it was over awoke to find we'd been fined and censured by our peers at AFTRA. That produced new shockwaves, reprimands, countercharges and further elaborate rhetoric. The controversy drags on. The fines were appealed, are still in litigation, and the end is neither certain nor in sight. Whatever the outcome, it offered another grand opportunity for one of the Bennett clan to join in battle. I'm not promising it's the last one.

Once, referring to actors, my father said, "We are vagabonds to the heart and we are not ashamed of it." Well, I'm still a "vagabond" and I'm shamelessly proud of it. At this point in time, I've done about everything there is to do in the entertainment field: Broadway theater to summer stock, films, radio and television. The only things I've missed are a magic act and the trapeze, and I'm not altogether certain I won't try those sometime in the future.

At present, my life is filled with *Dark Shadows* on Channel Seven, TV commercials, guest appearances, and tours of the summer theater circuit, and whatever time is left to me is spent with my family and friends. My four daughters, Ditty, Mims, Stephanie and Shelley, and my nine grandchildren remain my greatest pleasure and fulfillment. Shelley is in her final year at Sarah Lawrence College. The others are married and involved with families of their own, but if they think they can escape my loving attention any more than they have in the past, they're very much mistaken.

Though I have a tendency to groan about the pressures of a busy schedule, I abhor idleness and think I'd fall apart if my days weren't filled to the brim. My friends, the best ones, tell me I'm a monument to youth, stamina and physical fitness, and if there happens to be a shred of truth in that overwrought view, I can only think it must be due to a busy life, a young viewpoint, and an endless curiosity. I guess I just hate the thought of missing anything. I've spent forty-two years in the entertainment world and, so far, haven't given the slightest thought to retiring. Anyway, actors don't retire. They just work or are between engagements, no matter how long they live.

Actors are a singular breed. As I look back on the fabric of the past and the five generations of Woods, Morrisons and Bennetts, I'm aware of the priceless privilege of having been born into the theater. Although it was a career I rejected at first, the profession has given me an incredibly varied life and more than my fair share of success and failure, laughter, love and despair. I've not a single regret for any of it, and if, at some transcendental point, I am again involved in a theatrical world, then I will be overpaid.

I've no wish to dwell any more on the past. It isn't my

custom or nature to look back, and except for the period of writing this book, I've not given much time to retrospection in my life. The world is too filled with wondrous things, and the future is far more provocative. What it will bring to this strolling player is anybody's guess. I can only hope my father was right, when he said once, "You never can tell about Joan. She has all kinds of possibilities!"